TIDES OF CRISIS

TIDES OF CRISIS

A PRIMER OF FOREIGN RELATIONS

By Adolf A. Augustus Berle, Jr.

REYNAL & COMPANY • **NEW YORK**

CONTENTS

INTRODUCTION   13

PART I

One: THE UNITED STATES IN WORLD LEADERSHIP   39

Two: INTER-AMERICAN WORLD: ORGANIZATION FOR
     DEFENSE   63

Three: MID-CENTURY DILEMMA IN EUROPE   90

Four: CRISIS AREAS: MID-EUROPE   128

Five: CRISIS AREAS: MIDDLE EAST   151

Six: CRISIS AREAS: ASIAN COAST AND
     "COLONIALISM"   180

PART II

One: BATTLE OF THE PAST AGAINST THE FUTURE   219

Two: PEACE AND ITS INSTRUMENTS   238

Three: ECONOMIC TOOLS FOR PROMOTING PEACE   269

Four: RETHINKING AMERICAN FOREIGN POLICY   297

FOREWORD

THIS BOOK IS ENTITLED a "primer" and it is intended to be just that. Need of a non-technical, somewhat conversational introduction to problems of foreign affairs is, I think, manifest. The very lives of all of us may be at hazard; in any case, the lives of all of us are powerfully affected by foreign affairs every day. The forces at work and the resulting conflicts are those which made the Twentieth Century a century of crises.

As the year 1956 closed, we seemed to be moving into a new high pressure area. Mishandled, any of these crises may result in wars, little or big; at worst, they could provide an atomic convulsion capable (literally) of tearing the planet to pieces.

A terrifying fact is that the men who grapple with these crises are dealing with forces of which most other people are unaware. Often they must seek solutions for which the prevailing politics and public opinion of the United States are unprepared; and the only way politics and public opinion will ever be prepared is when enough people have general awareness of the underlying considerations and facts.

This volume is hopefully designed to add to that awareness.

Brutal necessity for some attempt along this line is daily apparent to anyone who works in the foreign-affairs field. He labors with his colleagues or fellow-experts taking account of past history, analyzing a body of facts, considering possible solutions, often reach-

ing for innovations or new devices—not because he likes to but
because he must. Then he leaves that circle, and talks to his friends,
to his business associates, to men in day-to-day politics, to students
in colleges and schools. He is struck with the vast gap between the
generally current information and thinking on the subject and the
actual information and thinking of the men who are obliged to
understand, have the job of meeting the crises, and are responsible
for the results. No wonder they can not expect to get, and often do
not try to get, agreement on policies they know are necessary, or
on measures they know to be essential. They are like the doctors
who first tried to explain that malaria came from mosquitoes when
everybody knew that it came from the evening mist; who insisted
that tropical houses needed screens, when everybody knew that you
should wrap a muffler around your mouth in night air.

For example, you go to attend a session at the Air War College, attended by the highest air officers charged with American
defense. These men know that air defense of the United States is
impossible unless the United States is in some sort of international
arrangement giving the Air Force ready use at least of the geography needed for their air bases and interception system. (Naturally,
since their air squadrons may start in Kansas, refuel in Iceland,
the Azores or Africa or Germany, thence to proceed on their mission.) They know that this means building a system of foreign
relations to match.

A day later you meet a group of entirely intelligent businessmen
at lunch or you read a commentator in a supposedly well-informed
newspaper. The talk runs on the absurdness of a powerful country
like the United States wasting time and money on the affairs of
Iceland, offering "give-aways" to Morocco, coddling Germany—
and so forth. It takes time to explain that without the radar line
in Canada, the air base in Iceland, or Frankfort or Morocco or
wherever, the United States would be wide open to attack. It takes
more time to explain that the relations between the United States
and Canada or Iceland or Germany or Morocco have to be such
that these countries and their peoples will be not only willing but
glad to have American installations there.

Still more disconcerting is the realization that the younger group, already of late high school or college age, have only the slenderest familiarity with the series of events which have involved us in crises for the past twenty years and will necessarily go on involving us in crises during the foreseeable future. Many wonder why we are mixed up in them at all—as though it were any longer our choice—as though we could secede from the planet, as though we could forget about the fact that radio communication from Moscow or Budapest reaches us in a split second, that a hydrogen bomb could reach us from either of those places within a relatively few hours, and that there is absolutely nothing we can do to change those facts. Still less can we change the history of the past few years.

In my seminar at Columbia Law School I have from time to time referred to major events in World War II, eliciting only blank confusion. It requires effort for the older of us to remember that when Hitler swaggered across the earth, when Stalin seized half of Poland and later half of Asia, when Japan attacked Pearl Harbor, and when the United States army captured Paris, this generation were children in primary or grammar school. The epic course of events which framed the lives of mature men was no more real to them than the Spanish-American War is to me—remembered chiefly because as a child I patted the nose of my father's cavalry horse, and saw Admiral Dewey parade triumphantly through the streets of Boston.

Yet the concern and interest of these young people is real. Their daily routine has been powerfully changed by the continuing momentum of these vast international movements. The young men are liable to draft just when they get ready to marry the young girls of their age. Headlines of foreign policy thus have direct personal impact. Quarrels over possession of far-away Formosa, Arab attacks on Israel or vice versa, Egyptian seizure of Suez, disputes over independence of Algeria or Morocco, or revolt in Argentina, may immediately affect their individual lives. In good American tradition, they rightly have a feeling that somehow America must take part in guiding events if the world is not to blow itself to pieces. Most of them want some background and, if possible, some sense of direction.

The "problem of foreign relations" actually is the problem of life in the modern world, though with special reference to those phases of it compelled by the fact that the United States lives, and now can only live, in some sort of continuous contact with most of the rest of the earth.

The explanations I have given under these circumstances had to be in the simplest terms; there will be little new here for specialized students. It is perhaps worth while to collect these explanations for the pleasure of some and the possible use of others, to introduce the new generation to the problems bequeathed to them by a predecessor generation.

The world conflict of our time was obviously not suddenly projected on to the twentieth century from a vacuum. Each problem in it represents a current climax of earlier developments and forces, many of which have been in progress for many centuries. Yet the fact that each of them involves most of the world is, of course, a relatively new, typically twentieth century phenomenon. The vast increase of world population in the last century and a half, the great increase in productive power occasioned by modern technology, the shrinking of the world through immediate modern communication like radio, rapid air transport, and the ability to deliver benefit or destruction through medicine or atomic weapons over vast distances, have unquestionably changed matters. Few international conflicts today can take place in comparative isolation —as did, for example, the Spanish-American War, the Boer War, and the Russo-Japanese War in my childhood. Nevertheless, despite the intensification and general involvement due to this outstanding twentieth century factor, it is still true that the essential forces behind each situation are those developed out of history, and solutions are primarily worked out in localized terms.

Regrettably, American schools do not as a rule teach world history or geography (some say, do not teach any history or geography) with sufficient scope and accuracy to give American young men and women enough background even for elementary understanding. I have endeavored to put in a little stage-setting in these pages. It is not to be confused with solid history: rather, it is as though, standing on a hill in current affairs, one took a rapid glance through a telescope at the long trail by which one arrived. It may be hoped that in some of the more interested readers this may stimulate a desire to read history more widely and to look at a globe. There is an unpleasant amount of truth in the aphorism that a nation which knows no history is condemned to repeat it. In the twentieth century, it is all too plain that we can not afford the luxury of repetition.

I can not, obviously, write without some bias—not, I hope, of the emotional type, but simply because I have had some personal contact with great areas of world affairs since 1918. Indeed it is difficult for me to write without evoking pictures. The picture of Woodrow Wilson entering Paris in December, 1918, with the pale winter sunlight falling on a hundred thousand or more people massed in the Place de la Concorde, weeping at the fact of present and hope of future peace. Or that of riding on a captured German gun down the Paris boulevards as all France celebrated the signing of the Treaty of Versailles. Or the hopes raised by the Washington Disarmament Conference of 1922; or the sullen faces of men on the dole in England or, later, wiped out in West Indies or South America by the economic crash of 1929. Or again, President Roosevelt's knitting together of the American hemisphere in Argentina in 1936; of the group of anxious men in the Department of State (we called it "the death-watch over Europe") which scanned the cables as moment by moment brought World War II closer. The disaster-stricken diplomats bravely putting on hopeful faces who filed through my office on January 1, 1942 to sign the "Declaration by United Nations," which constituted the Grand Alliance in World War II. The closing days of the Chicago Air Conference in 1944 which opened the airways for the free world. The massive enthusiasm of Latin American statesmen for Western Hemisphere union at the meeting of American countries in the old castle at Chapultepec. The silence in the Embassy garden at Rio de Janeiro as thousands filed through it, many in tears, when news came of

Franklin Roosevelt's death. Obviously, an actor however minor can not write with complete detachment. Attempt has been made none the less to evaluate evidence and reach fair conclusions.

A book like this does not purport to be complete. The world is a large place. Particularly in the Far East, the evidence is not yet in. All that can be hoped is that for those who are beginning to study and for the millions who, with little background, recognize the need of trying to understand current crises, this may prove of value.

I am indebted to Miss Margaret Poole who has struggled with the manuscript; to my friend, Professor C. Mildred Thompson who was kind enough to discuss many phases of it; and to my colleagues in Radio Free Europe and the College de l'Europe Libre at Robertsau, Strasbourg, who follow the Mid-European crisis area. The substance of the chapter, "Rethinking American Foreign Policy," appeared in *The New Leader,* which kindly gave permission for its use here in different dress.

ADOLF A. BERLE, JR.

Columbia University
New York City
January 1, 1957

INTRODUCTION: WHAT ARE MODERN "INTERNATIONAL RELATIONS"?

1

As WORLD WAR II fades into history, American strategists, schools of economics, and even newspaper readers, become uneasily aware that the traditional base on which international affairs were conducted has changed.

Technically, international relations are relations between "States" —which are defined as "sovereign political unities." These have fixed geographic boundaries which are the result of history. A sovereign political State may be tiny, like the Vatican State, which surrounds the Vatican inside Rome, or the minuscule States of Monaco or Andorre. Or they may be vast like China, India, the Soviet Union, Canada, Brazil or the United States. Each has been brought, also by process of history, under one government which maintains order in and can claim to speak for the State. These are, in theory, the units with which the Department of State and its equivalent ministries in other countries, and their embassies and diplomats have to deal. This condition has existed for practical purposes since the end of the feudal system (say, the seventeenth century) when royal houses and their possessions were the real units in the international game.

Only—here the changed base—combined technical and economic expansion of the twentieth century has undercut this classic and simple framework of States. From the sixteenth to the nine-teenth centuries, even a tiny country or State could claim with some plausibility to be master of its own destiny. A small army, if determined, could put up a very stiff fight for defense. Before the rise of modern technology, most States were more or less self-supporting; at any rate they were close enough to it to be able to exist for considerable periods of time even when cut off from the outside world. Those were the times, of course, when population was relatively sparse, when living standards were low, and when the agricultural product of most countries yielded a more or less adequate supply of food. Household crafts and hand labor supplied the products we today know as "manufactures." The number of articles which had to be obtained from abroad was not great; the really valuable foreign trade dealt in luxuries rather than necessi-ties.

The explosion of technical progress occurring in the latter part of the mid-nineteenth century which vastly accelerated during the first-half of the twentieth, changed this in two respects: economic and military. Economic problems multiplied with an enormous rise in population. Europe, since 1815, more than quadrupled in popu-lation. The United States in a similar period multiplied itself more than ten times. A somewhat similar increase went on in a great many countries. This meant more mouths to feed and more families to rear. The old primitive handcraft life, besides being insufficient to meet the need, no longer answered the general desire. To satisfy a population meant vastly increasing both scope and intensity of economic operations. By the close of World War II, if not before, the need of few if any States could be fulfilled from within the frame of their accepted geographic borders. This meant, in sub-stance, that every State with the possible exception of those falling into two categories, was compelled to exist not only as a "sov-ereign political unit" but also as part of some sort of international community, formal or informal, making it possible to exchange on a large scale goods and services with other nations as well. The two possible exceptions are, of course, the extremely large countries— if, indeed, any of them are capable of territorial self-sufficiency—

and the surviving, remnant States living on an aboriginal basis. The few, if any, aboriginal States left in the world scarcely count in the balance. Meanwhile even the largest territorial States can hardly exist if limited to the economic resources found within their boundaries. The United States, for example, a large State as nations go (though smaller than either Canada, the Soviet Union or Brazil) could seriously think of itself as self-sufficient before World War I. But today the United States must have certain necessaries—not to mention luxuries—from abroad if it is to maintain itself on anything like its present standard of living. It must draw copper and manganese from South America and Canada, uranium from the Belgian Congo, sugar and bauxite (the raw material for aluminum) from the Caribbean, natural rubber from the Far East or Brazil, tin from Bolivia or Malaya not to mention luxuries such as coffee, spices, and so forth. Even our basic steel industry relies now on Venezuelan and Labrador ore, and we should be close to the danger line if not beyond it if we were to rely only on domestic production of petroleum.

Countries less favored than the United States either because they have smaller land area (such as Great Britain or Italy) or because their large areas must support a huge and dense population (such as India and China) are in worse shape. Cut off Great Britain from access to some international system (the Germans nearly did this by submarine warfare in World War I and World War II) and a fair proportion of Britain would probably starve. Isolate India or China from the rest of the world, and the ensuing pressures almost compel explosion.

In result a State, though "sovereign" can *only* exist on a basis satisfactory to its population—even in time of peace—as part of some international system assuring access to economic resources of other States. The accident of history which determines geographic frontiers has endowed no State with a complete kit of supplies.

Militarily, this modification of sovereignty is even more drastic. It was possible, in older times, for a country to defend its frontiers in a land war where its men and women were determined and its armies were resolved. One way or another, a hostile force could be beaten off. In any case its operations could be made so expensive that defense more or less matched offense. A determined though tiny Netherlands could and eventually did beat off the armies of the Spanish Empire in the sixteenth and early seventeenth centuries when the Spanish Empire was one of the most powerful States in the world. A struggling United States could and eventually did expel British armies from the thirteen original colonies. Today, few strategists would support the proposition that a country materially weaker in population and economic resources could alone seriously hope to beat off a serious attack by a country which had much larger reserves of manpower backed by modern arms and resources.

Actually, in modern war the geographic frontier of a Nation-State has lost much of its significance. True, there is still a frontier line on every map. It can be fortified with barbed wire and with Maginot Lines of concrete. But this means little now to a flight of airplanes, navigated at or near sonic speeds, at altitudes of 40,000 feet and up. Frontier lines will mean still less tomorrow to the guided missiles which are beginning to make their appearance. Thus, serious defense today can not depend on a national system. It demands an international system permitting detection of attack hundreds or thousands of miles outside the national frontier, and interception facilities in depth all the way back; and there is no certainty that even these will suffice. At the least, defense of any State requires cooperation of many other States merely to have access to the necessary geography.

Obviously, also, war implies a vastly accelerated consumption of the most complicated combination of materials. To maintain either sustained defense or attack under conditions of mechanical warfare necessitates a whole variety of esoteric materials—for example, industrial diamonds and mica; uranium, cobalt, strange metals. The economic demands of peace are limitlessly multiplied.

To state the second conclusion technically: no modern State can hope to defend itself for any sustained period, *except* as part of a system embracing a number of other States.

It must be added that the system which provides the economic base for peaceful existence of any State is not, necessarily, geographically the same as the system which provides the base for its sustained defense. Conceivably the United States might operate a peacetime economy without recourse to the resources of Canada, though happily for both countries we do not have to do so. But it would be entirely impossible to conduct the air defense of the United States in event of war with the Soviet Union if we did not have access to the geography of Canada for detection, interception and defense in depth.

The result is that foreign policy everywhere in the world seeks to build international and supra-national systems. Failure to do so would be suicidal either in maintaining peaceful civilization or in carrying on effective defense. There is as yet no norm, no accepted method of working out a supra-national system. In older times, strong countries simply conquered the geography they believed they needed and called the result an empire. But empires, besides being out of fashion, have proved impossible to operate. Alliances constitute another method. But alliances have proved transitory, and history as a general rule shows them unreliable. The interest of any member of the alliance may change at any time. A simple system of "friendly relations" with most States worked fairly well through the nineteenth century; but "friendly relations" depend entirely on the mood of the countries involved. Today, the change of mood of a country might shatter economic and military relations to a point which imperiled the life of one or more of them; and nations, if they can avoid it, do not trust their lives to the moods of other peoples.

The problems of force relations in a crisis, later discussed, are in large measure problems arising from this change of base. The statesman knows and the peoples suspect what the language of ordinary American politics has not yet comprehended: that "sovereignty" can no longer mean "go-it-alone." Every sovereign, even a State as powerful as the United States or the Soviet Union, must find common ground with a large group of other States or must walk in peril of its national life.

2

Politics in any State necessarily speaks in terms and uses arguments
that its people understand. This means that in considerable measure, it talks the language of the past, for who understands and who
can demonstrate the unknowable future? For the past four centuries politics everywhere has talked the language of sovereign nationalism based on "national interest." But, suddenly, the "interest"
of countries, especially the greatest, becomes unclear. It has become
a "national interest" to find common ground with a group of other
sovereign States. But these have their "interests" too, and the only
way of creating a group with any hope of success is to base it on
common interests. Purely nationalist terms are commonly popular
at home. They may be disastrous in holding together a group; and
disaster to the group becomes itself a national disaster to each
member. The most honorable politician working in the foreign relations field has therefore a dangerous role to play. Anything he
advocates must be introduced to his constituency as conducive to
its national advantage. The diplomat must persuade a group of
other countries that it is their national advantage as well. Nationalist politicians frequently have to go farther; they have to persuade
their supporters that their countries are getting the best of a deal,
implying that the associated countries have somehow got the worst
of it. International arrangements do not flourish against that sort
of background. This phase of political debate—it exists in all countries—is probably passing. Our generation may be seeing the end
of it. The youth now being educated probably understand better
than the preceding generation the amazing interdependence which
modern development has forced on the twentieth century world.
If the fact is not clear to any groups now, the sheer pounding
growth of the world's population, the demands on its resources and
the increasingly intricate dependence of every national economy
on every other national economy will be convincing within a decade
or so.

One can thus forecast the outlines of future political debates on
foreign affairs with reasonable safety. Pressure for group action

will mount. Groups of producers will want a certain outlet or market for their product—as our cotton and wheat farmers want overseas markets. Groups of manufacturers will insist on supplies, as our electronics factories are demanding more copper, but they will also demand protection from foreign competition. Groups of exporters will demand help because less-developed countries to which they sell have not American dollars to pay for their product. Other groups will demand that safe and certain lines of communication may be developed, so that they can bring in their bauxite or their oil, or supply manufacturers in Brazil or Britain with their product. The economics may well become insoluble within the conventional national frame.

Politicians or statesmen will then propose solutions. Some of them will be novel, perhaps sweeping. They will immediately be attacked by the opposition. Insistence will be made that the solution "impairs the sovereignty" of the United States. Or, perhaps, that it involves a give-away of American resources. Or, possibly, as our aviation industry is unwisely doing now, that the United States ought to get clear from all entanglements and make sharp bargains as and where it can. Opportunist solutions will be tried and they will break down, as opportunist solutions usually do. Increasingly, economists with their figures, merchants and farmers with their problems of markets and supply, bankers with their problems of foreign exchange, processors with their problems of raw materials, will slough off the individualist approach in order to get toward a working solution. One can expect that exactly the same debates will be going on in other States throughout the world. Everyone will be seeking some sort of framework within which an acceptable life can go on; and that means a system comprising other sovereign States. Theorists will have raised the question whether "sovereignty" really exists in a modern world—indeed, this has been done already. Realistic thinking will ultimately prevail; but it will, surprisingly, be found that realism and idealism are not always as far apart as is sometimes asserted.

In current politics this will be assumed to be revolutionary. To a historian, that assumption will be less valid. There have been times in the history of the world when nationalism was not the primary political force; indeed during much of history international affairs have been strongly influenced if not dominated by supranational influence. Two illustrations will suffice: one from the Middle Period—the fourteenth century—and one from a still earlier period—the ninth.

Americans study the history of England as the history of an individual country—as though England as a nation was there from the beginning. But the fact was otherwise. In 1066 William the Conqueror, a Norman Duke, overcame the Saxon kings; he then made England a dependent province of his powerful French Duchy. The real capital of England was at Rouen, France. Presently the throne of England became merely one of a string of thrones held by the great feudal house of Anjou (known in England as "Plantagenet"—"heathersprig," with which the Angevin nobles adorned their helmets). The "English" heroes of that history—for instance, Richard Lionheart, and his great mother, Eleanor of Aquitaine— were certainly kings and queens of England; but their language was French, many of them spent most of their time in one or another part of the empire of the house of Anjou whose base was in France and which at its zenith ruled kingdoms in Italy, central Europe and the Holy Land as well as England. When there was a struggle over the English crown, a French army was quite often imported; it was, for example, a French army that helped to overthrow Crookback Richard III. The real independence of England was perhaps not solidly established until the time of Henry VIII; and even then, his daughter, Queen Elizabeth, had to fight a powerful group of local nobles working with the French and sometimes Spanish kings whose candidate was Mary Queen of Scots—partly French and partly Stuart.

There was, of course, plenty of nationalism in England and it was steadily making its way to the fore. But the fact that the real struggle for power was a struggle by continental European feudal houses shocked almost no one. This was normal. Loyalty ran, not to the nation, but to the reigning house; the object of the reigning house was not to develop any particular England, but to be a sort of holding company for as many kingdoms, dukedoms and counties as it could gather by conquest, marriage or intrigue. Fundamentally, it was Queen Elizabeth I who planted herself squarely within the geographical bounds of England. It was Shakespeare and the Elizabethan poets and writers who finally established England as a cultural reality. Before that era, international relations were not the relations of sovereign states. They were the relations of sovereign families, who were, on the whole, the most convinced internationalists (in an older sense) Western history has yet seen.

A second illustration comes to mind. Europe had been briefly, though very imperfectly, united under the single crown of Charlemagne in the year 800. This did not mean that the areas we know today as Germany were really united to the areas we know today as Italy, France, Hungary, and so forth. It meant that the armies and chieftains in these countries acknowledged this great leader as their overlord. He, with a surprising wisdom, knew perfectly well that mere military expansion of his rule would not do very well or last very long. To bring some unity into the picture, he called in the Catholic Church and where the Catholic Church did not exist, he imposed it by force. This gave him at least a single philosophical and cultural center. When his empire was divided among his three sons, and gradually broke into fragments, they were really the result of revolts—the unity of the empire ceased to exist.

Then arose a real international influence. The Mohammedans in the East were attacking and threatening to seize all Europe, much as the Soviet Union threatened to do in 1947. Their forces were in the Balkans, in North Africa, in the southern part of Italy, in Spain. A German, Otto of Saxony, known to history as Otto the Great, succeeded to a mid-German kingdom which included a substantial part of what today is known as Austria. It was a fairly solid kingdom—but in no shape to defend all Europe against the tide of Moslems which was rising once more. (That tide had only been stopped from seizing all Europe because Charlemagne's grandfather, Charles Martel, had defeated a Mohammedan force at Poitiers seventy miles south of Paris in the year 732.) Otto called in his counselors to consider the situation. Their advice and his conclusion was that he should try to reconstitute a supra-national combination—the ancient "Roman Empire"—and use that as a nucleus to gather in one combination the kingdoms of Europe which were still independent. His representatives broached this idea to Pope John XII. This Pope knew the danger quite as well as Otto; it was in fact already loose on the Italian peninsula in the form of a Moorish army which was rapidly establishing an infidel kingdom. He accordingly agreed and in 962 A.D. crowned Otto "Roman Emperor" with suzerainty over all countries which were Christian or had been Christian and had been conquered by the Eastern enemy. With that as a base, Otto worked up the combination of nations which a century later became known as "The Holy Roman Empire." It was far from perfect and perhaps never was an administrative success. But it was good enough to pull the situation together, maintain a moderately effective defense and even establish a loose working relation with what was left of the classic Roman Empire in Byzantine Constantinople (the Istanbul of to-day). The Holy Roman Empire lasted for more than eight centuries; it was only demolished in 1806 by Napoleon.

This empire was strictly supra-national. There was a whole constellation of kingdoms, duchies and principalities, most of them tough in their independent life. But they worked within the framework of the dream of a universal empire to which all Europe paid heed, and in which most of Europe acquiesced. Loose as this conception was, it was good enough to draw great parts of Europe into a degree of common defense when absolutely necessary, and to answer the deeper need of a common ideology—through the doctrine of the Catholic Church and the canon law.

Translate this into terms of today. The Communist world claims a common religion—Marxian Communism. This is interpreted from time to time by Communist congresses—such a congress was held in early 1956. In Communist theory, the Soviet Union is the Soviet Union. Communist Poland, Czechoslovakia, Hungary, and so forth, are independent States—but they must act within a common ideological framework—that of the Communist lay religion. Theoretically, the political sovereignty of these States is apart from this: the Soviet Union is merely the largest and most powerful national sovereignty within the combination, though it claims seniority and prestige from the fact that it has been Communist longer and has had the greater success and power.

Obviously, Communist political rulers—the custodians of power —intermix as powerfully as they can with the Communist Party people—the custodians of ideology. Most experts believe that the Soviet power machine uses the Communist Party; the Communist Party does not use the Soviet political machine. This was indeed the principal achievement of the dictatorship of Josef Stalin; he made himself Secretary of the Communist Party as well as the dominant figure in the Soviet power apparatus. In this respect, the method he followed was very much like the methods which the Hapsburg emperors of the sixteenth century (notably Charles V, and later Philip II of Spain) evolved in their own conquests, though no Holy Roman Emperor ever went so far as to try to make himself Pope as well. He was generally satisfied with a title and position which gave him at least nominal control of such temporal force as the Church possessed or had the right to call upon; he was the eldest son of the Church or, at times, the Church's Generalissimo. He, like Stalin or the present Bulganin-Khruschev combination was using a supra-national ideological force to hold a disparate group of peoples together.

The word "supra-national" is a bitter one to nationalists in the United States as elsewhere. How, it is asked, can a man be a patriot if he believes in supra-nationalism anywhere? How can there be divided loyalty? How can anyone be honestly a citizen of his own country unless he believes in "America First" or "Great Britain First" or "France First," as the case may be? It is a far cry from Kipling's Englishman back to the days when that Englishman's ancestor, though he was proud of being English, expected as a matter of course to give his allegiance to a supra-national Plantagenet or Stuart.

Yet—here realism comes in—no solid combination of nations has ever existed except on the basis of a core of ideas which overpassed geographical frontiers of component States and went beyond the political ideas of each sovereign political unit. In the nature of things it could not be otherwise. Something had to exist to which all the men in all the lands subscribed and which induced them to common action. Actually when the "Voice of America" today proclaims the doctrine of "freedom" throughout the world to offset Communist propaganda, it is endeavoring to do just that: it is saying, in substance, that the human interest in "freedom" and loyalty to it is higher than loyalty to a country (like, say, Communist Hungary) which denies it. When during World War II Great Britain and the United States alike appealed to citizens of countries engulfed by Hitler's armies to overthrow puppet Nazi governments and enlist under the Allied armies, they were doing the same thing. The "sovereign" political unity of France was the Vichy government of Marshal Pétain. Americans and British saw nothing wrong with asking Frenchmen to deny their allegiance to that "France" and to fight for the supra-national values of "freedom." We said that without "freedom" no real "France" existed; that the sovereign political State had become meaningless unless certain supra-national values were established and maintained.

Despite the anger raised by the word "supra-national," it will be seen that the rule holds good even for America. Suppose, for example, that a Communist dictatorship were established in the United States by a combination of Russian force and Russian intrigue or subversion. The bitterest American nationalist would probably be the first to insist that this was not "America" because it violated and trampled on the freedom of individuals, and he would probably join with any foreign center of resistance just as the Free French and the Free Italians joined with Great Britain and the United States in overthrowing Fascist regimes.

In some ways the history of the twentieth century is much closer to the history of the tenth and thirteenth centuries than it is to the history of the eighteenth and nineteenth centuries. But in our case the impulse towards common units made up of many sovereign political States is backed more solidly than it was when the Roman Empire was reconstituted to resist the Saracens. Then the chief drive (it was not always successful) was that of common defense and common attachment to the Christian religion. Today, there is not merely the need of common defense and agreement on certain spiritual principles. There is also, as we have seen, the ceaseless pounding of economics.

3

Cast in these terms, the problem of international relations takes on a new aspect.

Sovereign States naturally will still seek the advantage of their citizens. They will still like to be topdog in power relationships—to have the largest military potential, the most advantageous position if appeal is made to force. They will, of course, want relations which give their citizens the advantage in economic bargains; which will make them rich and comfortable and safe. They will want to be able to sell their products at a satisfactory price and to buy their needs at will. Self-interest does not vanish in the slightest. But they will and indeed already do increasingly realize that these interests—they are quite human—can be achieved only if similar interests of other sovereign States in the combination can likewise be safeguarded and satisfied.

It will likewise be clear that for the first time in recent history, the solvent goes beyond either defense or economics—it goes beyond guns or butter. The greatest problems are spiritual, philosophical and cultural. The essential struggle is for values. The world will divide, if divide it must, along the line of value systems. The common denominator of any group of nations lies in those values all of them are prepared to try to realize and which in case of necessity all of them are prepared to defend.

This is not the common language of international relations, nor of ordinary politics. Much of the current discussion indeed has revolved around issues which are fundamentally secondary in importance.

For example, it has been said that the free world believes in "private property" whereas Communism does not. But well over half the free world States are in greater or less degree socialist. Great Britain—anything but a Communist country—has gone very far in eliminating "private" ownership of many enterprises—coal, for example. Rail transportation in most of Western Europe is State-owned. For that matter, the precise difference between State-ownership of a railroad or of a telephone system and widely diffused ownership in which many hundreds of thousands of shareholders have a piece of paper called a stock certificate and no other relation to the property whatever is open to question. If men were asked to accept the terror of atomic war solely to assure that railroads, steel plants and telephones would be owned by private stockholders instead of by the State, probably most of them would vote that the difference was not great enough to justify the agony. The chief difference, anyway, boils down to whether the American Telephone and Telegraph Company, the Union Pacific Railroad or U.S. Steel Company is to be managed by a self-perpetuating board of directors, or by a government bureau with the probable lowering of efficiency as a result. An American who considers the current contest as essentially a contest over the choice of operators, or the mechanics of operating, or even the division of the profits of great enterprises simply does not understand the issue. Soviet propagandists, for that matter, make the same mistake. There are people, probably, who see little point in fighting a war to impose "peoples' ownership" (in practice, State-ownership and control of economic enterprise). The real issue in each case is whether everyone has a reasonable share of the services rendered by transportation, or coal mines, or communication services, or manufacturing establishments and whether he can choose his life-development instead of having the State apparatus choose it for him. The issue is free individual will and social justice, not the mechanics of operation. The contest is over values.

The free world maintains that the life, the mind, the heart, individual perception and the soul of each individual is important for itself, and that any economic system, socialist or private, is tested by its usefulness in preserving and liberating that individual. Both the Communist and the Nazi philosophers proclaim that the highest development of civilization is a composite known as the "State"; that this alone is important and that all individual development is tested by its usefulness in promoting the interest of the State. Communists, of course, claim that in some distant Nirvana the State will "wither away" (this becomes possible, they think, with the disappearance of private property, after which in some unexplained way, civilization will be automatically operated). Between maintaining the value of the individual because he can possibly apprehend eternal values, and affirming the value of a State to which everything must be sacrificed, there is a limitless gulf.

This is why in any grouping of sovereign States, desertion of the accepted value system produces the most violent repercussions. The oldest grouping of States in the world is the Organization of American States—the United States plus the twenty American republics of the Caribbean, and Central and South America. Within that group there have arisen governments which denied the value of individual life—for example, Peron's Argentina. When the United States saw fit to cajole Peron's government with loans and favors, it outraged the sensibilities of much of Latin America. A common denominator of the inter-American system was shaken. This even led to the initiation of serious discussions by a number of South American statesmen as to whether the hemispheric system, built up over many years, should not now break up. The longer-headed Latin Americans defend the continuance of the system, doing so on the ground that few American politicians or diplomats would enjoy. They say, in substance, that governments can make mistakes and that the government of the United States has recently made a great many. But, they contend, the government of the United States in these respects does not represent the sound instincts of an American public which will eventually demand that the Department of State live up to a value system and will rectify past errors.

Difficulty arises from the fact that the United States has no formal or recognized institutional custodian of its value system. We do not have a semi-independent State church, as does Great Britain, whose heads sit in the House of Lords and are called the "Lords Spiritual." Not being a Catholic country, we do not look to any group of bishops or to decrees of any Catholic Council. We have had in our history independent Lords Spiritual whose wisdom and thought and statements had general acceptance: the late President Charles W. Eliot of Harvard was such a man in his time. It is difficult today to think of any university president who considers that serving the American value system is his major function; the intellectuals of the United States have not been thinking along this line and have not had the instinct of mobilizing their thought. In foreign relations the government of the United States is the chief— indeed almost the only—spokesman, possibly augmented by the supporting voices of the heads of great corporations. But as a rule neither politicians nor businessmen have been trained to accept the responsibility of Lords Spiritual.

Twice in recent history the United States has had politicians who did accept that responsibility. One of them was Woodrow Wilson; he elaborated a system of values in his war speeches and made them a creed under his famous "Fourteen Points." Being a politician, his ideas were unhappily involved in his politics and his regime came to an end in 1920 with an adverse vote against him. Value systems do not take their validity from a majority vote at any given moment. Their political validity lies in the fact that they become accepted over the years by most men and women as principles of conduct. Britain would not, for instance, submit the creeds and doctrines of the Anglican Church to an election, and discard them in case of an adverse vote.

The other exception was President Franklin D. Roosevelt. He was an out-and-out politician, and a master of the art. But he was vividly aware of the fact that the world combination he succeeded in building through war had been held together while it lasted, and would survive in future, on a broader basis than the temporary need of mutual defense. He therefore proposed, and Winston Churchill in his incomparable English drafted, the "Atlantic Charter"; and he later endeavored to crystallize the value system in the "Four Freedoms"—Freedom from Fear; Religious Freedom; Freedom of Information; and Freedom from Want: "to preserve human rights and justice" in their own lands as well as in other lands (Declaration by United Nations, January 1, 1942). It is not an accident that the two greatest combinations of nations in which the United States has played a leading part—the Allied and Associated Powers in World War I and the United Nations in World War II—framed their battle cry in a moral synthesis.

To ridicule this fact is easy. Nothing is simpler than to claim that moral maxims and the help of the Lord Almighty are invoked to cover the brutalities of war and to camouflage self-seeking operations. There is adequate historical precedent for this viewpoint. Religion has often been invoked as a justification for naked imperial seizure. But in international relations as in all human action motives are generally mixed. The historical fact is that the combinations and the empires, which were most faithful to an ethical conception, survived the longest. The most cynical realist must take account of this fact.

Perhaps also, on balance, it will be found that the combinations —even the empires—which had this fidelity to ethical conceptions and expressed it in administration of policy did more for the areas and peoples involved than was done by anyone else. Even today in the anti-colonial populations emerging from the old British Empire there is higher content of like values than in the case of most areas which maintained independent government. The real tie which held the British Empire together was the British conception of individual justice under law and an incorrupt administration trained to give a measure of fair play to all hands within its jurisdiction. Nations like men tend to become the servants of the ideals they profess.

Your true student of international affairs (if he is wise) does not attempt to compete with St. Peter. The ethical professions on which international affairs are based have often been motivated by selfishness. Many of the men who have uttered them may well be damned as hypocrites. But the problem is whether the conception itself has soundness and force. If it does, it will eventually dictate action even by self-seeking politicians. Still more certainly when the politicians depart from their professions of faith, the structures they have built are shaken, become weak, and may eventually dissolve, as Soviet politicians are discovering.

4

This poses the problem we here examine.

Governments in international relations are now, and for a long time will be, the sovereign political units we call "States." Their geographical frontiers are results of history and are increasingly incongruous in solving the twin problems of economic life and military defense in the twentieth century. They are, nevertheless, intensely important in maintaining the cultural, sociological and linguistic framework within which the peoples within these borders like to live. The Greek likes to speak and think as a Greek; so, he wants Cyprus within the geographical frontiers of Greece though Cyprus never was part of the sovereign State we call Greece; though Cyprus economically must live on commerce only vaguely related to Athens; though the Greek State could not defend Cyprus were it seriously attacked from the Turkish mainland forty miles away.

It follows that we are really searching for new dimensions in international relations. Greeks like the combination of language, customs, manners, religion and culture which we call "Greek" and will fight to maintain it, just as the United States likes its own way of life, and Americans will go out and defend it. This may be called the "social" basis of sovereignty. But to maintain Greece as Greece —or even the United States as the United States—requires an international fabric far beyond the borders of either country if Greeks are to eat, and if Americans are to live as they obviously like to live. This calls for a second layer—the economic system permitting each "sovereign" to have the material for its economic life, without which it could not maintain its socio-cultural life. To achieve this involves geography and communications which have nothing to do with geographic frontiers. Finally, no nation-State has established geographic frontiers which given even remote assurance that, in case of war, the country will not be bombed into a bloody pulp, especially as guided missiles become practicable weapons. It is probable that, eventually, this defense problem can be solved only by a world-wide organization of this planet, which is why the

United Nations is important. In the long run, the world will probably demand at least in this third layer a universal organization —a sort of "one world" in the sense that the short-wave radio has created one communication world already.

It follows also that when any international situation is examined, or when any politician discusses it, a student of international affairs must ask himself what layer is being discussed. A Greek may be right in demanding that Cyprus become part of the sovereign Greek cultural State. He may or may not be wholly impractical when he demands that it be included in the Greek economic State. He might be merely stupid if he insisted on its relying for defense on the Greek military State. To arrive at solutions, we should be steadily evolving new frames and new devices, unknown to the international law of recent history.

In blunt fact, it is as absurd to tackle twentieth century foreign relations in terms of eighteenth century concepts as it would be to try to navigate a modern liner like the Queen Mary with the sail of an eighteenth century schooner. Or, if you like, to erect a radio network on plans drawn for a semaphore system.

International relations are still relations between sovereign States. Each State has a Ministry of Foreign Relations (ours is the State Department) and maintains embassies in the capitals of other countries. Primarily each State makes individual arrangements by treaty or otherwise with each of the ninety-odd States which make up the inhabited world. These are outright "government-to-government" relationships; they are the daily grist of the diplomats' trade.

Yet within these individual relationships, great groups have already formed. One such group, comprising about half the world's population, is held together chiefly because its governments profess a common doctrine—the doctrine of "Communism." This group has a growing pattern of economic exchange; the Soviet Union is the acknowledged leader of it though Communist China is warily reaching for an equal position, probably with an eye to supremacy at some future time.

Outside the Communist bloc, the oldest and largest geographic group is the American world—the United States plus the other twenty American Republics we commonly call "Latin America." The name is a misnomer, because Haiti is a Negro Republic, while both Mexico and Bolivia are predominantly Indian. These twenty-one States profess a common doctrine—that of the rights of man—and are organized into a League—the Organization of American States—and into a mutual defense alliance under the Treaty of Rio de Janeiro (1949). The United States claims no supremacy, but having nearly half of its total population—about 341 million—as well as a preponderance of military and economic strength clearly is the strongest member.

The inter-American combination overlaps another combination —the so-called "North Atlantic Treaty Organization," emerging after World War II. The United States is in this; so also are Canada, Great Britain, France, Italy, Greece, Turkey, and a number of other States. Like the inter-American defense alliance this is an organization primarily in the defense layer of international relations; it is registered as an agreement for collective defense with the United Nations.

Within the North Atlantic Treaty Organization there are smaller groups working on the economic layer. For example, most of the non-Communist West European countries are members of the Organization for European Economic Cooperation (OEEC), designed to assure economic cooperation in postwar recovery. There is even a hopeful if hitherto languid attempt to assure a degree of political and cultural unity for West Europe; this is the statute of the "Council of Europe" which came into existence only in 1949 which looks toward the eventual creation of a united Federal Europe, though its success has thus far been extremely limited.

Elsewhere in the world, the rising Arab States (Egypt claiming to be "Arab" though racially it probably is not) maintain close relations under the name of the "Arab League." Action in respect to any one of the Arab States is pretty apt to involve the others. This probably acts primarily in the defense layer though it is beginning to work in a crude sort of way at the economic level as well.

The Arab League overlaps, dubiously, with another combination at the defense level: the collective defense agreement (Baghdad Pact) between Turkey, Iraq, Iran (formerly Persia) and Pakistan which thus far is an arrangement primarily intended to develop common military defense in case of Soviet or other aggression.

In the Far East the groupings are still indistinct. There is, of course, the Communist combination which includes with the Soviet Union Communist China, North Korea, the Vietminh section of Indochina and the nominally independent though actually Russian or Chinese dominated Asian countries of Inner Mongolia, Outer Mongolia and lofty Tibet. On the free world side there is the still undeveloped "SEATO" (South East Asian Treaty Organization), including the Philippines, Pakistan, New Zealand, Thailand and Australia, with the United States, Britain, and France as parties. This last is again chiefly on the defense level, designed to protect its Asian members against aggression by Communist China, though it can also be developed as well at the economic level.

One of the most interesting groups on the economic level is the European Coal and Steel Community, with its capital in Luxemburg. This, interestingly enough, cuts straight across the old geographic idea of "sovereign" States. It is in terms designed to set up supra-national planning and a total European market for coal and steel, and it includes France, Germany, Belgium, Luxemburg and others; more recently Great Britain has joined it. The "Community" has a certain scope of action without reference to governments. It is a "thing" by itself: the United States sends an Ambassador to it; a purely supra-national body, it depends on a particular kind of activity rather than on geography though the component States still have, without doubt, physical capacity to terminate it should they really desire.

What really goes on here is a slow change of international relations from those of State-to-State to relations within groups and of group-to-group. The strict nationalist relations of one country to another are, as often as not, consultations to find out how they will work or vote in one or more of these particular groupings.

There are, of course, endless smaller groupings around particular economic or military problems. So, there are groupings to stabilize markets for wheat, to deal with the problems of marketing sugar, to deal with the navigation of the Suez Canal, and so forth.

One of the greatest (it is also the least defined) groupings of States is the British Commonwealth of Nations. Aside from Great Britain, its members were at one time or another colonies or possessions of the British Empire. These members are now, to all intents and purposes, independent States: The United Kingdom, Canada, Australia, New Zealand, the Union of South Africa; and also Pakistan, India, Ceylon. Emergent British-African communities like Nigeria and the Gold Coast will presumably enter in time. As originally designed, the single common element was a recognition of allegiance to the symbol of the British Crown; but some member States like India do not even accept that. It has been said that only a poet could understand the British Commonwealth of Nations. Diplomats nevertheless understand that in time of war the member countries, or many of them, will come to the aid of Britain just as Britain would assist them; and the Commonwealth affords opportunity at least for common consultation on economic policy.

This is not to say that the old diplomacy is dead. At long last, probably none of these groupings could really retain within it any member which wished to secede, or force a course of action on a member which really wished to nullify. Great Britain and the United States are both members of NATO, yet, conceivably, a dispute so great could arise that either might withdraw; indeed, that the two might fight each other, though this last seems happily, and substantially, out of the question. Power relationships—that is, physical ability of the component States to mobilize arms and sustain their action—remains (one supposes) the ultimate fact, just as in the eighteenth century Masters of Ordnance wrote that their cannon were the "final argument of Kings." The crucial point is that, increasingly, individual use by any single State of this ultimate power factor has become substantially impossible for any small State, and increasingly difficult for the large ones.

Further, international relations are no longer carried on primarily by Ambassadors and diplomats. Every country has some sort of a press and radio service. There is a degree of penetration of each country by each other country. American papers carry dispatches from Russia and print the substance of the more interesting articles in the Russian press. The Russian press carries, though frequently with distortion, at least a modicum of the news from the United States. Between countries of the free world interpenetration both of ideas and individuals is considerable. The press conference of a prominent American politician will be immediately reprinted throughout France, England, India and Greece, as well as in South America. To some extent, the news from all these countries reaches the United States. What is said powerfully affects relations, not always between governments, but certainly between peoples.

Increasingly also scientific thought and academic study cross national lines. Thousands of students come to the United States from other countries; thousands of American students cross the Atlantic and Pacific to study abroad. Though it is pitifully small in terms of the necessity of common understanding, a substantial degree of knowledge exists in most countries about most other countries. In other words, foreign relations are gradually becoming "people-to-people" relations as well as government-to-government relations.

This may or may not make for peace and good-will. Professor Hans Morgenthau of Harvard and Mr. George Kennan rather wonder whether so high a degree of contact will make for friendship or hostility. We can not tell: the extent of interchange through news, academic contact, tourism, and so forth, has not been great enough nor has lasted long enough for anyone to give a verdict. Clearly an ill-mannered tourist, an unthinking politician, fiercely hostile newspaper headlines or the like can create difficulties. On the whole, despite the opinion of very well-informed men, the writer believes that the contact is good. Foreign relations are not served when one or another people lives in a world of its own, or has a dim or completely false picture of the facts of life in other countries. If, as is here suggested, we are fated to live in groups of nations, some common denominator of thought and action has to be established. Communication is the only way by which this can be achieved.

5

Finally, there are the vast problems emerging as group conflicts with group, or as a conflict between States threatens to shatter the structure of existing groups. Problems arise as new nations emerge from the ruins of old colonial empires. At long last, the problem of world peace depends on solution of these problems more than on any others; and many of these problems could not be solved within groups but must be solved either by war or by some appeal to an organized world.

This is the real reason why the United Nations exists; why, if it were dissolved tomorrow, the world would be obliged in travail to invent it anew.

The United Nations is still an organization of States. The views one hears are not the views of peoples but the views of governments. A government may, or may not, represent its people, but its view has to be heard because it is or at least may be in a position to resort to the "last argument of Kings," mobilize its forces, nullify group decision, even attempt military action. Nevertheless, and despite its shortcomings, the United Nations more nearly permits solution of world-wide problems than any organization which has yet existed. It is an institution in process of development. Its real functions will become more apparent twenty years from now than they are today. One can fairly say that the apparent trend of world forces is almost certain to increase its importance and emphasize its necessity.

The foregoing explains why the conduct of "foreign relations" is essentially a substantial part of life. It explains why in the Department of State you find men working on every phase of life, from distribution of Salk vaccine to determining policy in connection with the Suez Canal; why there are specialists in international organization, in civil aviation, and in the exchange of college professors; why there are economists working on problems of foreign exchange and of the sale of wheat and military specialists working on problems of disarmament; why, in a word, most phases of life are affected by and eventually become matter of foreign relations in greater degree or in less.

TIDES OF CRISIS

THE UNITED STATES IN WORLD LEADERSHIP

1

WORLD LEADERSHIP among nations as the twentieth century passed its half-way mark unquestionably was held by two very great nations. One was the United States, the other the Soviet Union. The oft-quoted prediction of Alexis de Tocqueville had been fulfilled. Of the two, most dispassionate observers would probably have conceded primacy to the United States. American philosophers, American politicians, and American commentators, not unnaturally, have conceded primacy to the United States as a matter of course.

Yet, while it is clear that the two countries were and still are primary contenders for leadership, two bitter observations must be made.

The first is that world leadership can be singularly transient. Shortly after World War I the classic historian of American diplomacy, John H. Latané, wrote a book entitled "From Isolation to Leadership," claiming world primacy for the United States as a result of her participation in World War I. But the election of 1920 ended the Wilsonian era of diplomatic leadership; American private participation in overseas economics was a resounding failure; American public opinion reacted against any entanglement with world problems. It was fairly arguable that there was no adequate economic or military base for world leadership; no psychological or political preparation; even, that the population of the United States at its then productive capacity was far too small and its social problems far too great to permit America's assuming the obligations or exercising the authority implied in the Atlas task of world primacy.

The second observation is that while thirty years later in mid-twentieth century the claim of the United States to world leadership does have an economic, a military and a demographic base, her relative position in the international community may well become less rather than more powerful in the next two generations. Her absolute power will increase. She is quite likely in half a century to attain a population of 250 millions or more. Her productivity, *per capita,* is likely to be increased. Her military potential will be as great as her people agree to make it. But other countries comparable in size and wealth of natural resources are coming up even more rapidly than the United States.

The Soviet Union has now an area of 8,597,000 square miles which is approximately two and one-half times that of the United States. The present population is 200,000,000 which has been increasing at the rate of approximately 4 millions a year. Demographic predictions are no less hazardous than others; but it is not unreasonable to expect that at the close of the century the Soviet Union will have a population of well-over 350 millions in a huge territory as well able to support it as any area in the world. Industrially the Soviet Union is increasing her capacity at a rate more or less comparable to our own though she started from a far smaller base. Relatively, the economic gap should narrow; the United States may well be equalled.

A third contender is Brazil. With an area equal to the United States plus another Texas, a present population of approximately 60 millions and an annual increase of substantially 1½ millions a year, with a not inconsiderable power of organization, and natural resources known to be comparable to the United States, she should end the century with a population of, say, 125 millions, with an economic potential comparable to the present potential of the United States, and a predominant position in the Latin world, European as well as American.

The other competitors are, respectively, China and India—with China far and away the more likely candidate. She claims a population of 600 millions—although the figure is probably exaggerated by at least 20%—and a land area half again larger than the United States. Her territory is large, her industrial resources great though largely unexplored. Her ability to organize her masses is certainly considerable—the Korean war demonstrated that. Sheer weight of numbers gives her a variety of military potential, capable of being matched against the higher economic and organizational factor of the less populous nations. India, of course, with 360 millions of population and an area two fifths the size of the United States remains an enigma: the problem of organizing one choate nation from the diversity of language and race in her subcontinent is probably crucial.

In any case, time and technology probably work toward the appearance of nations basically able to claim equality, if not primacy, in the power politics of the world. From being one of two leaders as at present, American policy must assume at least the possibility that, when our grandchildren come to late middle age, she may be only one among five or six contenders.

That is, unless the organization of world affairs changes form. Our habit of assuming national units is still strong and so deeply rooted that it is difficult for Americans to think in any other terms. Some extremists regard it as almost treasonable to discuss the subject frankly. Yet as we have noted national units—nation-states based on people as we think of them today—have only arisen in the past four centuries. Before then, very great empires indeed were constructed by dynastic nuclei which organized many separate peoples—the Hapsburg Empire of the Emperor Charles V which held acknowledged world leadership in the mid-sixteenth century is an illustration. But nation-states are the base of present international affairs. True, European intellectuals have for years talked about an "integrated" Western Europe, and United States policy attempted to build such an integration when it supported the European Defense Community in 1954–1955 whose cardinal expression was to be a united European army. Had this been attained—or, perhaps better, when it shall be attained for it would appear that despite political setbacks, underlying forces almost compel it—a regional organization multi-national in composition but integrated for the purposes of military, diplomatic, possibly even economic, action would appear. Such a combination would have over 200 millions of population including some of the most highly disciplined, highly organized and highly productive peoples of the world. The nation-state system could change. It has not done so yet.

World leadership can, of course, be maintained despite the fact that there are other national or regional units of comparable or greater size, productivity, military potential and capacity for organization. For one thing, the United States might in itself take a major part in bringing into being a great regional combination of nations, and by soundness in policy and forwardness in thinking be the greatest organizing force in a multi-national group. But this lies ahead, and no one can predict. The important consideration is the fact that American leadership based on her present situation can be counted on only for the next generation. Beyond that, we are dealing in the realm of speculation.

2

If, as the famous remark goes, Britain picked up her nineteenth century empire in a fit of abstraction, the United States acquired world leadership in a fit of indignation, largely as the accidental result of her emotional idealism. Certainly no American Administration or State Department sought it, still less thought out and endeavored to produce the series of events which led to it.

It was, primarily, American anger at the Spanish methods of dealing with her Cuban revolt which laid the base for the Spanish-American War in 1898. In that atmosphere, the incidental explosion which sank the battleship *Maine* opened passionate flood-gates. When the Spanish-American War ended a few months later, the United States without having seriously considered a policy found herself successor to the remainder of the Spanish Empire —including Guam and the great Philippine Archipelago. The extent of this vast area is hardly realized by most Americans even now; the geographic fact is that if it were superimposed diagonally on the continental United States, with one end of the archipelago placed in Oregon, the other end would lie in Florida. Briefly, the United States overnight became a Far Eastern power. A brief and vigorous controversy ensued: would the United States accept imperial position or would she refuse colonial ambition and turn the conquered territories into independent nations? The anti-imperialist view prevailed; Cuba shortly became independent; a pledge to prepare the Philippine Islands for similar independence was made and implemented in the year 1943.

Even more surprising in the light of after history was the second explosion. The slow process of European politics and European diplomacy ground implacably towards World War I as the German-Austrian imperial *bloc* crossed the path of the Russian imperial ambitions in the Balkans and the Near East. But the Russians were then allied with the French and British. The latter particularly feared a continental Europe dominated by a Germany heavily influenced by the ambitions of the German General Staff. World War I was, perhaps, the last of the nineteenth-century wars; the chief stake was primacy over Europe and particularly West Europe carrying with it control over much of Asia and substantially all of Africa which had been parceled out in great colonial areas. The United States conceivably could have stayed aloof —she actually did so for three bloody years.

American public opinion rather rapidly veered to the Anglo-French-Russian side. This was partly anger against Germany, believed to have been the instigator of the war. It was partly an equally violent reaction against the violation of Belgian neutrality and against the alleged brutality of the German armies in that country. In considerable part, it was an instinctive feeling that American national interests were bound up with the effective defense of Britain and France. But the correspondence of President

Wilson indicates that his mind eventually ran towards American intervention in World War I for the purpose of giving the United States a solid stance from which she could influence the making of an eventual peace. Particularly he wanted a world political and diplomatic situation which would serve as guarantee against future wars; and his particular preoccupations were moral. Granted self-determination of nations, control by peoples of their governments and a central organization of nations devoted to suppressing war, he thought the world and with it the position of the United States would be vastly improved.

From the point of view of actual warfare, American participation was more in the way of romantic interlude than serious struggle, though this could not have been foreseen. The total American casualties—126,000 dead, 234,300 wounded—and a total economic participation roughly measurable by the 22 billions of debt incurred in preparation and hostilities were not very much greater than the expenditures of life and treasure in the Korean fighting of 1950–1954—though Korea was regarded as a minor matter while World War I is assumed to be a major struggle. The fact nevertheless was that though the American participation was late, and in terms of conflict relatively little, it proved the decisive margin, partly in and of itself and partly because it made plain to the Central Powers that an infinitely greater potential would be forthcoming if necessary.

For a few brief months in 1919 the United States had world leadership as nearly as it has ever been possessed by a single power. Certainly the policies insisted on by President Wilson at the Versailles Peace Conference were in broad outline accepted (albeit with reluctance) by allies and enemies alike. It is possible that the position might have been maintained had the United States followed up with diplomatic, military and economic participation in European affairs, in the League of Nations and in the assorted questions which promptly arose as a shattered European system desperately tried (and eventually failed) to reconstitute itself. But the United States was unwilling to be involved in the settlement of foreign problems, was preoccupied with an insufficiently organized economy of her own, and was passionately anxious to disarm at once. Her almost total inexperience in the realm of international finance and her lack of sophistication in international economics rendered abortive her economic efforts through private and foreign loans, international export combinations and so forth. Lingering influence maintained itself through the Washington Disarmament Conference of 1922 presided over by Secretary of State Charles Evans Hughes. But isolation was then the shibboleth of Republican and Democratic politicians alike. In retrospect, it is by no means certain that America then had the basic materials for world leadership. Even if she had, the will was lacking. She did not exercise, indeed passionately rejected, whatever opportunity for leadership she then had and devoted herself to problems of internal development and technological progress.

World War II, the third American incursion into world affairs, is essentially the same psychological story repeated, though this time there was consciousness that results must be more fundamental, and the clash of interest was real. In this case, the historical record is far clearer than in the case of World War I. Hitler's program was one of frank aggression, using force where the immediate target nation did not promptly surrender to his will and his domination. He did intend dominating the world, including the American continents. His companion dictator, Mussolini, joined in supporting this. World War II was plainly Hitler's object, his intent and his creation. American indignation had already been whipped up by Nazi brutality—this time not merely alleged but proved, and indeed asserted with scornful arrogance by Nazi leaders as an intended instrument of terror-policy. They were not backward in asserting that their objective was world supremacy. Even so the American public and the Administration of President Franklin Roosevelt then in power did not favor entry into war, though awareness rapidly grew that war might come to the United States if the United States did not go to it.

We have been treated to bizarre contrary theories by some less reputable historians of the extremist political wing. These assert that the Roosevelt Administration fomented the war by endeavor-

ing to check Japanese aggression against China; that President
Roosevelt's personal ambition was to be a world arbiter; that he
therefore provoked a situation in which the Axis Powers eventually
declared war on the United States. These theories may be dismissed for the nonsense they are, and the historical record by
now is complete enough to document this conclusion. The fact
was that the extremist military party in Japan wished war with
the United States. They wished it so badly that (as American
Ambassador to Japan Joseph C. Grew surmised) they altered
Secretary Hull's final telegram to make it appear to be an ulti-
matum. This only became known with the publication of Prime
Minister Yoshida's Memoirs in 1955; the Japanese militarists
had followed the famous precedent created by Bismarck who
altered the famous Ems telegram in 1870 to assure outbreak of
war between Germany and France.

In point of fact, the United States, being a Far Eastern Power,
did attempt to check Japanese aggression against China. History
will form varying conclusions as to the necessity or wisdom of this
procedure; but back of it was a solid desire not to permit a Far
Eastern situation to arise in which a powerful, militarist and race-
conscious Japan, backed by all the resources and manpower of
China, might one day contest with some probability of success for
mastery of the whole Pacific Ocean. As this was precisely what the
militarist extremists in Japan intended to do, they were led astray
by the hope of rapid and cheap victory resulting from a surprise
attack. Pearl Harbor was undoubtedly a surprise, but victory did
not result. Hitler, bound by treaty to his Japanese ally to declare
war in case of Japanese involvement hesitated momentarily, but
forty-eight hours later declared war on the United States. He had
previously committed the major blunder (from the point of view
of his military strategy) of attacking the Soviet Union. Now he
conclusively changed the balance of force against him by attacking
the United States.

And yet, behind the entire situation was the fact that America,
morally, was as indignant against Japanese and Nazi aggression in
1939 as ever she had been against the aggression laid to Kaiser

Wilhelm II in 1914. This time there was an element of fear mixed with anger: a victorious Germany might have executed the design which Hitler's government actually had conceived of attacking the Western Hemisphere. In 1945 American participation was again decisive and this time it was based on the exercise of a very considerable amount of the American war potential, the exhibition of an appreciable amount of military capacity, not to say genius, and the sudden development of the atomic bomb.

But in the twenty-four years intervening between 1917 and 1941, America had enormously increased her total capacity. To document this would require a volume in itself. It is enough for this purpose to say that her population had increased from approximately 100,000,000 in 1917 to 133,230,000 in 1941; that her ingot steel capacity had increased from 55,567,555 net tons in 1917 to 85,158,150 net tons in 1941; that she had successfully wrestled with the problem of bringing a substantially unorganized finance and production system into a more or less choate governmental organism capable of organizing and directing effort, and had —unknown even to herself—accumulated an astonishing reserve of additional energy.

Faced with the exigencies of preparing for possible war in 1940, and prosecuting that war from the end of 1941 to the Summer of 1945, she proved able not only to swing that load, but to increase the standard of civilian life as well. She almost doubled her total productive capacity—and still more importantly—acquired the technical knowledge and skill for doubling again in the ensuing decade. Her military potential had been demonstrated and in some degree at least was maintained with the added augmentation of the atomic bomb, a weapon over which for a few brief years she maintained a monopoly. By comparison with any other power in the world, she was far ahead in everything save the number of soldiers she could maintain in armies. There, America had lesser potential than the highly organized Soviet Union. But this could be compensated by her far greater ability to provide fire power, mechanized transport and weapons, naval support and, above all, air armament.

Perhaps more important even than these necessary material bases was the decisive fact that the United States had acquired a will to exert at least a degree of leadership. Unsought as the leadership position had been, a preponderance of Americans (perhaps not overwhelming but still substantial) felt that the safety of the United States demanded her continued participation in the great theatre of world politics. Part of this was and still is based on moral considerations: the United States has a duty to seek and endeavor to create world peace; a duty to join in preventing aggression; an interest at least in preventing brutality and tyranny from becoming an accepted primary instrument in the administration of peoples. More importantly perhaps there was—and is— awareness that it is no more difficult for foreign powers to send armies across the broad seas against us than it was for the United States against Asian and European enemies. The invasion of North Africa, the landing in Normandy and ensuing reconquest of Western Europe, the crossing of the Pacific, made it sufficiently plain that neither Atlantic nor Pacific was an impassable barrier. In any case, developments in air warfare and the now clear feasibility of guided missiles, either of which could let loose atomic bombs, underlined the fact that the United States was no safer than any other part of the world. Clearly, indeed, her continued safety rested primarily on a state of world affairs in which world war or in fact any war did not occur.

Emphasis must be given to these two separate currents in American public opinion. They are continuously reflected in American politics and as a result in American Administrations. The moral current loosed by President Wilson remains continuous. It fluctuates in political power. It is vigorously attacked as fuzzy-headed altruism, but in the decade since World War II, it has remained a current which most American politicians do not care to oppose. There must be, in this line of thinking, world peace. To have this, there must be minimal enforcible standards in the conduct of international affairs. To have such standards, there must also be certain minimal civilized conditions which prevail in the relations between the government of any nation and the people of that nation.

Therefore, the United States must participate in world affairs, must assume responsibilities comparable to its capacities; must endeavor to exercise an influence for morality and civilization.

The second current comes to the same conclusion from quite different premises. Calculating the mathematics of economic life and military potential, realists are aware of the fact that American safety could be jeopardized at any time by properly organized attack of a power of comparable strength. The Soviet Union, which until the Geneva Conference of July, 1955, made no secret of its hostility to the United States, has the potential of being such a power. In another decade or two, China or a unified Western Europe might enter the lists. The United States as an isolated power no longer has the geography necessary to prevent atomic bomb attacks from the air by plane or rocket. Her huge productivity increasingly requires command of materials from outside the United States, as the so-called Paley Report of the President's Materials Commission first demonstrated in 1953. Effective defense, and continued economic development, requires some adjustment of world affairs which shall steadily diminish the possibility of war. Having played a decisive role in two world wars, it would seem unlikely that in any new upset the principal opposite power will leave the United States undisturbed; rather, she will be the first target at least of air attack. Participation in world affairs, steady attempt to ease tension and growing effort to create a world situation in which no government can seriously consider using war, is in the view of the "realist" group a deadly necessity.

The two currents of opinion thus reach the same conclusion, though they are rarely harmonious. Realists not infrequently accuse the moralists of being starry-eyed. The moralists are frequently unwilling to accept the conclusion that American participation in world affairs does involve the grim business of maintaining a necessary norm of armament, and of being willing to accept the hazard that it may have to be used. Since morality is frequently realism with an extremely long view, it seems at least possible that the two currents may eventually coalesce. Taken together, they supply a continuing element of will. From Pearl Har-

bor onward, the United States, thrust by its emotions to a position
of leadership, has continuously endeavored to exercise according
to its collective wisdom some degree of the authority and to assume a considerable measure of the obligation which leadership
entails.

3

Exercise of leadership invariably presents problems. Puzzling at
best, they are even more puzzling when presented to an involun-
tary-leadership country. A nation which has sought and achieved
world leadership usually has made its choice of method in the
course of its ascent; a nation thrust into that position without having aspired to it must think through the problem from the beginning.

The first and fundamental problem is essentially philosophical.
What is the end really desired? Obviously leadership implies associates if not followers willing to act in accord with the orders, the
direction or the guidance of the leader; else the leader becomes a
general without an army. Yet to achieve this a common denominator must be secured. The old empires relied primarily on force;
their followers or sub-nations obeyed their will in matters considered essential by the leader because failure to do so could mean
the relatively prompt appearance of the leader's army on its
borders. But since military domination produces only limited or
at least temporary results, empires, new and old from the days of
Darius the Persian, to those of the Soviet dictator, Stalin, sought
to erect a body of magic, or mystik, or philosophy predisposing
the subject nations to political organization and political action
concerting with the will of the dominant empire. Superlative efficiency in this form of organization made it possible for the leader
to reserve his armies and military potential primarily for foreign
conquest or, if need be defense, instead of having to disperse them
throughout his dominions to enforce their loyalty and their compliance with his will. Even so, the ultimate reliance was force:
then—as now—the minimum requirement for any leader nation

was an ability to intervene decisively for the maintenance and defense of the sub-countries.

At the opposite extreme, the common denominator of action may be provided by a body of common doctrine kept effective by common consent, leading a community of component nations to take common cooperative action for the protection and well-being of each according to their respective abilities. This, a far more difficult but probably far more permanent form of organization, has been the aim of the United States in those relatively rare moments when American statesmen have endeavored to think through and explain their policy. Somewhat surprisingly in the long course of history the apparently weaker form of leadership by common consent has been successful when challenged militarily about as often as the old imperial form. The League of Greek cities in 432 B.C. tore to pieces first the navy and then the army of the Persian Emperor, Xerxes; the armies of the Roman Republic in the days of its freedom proved more than a match for the empires of Egypt and Carthage. In our own time, leagues of free nations have defeated highly organized empires in World War I and in World War II. Without reviewing the long historical record (it would take a large volume), it is fair to say that the classic technique of empire, despite its solid achievements, has not a record so outstanding as to dictate its choice.

It is an odd footnote to history that precisely this point was discussed by Secretary Cordell Hull with Josef Stalin and Vyacheslav Molotov when Mr. Hull visited Moscow in 1943. The conversation turned on post-war relations. Mr. Hull was perfectly informed of the Communist insistence on world revolution carried out by the Communist Internationale, backed by the resources of the Soviet Union and leading eventually to a thinly disguised Muscovite empire. He was pointing out, tactfully, that while the Communist Internationale existed, every country in the world would feels itself attacked. He took occasion to observe that in 1776 the United States had set up a great democratic republic in a world of empires and king-states, and that in the century following most of the world had followed its example, largely owing to the appeal of the central core of ideas which the American state had endeavored to embody in its government. The American experiment in democracy stood or fell by its internal success; this had been great, other peoples had followed, adopted or evolved the essential principles with like success, and the democratic revolution had triumphed in most of the world. This, he pointed out, had the advantage in international affairs that like-minded nations could achieve programs of common action. He suggested, therefore, that the Soviet Union might well consider in its own interest the achievement of a great and happy and strong Russian people in which case he imagined they would have little lack of imitators.

The Russians made little comment: they were probably not greatly impressed since the Leninist doctrine heaped contempt on "liberal" ideas. Factually, the immediate post-war policy of the Soviet Union was to foment revolution leading to Soviet seizure of power by the direct intervention of their armies. With one exception, no Communist government has been set up in any nation save as a result of direct intervention by Soviet (or in the case of Indo-China, Chinese) troops operating on foreign soil. Even the exception—Czechoslovakia—is apparent rather than real; Russian troops were assembled on three sides of her vulnerable borders and this threat was the chief, perhaps decisive, factor in the success of the Czechoslovakian Communist revolution of 1947.

Between the two extremes of direct military conquest and the setting up of a community of nations, there are, of course, all degrees of possible action. Pure military dictatorial empire is not possible over great areas save for a relatively short time, if only because the leadership-nation must devote and exhaust its resources both of men and material in maintaining and applying force beyond its own borders. In politics, as in geometry, the area of a circle increases by the square of its radius. No nation has yet appeared populous enough, rich enough and with great enough reserve to combine the necessary military and administrative ability to maintain alone a huge empire through a long period of time over unwilling peoples of comparable technical development and ability.

There is in mid-twentieth century an added reason joined to the obvious numerical difficulty.

For the twentieth century offers a picture quite different from that in which empire at its greatest was conceived. Probably the largest single empire attained in recorded history was that of Genghis Khan. From a simple Mongolian chieftain attaining tribal leadership about the year 1200, he had in twenty-eight years made himself and his Mongolians master of an empire roughly equivalent to the Soviet Union and Communist China combined. But great parts of it, especially in the vast Siberian plains, in Central Asia and even in what is now mid-Europe were then inhabited by more or less primitive peoples. Also the warfare of the time permitted armies to supply themselves by ravishing the conquered countries as they went along; the conqueror was not faced with the problem of a continuous service of supply from the central or leadership country to his armed forces on the periphery of his empire. A modern empire has no such luxury; its men, its ships, its airplanes, its machines, its oil and, importantly, its food, must be created and transported from the leadership country. Vastly greater organizational and economic strength is required of an imperial leader now than was required in the days of Rome or in the days of Genghis Khan.

Actually, the burden has grown decisively since the nineteenth century and in our own lifetime. The British Empire of the late eighteenth, nineteenth and the early twentieth centuries was based primarily on British sea power. The residuum of force needed to maintain order, to defend the Empire, to assure the economic functioning of this, one of the very great empires of history, was transmitted by sailing ships, and later by steam. But naval power, especially in the sailing-ship days, was one of the least expensive forms of applying long-range force known to history. In the greatest days of her naval power—1900—which was also perhaps the time in which the British Empire held its greatest extent of territory, the government of the leadership state, Great Britain, applied only six per cent of its national income to maintaining its army, navy and supporting forces. Though a relatively small country with a relatively small population—she had then about 30 millions—with her remarkable resource of human administrative ability and an enlightened development of political doctrine, Britain could fairly claim to have solved the problem.

The imperial aspirant of half a century later could expect no such good fortune. Naval power, like sea transport, though now expensive, is still the cheapest form of transmission. But its essential companion, if not its substitute, air power, is, in the present state of the art, one of the most expensive. Cost figures change almost momentarily as the technique of air warfare incessantly shifts and expands. At date of writing (1956), the cost of the newest jet fighter runs to $4,500,000 per plane. What the cost will be when guided missiles of intercontinental range with atomic warheads or captive satellites accompany or replace planes, is matter of surmise. In the foreseeable future, the cost of developing, maintaining and (if need be) of applying force will continue to be great, and almost unquestionably will continue to increase. The cost, or to put it differently, the drain on national economy of force requirements, therefore make leadership a luxury reserved to rich and highly productive nations. It is fairly questionable indeed whether any country, by itself, could long sustain the burden of maintaining leadership by pure force.

The possibility, however, must not be entirely ruled out. The ability of any given stretch of territory to produce, granted a high technical development, has dramatically increased in the past thirty years. There is reason to believe that the increase will be still greater in the coming generation. Theoretically, it is possible that the United States might be so rich, so productive and so well organized and educated that from its own resources it could equip, maintain and where necessary apply force all over the world through modern machines, just as Britain was able to do so with her naval establishment half a century ago. The possibility, if it exists, remains for the future to demonstrate. The United States could not do it today without changing the habits of her population. It is questionable whether she could do it a generation hence. And it is probable that the Soviet Union, were she to continue playing that game, would encounter at least as much difficulty, if not more. This perhaps was behind the asserted change in policy of the Soviet Union in 1955, and her alleged attempt to seek a measure of disarmament for herself as well as (of course) for her opponents.

The degree of force needed to maintain an empire is diminished in almost direct ratio by the amount of assent gained from its component peoples. Some measure of that assent indeed is necessary to operate any empire—armies themselves are held together by the assent of the soldiers in them to their central organization. Consequently, even realistic and wholly amoral imperial masters or oligarchies have paralleled their force mechanism with a philosophy designed to command support and assent. The Fascist empire of Mussolini and the Nazi empire of Adolf Hitler attempted to create an ideology, a mythology, and a philosophy commanding moral allegiance as well as physical conformity of a substantial number of their respective subjects.

In no case has the process been carried farther than in the Communist empire. The Leninist version of Marxian philosophy was manufactured into a body of doctrine which the English philosopher, Bertrand Russell, rightly called a "lay religion"; groups were created wherever Communist territorial jurisdiction or propaganda opportunities permitted. The central core of ideas was put forward as one for which men and women should willingly give their lives. The central Communist authority in the Soviet Union was set up as the final authority on this doctrine; its orders must be followed not merely because violation meant punishment or reprisal, but also because failure to obey was a betrayal of the Cause and of the people's personality. Interpretations and directives given were, of course, calculated to strengthen the power position of the rulers of the Soviet Union. Lenin had taught that religion was the opiate of the masses, blinding them to the real motives and objectives of their masters, and making them willingly subservient. As not infrequently happens when a man attacks another system, he gave the most faithful analysis of Communist doctrine itself and of its effects.

But our quarrel is with the doctrine, not with the principle that doctrine must parallel power leadership. The British Empire could not have existed had it not been that British ideology went with it. British ideology included such great and universal conceptions as that of impartial justice, incorrupt administration, an increasing degree of freedom of knowledge and information, and a high degree of respect for the individual thought and life of men and women. In its own time, Rome had carried into her empire the conception of a universal and relatively just Roman law as the times then considered justice. Peoples conquered by Rome more often than not found her administration more attractive than their previous systems. The result of British imperial rule was a sufficiently high degree of assent so that relatively little force was necessary; indeed, where the British Empire has withdrawn, as in the case of India and Pakistan, the British conception of administration and of justice still survives in the liberated states. In vast areas, especially those populated by peoples of English background, force not only was unnecessary but the areas were prepared and even anxious to contribute force for the assistance of the leadership country.

At this point empire stops. It is no longer necessary. In the British case, it turned into the British Commonwealth of Nations, a vast family of peoples held together by assent to a common body of principles and by the advantages, economic and military, of a mutual alliance, with varying degrees of loyalty, under the symbolism of the British crown. Though the experiment is relatively new (the constituting Statute of Westminster was passed in 1931) and its ultimate tensile strength can not be historically judged, it unquestionably did produce a high degree of common action when Britain entered World War II in September, 1939. Unity of the Commonwealth tended to increase rather than decrease in Britain's darkest hours in 1940 and 1941.

The United States for practical purposes possesses no empire and has rejected every opportunity presented her to acquire one in the past century. It is equivocal to insist that the American policy in the nineteenth century—"Manifest Destiny"—which took her from the Atlantic to the Pacific was "imperialist." Perhaps it might have been so had North America been an inhabited continent in which thirteen states constituting the American union would have been obligated to conquer other peoples in order to expand. The fact was the successive acquisitions at the expense of Spain in Florida, at the expense of Mexico in the Southwest and California, at the expense of France in the Louisiana territory, were all empty lands. The problem was not how to dominate other peoples, but who should have the first privilege of occupying empty territory. The first opportunity really presented was that offered at the close of the Spanish-American War of 1898. But, as noted, American public opinion demanded that the territories thus acquired should be promptly offered independence. The single substantial territory which did not opt for this was the present Commonwealth of Puerto Rico; this island, after passionate political discussion, determined upon co-existence as a free "Associated Commonwealth." Of the great territories of which she has had possession as military master, America elected to keep only a few relatively insignificant islands, of which may be mentioned Guam, and Hawaii, the last named having sought not independence but integration into the United States.

Historically, modern America has no interest in creating or being an empire. Her public opinion dislikes the principle. Her people have displayed no interest in exercising the functions of colonial government with its attendant burden of life outside the United States. She has had no body of avid adventurers comparable to the sixteenth century Spaniards who sought to carve out provinces for themselves in the West Indies and in Central and South America. She has had no group of men willing to make permanent careers in colonial administration comparable to the Civil Service Britain sent throughout the world. She has indeed had only a tiny group of men and women who were prepared to dedicate their lives to the service of education or religion in foreign lands—no group comparable to the Franciscans or Jesuits whose far-flung work paralleled the conquests of Spain and Portugal.

She has not—it is perhaps her principal weakness in the field of leadership—any well codified body of doctrine capable of ready explanation to peoples other than her own. Not that such doctrine does not exist, clearly it does. The most significant single fact about American experience with alien groups coming into her fold has been that no substantial "minority" people has ever grown up within her borders. No group of non-American ancestry and background has failed to be absorbed within the space of one generation, or has seriously sought to relinquish their membership and participation in the organism that is the United States. This is not accidental. Within the United States approximately 25 million Americans are of German blood and heredity. During the Nazi period, the greatest propaganda effort was made to galvanize some part of this group into a consciousness of Germandom as opposed to Americanism. The bait offered was perhaps as high as imperial bait can be: in the event of German conquest, the Germans were to be the master race, all others being relegated to various degrees of subservience. Somewhat similar attempts were made, though less efficiently, by the Fascist regime of Mussolini. The results obtained were inconsequential. The absorptive power of American doctrine, its ability to command a high degree of assent from populations of wholly disparate blood, language and tradition within its borders has been perhaps the outstanding achievement of the American system. A famous Brazilian Minister of Foreign Affairs, Dr. Osvaldo Aranha, commented that the United States, beyond any other nation-state in modern times could claim the title, "nation of nations."

But doing this is one thing; explaining it is something else. True, the literature of the "American way of life" is endless. Explanations of its results both by Americans and foreigners are not wanting. But it would be impossible to point to any single volume or group of volumes outlining in form comprehensible to an outsider the American system.

This must be contrasted with the relatively clear-cut embodiments of doctrine which other world leaders have had and have used. Rome had her Tables of laws and her Pantheon of religion, replaced in the fourth century by Christianity. From the middle of the seventh century, the Mohammedans had the Koran. The Spanish-Portuguese empires had the settled doctrine of the Catholic religion. In the case of Spain this was flanked by a remarkable body of legislation, "The Laws of the Indies," which remain a landmark of enlightened colonial administration and legislation in the context of its time. In these cases, there was no question about it: the flag went with the conqueror, the doctrine went with the flag, and the administration, military and civil (for better or worse) accompanied both. In the case of the United States, the flag went with the army; but there was no necessary assumption that either army or flag would stay. The United States Supreme Court (in the case of *Balzac v. People of Porto Rico*) decided that the Constitution did *not* follow the flag. Methods of administration were improvised as we went along, sometimes with grotesque results. Perhaps the single common factor in all American expeditions into the imperial field has been a great predilection for immediate order in the area, a desire to give the downtrodden a break, and an almost equal insistence on instituting a system of public education. In practice, providing a reasonable road system and a public school system seemed to be the chief practicable result of American occupation—all of them designed for the purpose of being turned over to the population of the region as soon as the Americans could arrange to go home. This is hardly a body of doctrine, let alone an explainable lay religion.

Yet, in outcome, the United States has fared surprisingly well.

For the United States, despite the absence of doctrine, has maintained an adequate if not perfect leadership in the Western hemisphere without empire, and with only the barest minimum of force, through the Organization of American States discussed in the next chapter. The ideal of a possibly unified American group had been actively pursued since Simon Bolivar threw it up as a great dream in 1820; it has activated a fairly high factor of common action. It takes form from a pact of mutual defense, the Treaty of Rio de Janeiro (1949) and from the "Organization of American States," set up by charter adopted in 1948 at Bogota, Colombia; of both pacts we shall hear more later. The Organization of American States has not yet had to stand the test of a major struggle. It can be said that it, and its predecessor organizations in which American economy and military potential was unquestionably predominant has given the Western Hemisphere a measure of peace and security unknown in any other part of the world. Certainly, even in its present state it has deterred overseas imperialism from serious attack.

This experiment is interesting because it is perhaps the only permanent organization held together by pure consent in which force is designed for external defense only. The value to any country, especially to the United States, can be gauged by considering the number of divisions, of ships, matériel, and so forth, which would be needed to obtain comparable access to the geography and resources of the region if it had to be conquered instead of being available through cooperation. Obviously, a leader-country's resources are vastly multiplied by the extent to which it can attain common action with peoples and nations outside its own borders.

There is a purely theoretical additional possibility. Conceivably other countries might join in a federal union with the United States. Some urge the United States and the British Commonwealth of Nations to attempt construction of such a "union" now. In future generations the possibility of this and other similar unions may emerge. At the moment this seems so far beyond the horizon of practicality as to need little discussion. Yet it must be remembered that as the geopolitics of the world have altered in one generation by airplanes and atomic weapons, they may be changed still more profoundly in the next by guided missiles, cosmic rays, and economic pressures. For this reason the dim, star-lit ideal of great unions of peoples in a common government can not be wholly dismissed. But the bases and plans required for national governments as presently constituted are complex and difficult in the extreme. Infinitely more is needed than writing out draft constitutions or formulae. While there are indications of vast, underlying forces, economic and military and perhaps even psychological, which tend in the direction of greater federal unions, and while no serious statesman would or could impede them, they have not in our time attained a point in which federal unions can be considered existing instruments of policy. We shall be examining this in more detail later.

One thing is clear. A nation in the position of voluntary or involuntary world leadership must constantly recognize the absolute necessity of attaining common action with other nations forming a group sufficient to meet any probable external threat. A Xerxes or a Caesar might possibly consider drawing a line around his existing empire (the Emperor Augustus actually did around Rome), and remaining unconcerned about the attitude of the surrounding territories and peoples. A modern State has no such luxury; certainly the United States has not. It must either exert its own leadership, join some other leader, or find itself in terrible danger.

CHAPTER Two

INTER-AMERICAN WORLD: ORGANIZATION OF DEFENSE

1

IT HAS ALREADY been made clear that America, suddenly thrust into the position of a leading world power, had only three alternatives. It could retreat at once into isolation—thereafter adapting itself to events as expediency dictated. This policy had been attempted after World War I. Or it could conquer an empire and be quick about it. This policy is totally out of line with American tradition, history and national instincts. Third, it could attempt the creation of a group or connecting groups of nations, working together. This last is, at date of writing, the declared policy of the United States.

Ideally, such a group of nations should be world-wide. If it were ever constructed, there would then be a world community of nations and the result would be world peace. This was the goal and the hope when the United Nations was constructed at San Francisco in the Spring of 1945; pursuit of that goal continued substantially until the Truman Doctrine declaration in 1947 and the overt prosecution of the Cold War. The goal of a world group of nations, for practical purposes, had really been defeated by a decision taken in Moscow not earlier than mid-Summer nor later than early Autumn of 1944; but the world and the United States did not know that, and indeed know it now chiefly by inference. When in 1947 President Truman threw down the gauntlet to the Communist group of nations and undertook the defense of Greece, he was recognizing a situation which did exist, and he abandoned the form of world cooperation for the substance of regional groups.

Construction of a group of nations is, however, more easily said than done. We speak of "the free world" or "the western world," implying that there is a group of nations in contradistinction to the tightly knit Communist group. Factually no such grouping exists. In reality, the United States has constructed or availed itself of a number of associations of nations interlocking in one way or another. Of these the three greatest functioning groups are respectively the British Commonwealth of Nations—which the United States did not construct but with which it is intimately allied through its relations with Canada and Great Britain; the NATO group, of which the United States is the most powerful member; and the Organization of American States or inter-American group of which also the United States is the most powerful member.

Of the three, the Organization of American States is the oldest, is organizationally the most highly developed and is, perhaps, the most important to the interests of the United States.

Paramountcy of its importance to the United States is matter of debate among students. Clearly, the substantial integrity of the British Commonwealth, including as it does Canada, Great Britain, Australia, New Zealand and other significant but less powerful elements is of great importance in maintaining peace throughout great areas of the world, of assuring a degree of equilibrium, and of permitting at least a modicum of organization of world economics. Plainly, too, the NATO group, extending from Great Britain to Turkey, though presently in bad disrepair (January, 1957) is the principal barrier to Russian seizure of West Europe; and the national existence of the United States would be seriously threatened if Western Europe could not only be conquered but also used for offensive purposes by the Communist imperialists. Yet, if the British Commonwealth were to break up it is impossible that Canada should not remain grouped with the United States; and in World War II the United States faced and overcame a situation in which all Western Europe was held by a then bitterly hostile power, Nazi Germany. In other words, the United States might survive, though with unhappiness, the break-up of these two groups.

But it is questionable whether it could survive the break-up of the inter-American group of nations which comprises all of the independent countries in the Western Hemisphere save Canada. Strategically the position of the United States would be precarious if it were cut off from any territory of the Western Hemisphere with the possible exception of Argentina; the sheer loss of its raw material would constrict American economy in time of peace and cut its potential below danger point in case of war. On straight naval and military grounds, the United States would be in severe peril if the political situations so altered as to permit a hostile power to establish bases in South America from which air strike could be made against the Panama Canal. Its hazard would be still greater if populations as large as those of Mexico and Brazil could be energized against the United States. Morally and politically, if the United States fails to make a viable organization of the Western Hemisphere its hopes of attracting groups of nations in other parts of the world—say the Near East, Southeast Asia or elsewhere—would go glimmering: few in that case would pay serious attention to American diplomatic conversation.

Unhappily (and wrongly), neither American politics nor American diplomacy has given adequate attention to the fact that the inter-American group is really basic to any American policy. The red signals prevailing are at least partly due to the American cultural lack. For a century and a half, Americans have, rightly, travelled to Europe from which our civilization sprang. They have, wrongly, assumed that the area outside the London-Paris-Berlin-Vienna-Rome circuit must be a vast, unorganized and uninteresting wilderness. European and Asian crises have made headlines. American politicians and American diplomats have made reputations and become known as a result of this spectacular, if unhappy, turbulence in these areas. Not only was life more vivid, but political fortunes seemed more probable in the great Western capitals. Secretaries of State, and their chief lieutenants, almost prided themselves on their relative lack of concern with Latin America—Cordell Hull and Sumner Welles being two conspicuous exceptions who knew better. Unhappily, the American hemisphere knew pretty well how American politicians felt about it.

Yet the actuality is that the United States' strongest claim to be well regarded as a world leader rests precisely on the fact that, in the main, she has been able under stimulus from her hemispheric neighbors to create an area in which there is substantial freedom from fear, and which offers some promise at least that there will be one day freedom from want; in which there has been a more or less continuous ideal of freedom of religion and thought, and in which there would one day be full freedom of information and expression. As long as this group holds together the United States could, if need be, face the rest of the world with a respectable chance of national survival. Should it break up, the United States, even if other groups like NATO and the British Commonwealth remain in existence, would become little more than a larger France or Germany required to follow a course of world affairs over whose guidance it could exert only secondary influence.

Because of this, the writer believes that the inter-American group of nations known now as the Organization of American States takes first rank in American foreign policy. It is also, by accident of geopolitics, the area in which the United States can do more to guide the events than any other area in which she exerts influence. The dream of an American group of nations is historically ascribed to that amazing and erratic genius, Simon Bolivar. In a famous letter, he sketched out the possibility of a Pan-American Union; the hope of giving it a capital probably at Panama; of endowing it with an intellectual life through a university. Then, he thought, the American nations born or in process of being born, having established themselves as a community, could make an alliance with the British

Empire. On that basis, he believed, a world community of nations might be established.

Actually a conference was called to that end which was held in Panama in 1826. The United States accepted an invitation, expressed sympathy and sent delegates. Unhappily in those sailing ship days the delegates never arrived at the conference and in any case it did not establish any permanent organization; but the United States had gone on record as favoring an American grouping. Later, Mr. Henry Clay, at the time Secretary of State, joined in reactivating the project and a later, likewise abortive conference was held in 1830. The idea of permanent grouping encountered many political difficulties. Its fortunes rose and ebbed through the nineteenth century; the dream nevertheless persisted. Actually, the first substantial if unspectacular progress toward realizing it came in the year 1890.

The Monroe Doctrine, supported by British policy, had screened the American hemisphere from the European colonial maneuvers which parceled out the entire continent of Africa among European countries. As a result, the field was clear for a grouping of independent nations.

The Pan American Union was formed, largely at the insistence of Secretary of State James G. Blaine, for the most limited purposes; its principal effect was to cause periodic meetings of representatives of the twenty-one nations, and with it to cause a habit of developing a common point of view. Though the Union encountered stormy weather particularly because of American armed intervention in Mexico in 1914, and in Haiti, the Dominican Republic and Nicaragua in 1915, the group did not break up. At its regular meeting at Montevideo in 1933, Secretary of State Cordell Hull interpreted the "Good Neighbor" policy in a manner which satisfied the fears of most of the American nations. In 1936 at a special meeting at Buenos Aires, President Roosevelt proposed amid general approval a pact of common consultation. Two years later, as war clouds hovered over Europe, this was further strengthened by the now famous "Declaration of Lima," subscribed by all twenty-one American republics at the initiative of Secretary Hull.

2

For practical purposes the inter-American community of nations became a functioning group as a result of the Conference of Lima in 1938. The shadow of Hitler was dark across the world. Czechoslovakia had been sacrificed to him in the hope of a peace of appeasement, but few outside Great Britain had any hope that war could be avoided. At Lima the twenty-one American nations declared that in case

"the peace, security or territorial integrity of any American republic is threatened by acts of any nature that may impair them, they proclaim their common concern and their determination to make effective their solidarity."

In plain English, the declaration meant that the countries would work together for the common defense of all of them should any of them be under attack.

As wording goes, the declaration was not too good. But it was good enough, when the European war broke out in 1939, to assure that substantially all the American states joined in declaring war on Nazi Germany. It was also good enough to suggest to all participants that a more highly organized, more powerful grouping was desirable in the post-war world.

As it turned out, the American countries south of the Rio Grande had a far clearer view of the post-war world than did the United States.

Even before the war's end, certain of the foreign offices, notably that of Brazil, warned the United States that the Soviet Union was not likely to cooperate in any world group. When plans were elaborated at Dumbarton Oaks in 1944 for the creation of United Nations, and as the pattern of those talks became known, the Latin American countries were frankly concerned. They considered that the existence of the inter-American group was not forwarded but threatened by the emergence of the world group. When it was learned that the Security Council was permanently to include four great Powers—the United States, Great Britain, Soviet Union and

China—each with an unlimited veto, and that the Security Council was to have power to deal with any situation involving a threatened breach of peace, they were alarmed. A United Nations, making decrees affecting the peace of the hemisphere through a Council in which the United States was only one of four—and in which the other three major powers were not countries in which the American public had much confidence—looked more like an aggregate of foreign masters than like a peace-keeping organization. At this point, Mr. Nelson Rockefeller (then Assistant Secretary of State for Latin American Affairs) with some assistance from the writer who had preceded him in that post, intervened to cause the calling of a special meeting of the American states to be held at Mexico City in February of 1945. The result of that meeting was a remarkable document known as the "Act of Chapultepec." This was in substance an agreement by the twenty-one American republics that they would enter into a treaty by which each would guarantee the boundaries of all the others, and that

> "any attempt on the part of a non-American State against the integrity or inviolability of the territory, the sovereignty or the political independence of an American State shall be considered as an act of aggression against all the American States."

The agreement had been directly authorized by President Roosevelt at the insistence of President Santos of Colombia.

The understandings of the Act of Chapultepec were later put into treaty form by the so-called "Treaty of Rio de Janeiro," signed on September 2, 1947. The operative provision is Article 3:

> "Art. 3.1. The High Contracting Parties agree that an armed attack by any state against an American State shall be considered as an attack against all the American States and, consequently, each one of the said Contracting Parties undertake to assist in meeting the attack in the exercise of the inherent right of individual or collective self-defense recognized by Article 51 of the Charter of the United Nations."

But between the date of Chapultepec and the date of the Treaty of Rio de Janeiro, a turbulent bit of hitherto unpublished history occurred.

The meeting at Chapultepec was unanimous in wanting just this provision. The stormy struggle occurred, surprisingly, within the American delegation. One important faction in the American State Department at that time wished that there should be no peace-keeping group other than the United Nations: there was to be either a world group or no group. It has been argued by some that the opponents of the Act of Chapultepec were activated by pro-Communist or pro-Russian motives, partly because Alger Hiss who came to the Chapultepec Conference with Secretary Stettinius on their way back from the Yalta Conference was opposed to it. There is no evidence to support this sweeping conclusion. More probably, the trouble arose from the doctrinaire ideas of the men who had been working on the proposed United Nations Organization and could see no alternative.

Their argument ran substantially as follows: Peace is indivisible. If war breaks out anywhere—say in South America—and any group of states undertakes to restrain that breach of peace, we have war. In any war, the United Nations must function. Therefore there must be no peace-keeping save the peace-keeping of the proposed United Nations Security Council. To which various Latin American diplomats, notably those of Mexico and Brazil answered forcefully: If ever the Soviet Union, Great Britain, China, intervene in South American affairs, even though acting in the name of the United Nations, we will become little more than pawns in European and world power diplomacy. Primary responsibility for restraining breach of the peace in American affairs must, therefore, belong to the American nations. After these have failed it is time enough to call in the non-American great powers. They closed their argument with a clincher: if this principle is not recognized, for our part we will not vote for any United Nations charter. How right they were has been sufficiently demonstrated by ten years of post-war history. In point of fact, the Act of Chapultepec (now the Treaty of Rio de Janeiro) was almost forced on an unwilling United States Secretary of State by nineteen of the twenty other American republics (Argentina being at the moment absent); and it was finally accepted by the American delegation owing to strenuous efforts by Mr. Nelson Rockefeller and Senator Warren Austin, by the American naval and military delegates and by the writer.

The incident should have ended there but did not. The United Nations Conference convened in San Francisco on April 25, 1945. The American delegation did not include anyone who had been at Chapultepec. The proposed United Nations charter did not include any recognition of regional groups. The text of the proposed charter indeed would have outlawed the arrangement made at Chapultepec. It was then naturally discovered that the Latin American countries were unwilling to vote for it. Mr. Nelson Rockefeller was summoned to assist in getting their votes; he pointed out that the American word given at Chapultepec after full deliberation had not been kept. Ultimately by enlisting the aid of Senator Vandenberg he was able to compel inclusion in the charter of the United Nations the famous Article 51 which provides:

> "Art. 51. Nothing in the present Charter shall impair the inherent right of individual or collective self-defence if an armed attack occurs against a Member of the United Nations, until the Security Council has taken the measures necessary to maintain international peace and security."

And again

> "Art. 52. Nothing in the present Charter precludes the existence of regional arrangements or agencies for dealing with such matters relating to the maintenance of international peace and security as are appropriate for regional action."

It is under these clauses that the Treaty of Rio de Janeiro, the North Atlantic Treaty Organization, and other similar agreements now exist.

The struggle in the American delegation at San Francisco appears to have been violent. President Roosevelt who had finally determined the point in favor of the Chapultepec agreement was dead. Secretary Stettinius apparently had been induced to agree that the Chapultepec agreement should not be carried out. President Truman was too recently in the situation to have been well informed about it, and the State Department had been entirely reorganized. The persistence of Mr. Rockefeller and of Senator Vandenberg eventually carried the day; and as a result, the present structure of American foreign policy has taken form.

The battle should have been over; but the group which disliked regional arrangements (and also the current of Russian propaganda) worked strong and hard. Mr. Stettinius was replaced as Secretary of State by Mr. Byrnes immediately after the close of the United Nations conferences. It had been understood that the treaty embodying the provisions of the Act of Chapultepec would promptly be drawn at Rio and the Brazilian government opened negotiations with the writer (then Ambassador) looking toward preliminary drafts. Whereupon the Department of State called off the whole proceeding. Since both the Secretary and his Undersecretary were new in the situation, and since neither of them knew anything about inter-American affairs, it remains a question whether they actually realized they had broken a given word, on the faith of which twenty American nations had joined the United Nations Organization. Of Russian hostility, there was, of course, no doubt whatsoever. The Soviet Union opposed the formation of the inter-American group just as it had opposed, and still opposes, the formation of any Western European or indeed any non-Communist group.

It was not until Secretary Byrnes had been superseded by General Marshall that his very able Undersecretary, Robert Lovett, reactivated negotiations so that the Treaty of Rio was signed on September 2, 1947. By then, of course, the Soviet Union had shown its hand, and the Truman doctrine of resistance to aggression had come into being. Erecting a world group of nations was revealed as a matter for the future: long and patient effort was needed before the United Nations could be relied on to undertake regional defense; the policy of interlocking regional groups was the only practical alternative. Rightly, such a policy did not exclude continued work toward their eventual integration in a world group; meantime it recognized and now recognizes realities. Somewhat ironically (in view of history) negotiations looking towards formation of the North Atlantic Treaty Organization were commenced along the lines laid out by the Treaty of Rio de Janeiro. The stone that some of the builders had attempted to reject had now become the cornerstone of the American international edifice. The North Atlantic treaty, signed in Washington on April 4, 1949, was witnessed by some Americans who, a scant four years earlier, had done their best to make it impossible.

3

Groups of nations as a rule require more than military clauses to give them permanence. In any case, the inter-American group had erected the military alliance of Rio de Janeiro not so much on the basis of common fear as on the basis of solid desire to work together in peace as well as in war. The old organization of the Pan American Union had long since been outmoded and this fact had been recognized at Chapultepec. Accordingly, at an inter-American congress held in Bogotá in March of 1948, to fulfill the understandings entered into at Chapultepec, the group drew an agreement of regional organization known as "The Charter of Bogotá." In substance, this set up a regional United Nations with a highly developed mechanism for dealing with common problems—political, economic, social and cultural. It created a permanent council which sits in Washington, to which appeal may be made by any American country. A number of specialized commissions exist including an inter-American economic and social council; and there is an "Advisory Defense Committee" composed of the highest military authorities of the American States. In substance this is the outline of an inter-American General Staff. There is thus machinery in existence which can not only discuss but (with good-will on the part of the participants) can enforce decisions of the community. On at least one occasion— that of the Nicaraguan attempt to subvert the Costa Rican government in the Spring of 1955—the Organization of American States with the help of the United States supplied force sufficient to prevent serious breach of the peace.

4

Maintenance of the bloc of geography, natural resources, manpower and cultural ability comprised in the twenty-one American nations is a geopolitical necessity for all concerned.

It is a necessity for the United States in time of peace, and doubly so in time of war. It is no less essential to other component American countries if they are to remain masters of their own fate.

Merely as a pool of manpower and human ability, the combination is at least respectable when compared with the more populous nations of the world. The aggregate population of the twenty Latin American States is probably slightly more than the population of the United States—a fair current estimate would be 171 million as against 170 million inhabitants of the United States. The population of a number of Latin American countries increases rather more rapidly than our own. A total of 341 millions of population compares with an estimate of perhaps 375 millions in India, and perhaps 480 millions in China. The density of population, of course, is infinitely less. If to this figure be added 16 millions population of another country—Canada—inevitably linked by geography and history to the American bloc, the comparison becomes clear: the American world, *if it sticks together*, does not need to be frightened by the sheer population masses of even the largest Asian countries.

In terms of natural resources, the interdependence is, of course, more marked. The Latin American Republics (excluding the United States) exported nearly 10.7% of the world total of exports in 1951, and absorbed 9.3% of total world imports. Trade between the United States and Latin America is roughly equal to the trade between the United States and Europe; only the recent rise in European economy drew trade relations with Europe slightly ahead. Latin America is one of the United States' best customers, if not the best customer; it is one of the United States' largest suppliers. The relation is reciprocal.

But this trade is not on an optional basis. The United States clearly can produce more than she needs in most staple food commodities, and in many manufactures. But to do this, she must have certain commodities from outside. Already the United States is running short on high grade iron ore; she is currently importing from the valley of the Orinoco in Venezuela. She has never had enough high grade manganese, essential in steel production; she is developing that in Brazil. There is at present something approaching a world shortage in copper; the excess needs of the United States are supplied chiefly from Chile, though the Peruvian production is coming up. She can use more lead; there are lead deposits in the mountain region of Argentina. One of the world's greatest deposits of very high grade iron ore is at the head of the Rio Doce valley in Brazil though at the moment only a moderate amount of production is generated there and most of it goes to Europe. Another is in Venezuela; it supplies American steelmills on the Eastern seaboard. The oil resources of the United States, though new fields are being discovered, are steadily supplemented by imports of oil, of which a great amount comes from Venezuela. The only great resource of tin in the new world is in Bolivia, and so forth.

In ordinary open-world peace-time economy, the United States draws heavily on Latin American resources for minerals and for the tropically grown products like coffee. In case of disturbance of world conditions American need would be vastly intensified. The Near East, for example, is a dangerous and troubled area; were it ever closed in by war, or by Soviet seizure of territory or the like, or (as now, by international disorder) the Latin American supplies of oil would become an absolute necessity not only for the United States but for America's friends and associates in Western Europe. Were Africa ever to be cut off from Europe, Latin American copper would become essential to the Western world. Were Malaya to be taken out of world commerce, the Bolivian tin and the Brazilian rubber potential would become of first importance. There is nothing of "favor" in inter-American commerce. It is a necessity for all concerned in time of peace. The necessity would become vital in time of war.

Defense of the region—or more accurately, the welding of this area into a smooth working community capable of defending itself —is thus no philanthropic project. It is matter of first concern to any serious student of American foreign affairs. For the fact is that the United States would have the grimmest difficulty defending herself if the rest of the area did not join. Equally the Latin American area probably would be torn to pieces if the United States were not a willing partner.

Carefully considered, either as defense or as formation of a community of nations, this can be accomplished only if the entire territory is included. During World War II, when plans were made for hemispheric defense some students expressed the view that the United States needed only to defend "down to the bulge," that is, down to the point at which South America juts out into the Atlantic toward the shoulder of Africa. This might have been adequate in the old days of land warfare, though the problem of holding a line running roughly from Natal (Brazil) south of the huge Amazon swamp (it extends four-fifths of the entire width of South America at its widest) to, say, Lima, Peru, seems insoluble; and few military experts would relish the task of maintaining adequate force with two thousand miles of the most impenetrable jungle in the world between them and their bases. Even if feasible, the sector thus defended would not include the resources necessary to defend the area. Practically, if a global World War III breaks out between the Communist world and the free world, one objective of the Communist world would unquestionably be disruption of the inter-American system and political seizure of great areas in South America. It is almost (though not quite) true to say that the United States cut off from any substantial part of Latin America would be too crippled to conduct a long defense of her own territory. It is certainly fair to say that cut off from the United States, no Latin American country could maintain itself for long if attacked in such conflict.

"Defense" is a misleading word in this connection. One thinks merely of repelling an attacking force; of throwing an extra-hemispheric invader back over the seas to another continent. But modern conflicts are not posed in those terms. Communist governments put into practice what the German militarists knew perfectly well. The objective of aggressive war is to set up political domination over conquered areas. Quite logically, therefore, the Communist plan of attack begins with political agitation and infiltration; force is then used; the end result is establishment of a government and political system responsive to its will. Mere military occupation of strategic ports, roads, lines of communication and production areas is not enough. Such purely military action may, indeed, deny the geography and the resources of an area to an enemy; but it will not make available the resources, production and manpower to the occupying forces. The Nazi armies discovered this in Yugoslavia where they held the cities, the railroads and the chief highways, but were unable to exploit the resources because the population was solidly against them.

It follows that "defense" means not merely excluding enemy force, but creating a political situation in which substantially all the population desires to work with the United States, or rather with the free community of nations of which the United States is presently the strongest single element. "Defense" thus includes the conception of political organization as well as military organization. Of the two, political organization is more important: military organization is merely a means to that end.

The geography of Latin America is almost ideally constituted so that much of the population could carry on as usual, irrespective of hostile military action. No power in the world has soldiers enough, or supply capacity sufficient, to hold down this area by force. Were the United States to attempt to secure production and resources of the area with its own armed forces, so large a body of men and matériel would be required—"pinned down" in the military slang phrase—that other operations would be almost impossible. To the contrary, our enemy might be satisfied, temporarily, by merely cutting communication and supply lines which connect the United States with the rest of the hemisphere. Successful military action without political success thus might be adequate for an attacker; similar domination would not be sufficient for the United States unless with it that measure of good-will which keeps the Latin American economy joined to the economy of the United States were achieved.

This alone would be reason enough for spending an infinite amount of time and pains in constructing a hemispheric system capable of engaging the good-will, the loyalty and the enthusiasm of the populations concerned. Political defense and the military defense for all concerned go hand in hand.

Or would, were it not for the fact that defense is essentially a negative conception. Sentiment for it rises in time of danger and falls when danger seems remote. The positive aspect—constructing a true community of nations with a system of thought, economics, social conceptions and culture is therefore essential. If anything is clear, it is that a system of "defense" can not be jerry-rigged in the twentieth century world; it can only be built around a positive construction.

This explains the endless search for an evergrowing common denominator of American civilization. It explains why there is an intellectual dream of ever-growing exchange between scientists, teachers, students. It justifies the limitless search by students of economics and trade for an integration in economic affairs which will spread the benefits of twentieth-century production more or less evenly over the entire area. It indicates why social thinkers never abandon the efforts to work out measures whereby every citizen of the hemisphere, peon, laborer, or share cropper, get a steadily increasing share of that production. The men who work at this sort of thing are often attacked as visionaries, or perhaps as mere do-gooders. The fact is that correlation of some part at least of their dreams is needed to create a true American civilization and this common civilization is the beating heart and blood circulation of any organization for hemispheric defense. The Charter of Bogotá which sets up the Organization of the American States, and the Pact of Bogotá which looks towards the creation of an arbitral tribunal is therefore accompanied by another document: "The American Declaration of the Rights and Duties of Man."

This Declaration is only a dream. It proclaims that men, being born free and equal in dignity and rights, should conduct themselves as brothers. It poses the duty of man to seek spiritual development as the supreme end of human existence. It sets out that culture is the highest historical expression of spiritual development. It therefore declares human rights of life, liberty, security, the right to freedom of investigation, opinion and expression of ideas, the right to education, the right to raise his standard of living, to be a useful member of society, to take part in the cultural life of the community. It sets up correlative duties: men must so conduct themselves in relation to others that each and every one may fully form and

develop his personality. It insists that every person has the duty to
acquire at least elementary education, and to obey the law and to
participate in military defense, and to pay taxes and to work for
his own livelihood or to benefit the community. The Latin American world, like the United States, does not live up to this noble
declaration. But it continues to strive towards it. The importance of
the document at present is less achievement than intent.

In this respect it must not be underestimated. A community of
nations which, together, wants to go somewhere, and has a vision
(however hazy) of where it wants to go, has the first essential of a
true political unity.

On such slender strands of thought, political parties are organized
in many of the component Latin American countries. They seek to
realize this dream of civilization in all kinds of diverse ways. Most
parties pay lip-service to the general ideal; some are activist in endeavoring to push towards it. The point is that a substantial and
growing majority of the population of the hemisphere is moving
towards precisely that ideal, and as it does so, moves into closer
working and cooperative relationship. Since the Latin American
picture is not materially different from the American ideal, a powerful force, imponderable it is true, exists to bring about that political
cooperation which makes a positive civilization in peace or defense
in war practical.

5

The drawing of charters, making of treaties, and setting up of international committees does not of itself accomplish anything. It is
indeed the tragedy of international action that peoples assume institutions can be called into being by diplomatic action whereas the
fact is that they must grow organizationally. For practical purposes,
the Organization of American States would have scant power were
it not for the fact that two or three American countries stoutly
insist that it shall be real and not paper.

Even within a community of nations the theory is that governments will handle their affairs by direct negotiation, calling on the
regional organization only in case of crisis. But it lends an entirely

different atmosphere to the situation when an appeal to a regional, or for that matter, a world, organization, will produce results. In the case of the Organization of American States, the United States has such a vast preponderance both of economic and of military power that in any major matter its support is indispensable. On the other hand, the existence of the Organization of American States gives an opportunity for the United States to enter a situation without being charged with intervention. It is one thing for properly constituted legal authority to move in to quell a riot or to give relief; it is quite another when a self-assertive neighbor moves in to mind other people's business. Action by the United States in any regional situation, concurred in or perhaps sought by other American nations, is acceptable. The will of the United States unilaterally imposed—even if benevolently intended—is resented. Even Soviet propaganda, deadly opposed to any group of nations other than the Communist is wary of attacking the Organization of American States: the sentiment of the American peoples in its favor is too strong. But the heart of it lies deeper than defense, deeper even than economics. It lies in a phenomenon which is perhaps peculiar to the new world; it is essentially idealist.

We noted the dream of Bolivar as the historical take-off point for the inter-American group. As good a case can be made against the diplomacy of the Western Hemisphere as against the diplomacy of any other part of the world. It is no less formalized, no less self-seeking, perhaps no less cynical. But, at long last, the most cynical North or South American diplomat knows very well that there is a current of opinion constant throughout the hemisphere which judges him as much by the ideals he claims to serve as by his opportunist successes. The very instabilities of Latin American politics have given increased importance to the continuing force of intellectual currents, and to an endless, agonizing search for men whose work justifies itself idealistically, as well as pragmatically. The greatest heroes in Latin America are not military men, or even politicians though they may have acted in one or the other capacity. They are men like Sarmiento in Argentina known peculiarly for his work in international law and in education; and like Rio Branco in Brazil who settled all of Brazil's vast territorial problems without war and by process of law.

By consequence, when, as in the Charter of Bogotá, the inter-American world subscribes, as it has, to a declaration of the rights and duties of man the realization may not be practical but the ideal has force. When the American States declare that all men are born free and equal in dignity and rights, and that culture is the highest social and historical expression of spiritual development, they mean just that. Violations may take place as far and as fast in Latin American countries as in any other, and in fact they do. But the politician always works against a background in which these ideals are persistently recalled. If violation has gone to extremes, the ensuing rebellion eliminates the politician. The most cynical dictator knows that; it is as though in the hour of his abuse of power he realizes that he writes his own death warrant.

The point can not be overstated, perhaps because it is so rarely understood. Citizens of the United States rarely deal in abstract principles; they, like their Anglo-Saxon exemplars pay less attention to theory than to practice. South of the Rio Grande the practice is frequently anything but good; but the theory remains a living standard, and a no less living reproach to the violators. Operating the Organization of American States is, therefore, a combination of hard-headed practical dealing with situations—and continuous statement and restatement of certain moral principles commanding the assent of the member states. Or, of the member governments, or if not of the member governments, then of the member peoples which in time constrain their governments to some measure of conformity to the principles they proclaim.

6

An international organization of states means, in practice, an organization of governments represented by Ambassadors or governmental delegations. This is true of the Organization of American States, just as it is true of the United Nations. At best, it is a difficult way of getting business done for two solid reasons. Before voting for anything, the delegate or Ambassador in such an organization must consult his government to obtain power to act. Governments do not always make up their minds rapidly; the United States government in Washington is no exception. It is sometimes said that intergovernmental organizations have the bureaucracy involved in any government multiplied by the square of the number of governments involved. None the less, intergovernmental organizations do get things done, and perhaps their frequent slowness prevents wrong decisions from being made.

The other difficulty is more deep-seated. The government of a nation is never quite the same as the people of a nation. In extreme cases it may not represent the people at all. A dictatorship, for example, such as that existing at date of writing (December, 1956) in Colombia, Venezuela, the Dominican Republic or Nicaragua undoubtedly commands control of the resources of the country, and can require the acquiescence of its people. But there is no way of knowing whether what it does is really acceptable to its people; this is especially true in respect of countries which do not allow a free press. Also, a dictatorship, or a weakly handled democratic government always stands in danger of being overthrown at some time (in the case of a dictatorship it is only a question of time though the time may be comparatively long). In such cases the group then assuming control may be directly antagonistic to the policies of the previous government.

The United States, in consequence, has to think not merely of the views of the government in power, but also of the views of the people of the country in question. Few serious students of Argentina believed that during the year 1955 the government of General Juan Peron spoke for the Argentine people.

It follows that the United States, in dealing with the other American governments must go below the surface of diplomatic negotiation and formal assent. It must at all times consider the stability of the government involved—and also the extent to which it really represents the people of its country. This is why, in ultimate account, the United States must hope for and can best deal with governments by representative democracy. At best, democratic government is stabler (the government of the United States is one of the oldest, uninterrupted, governments in the world, despite the fact that it only dates from 1787). Obviously agreements with non-representative governments are worth something; a dictator can make a promise and declare a policy, and he can keep that promise and enforce that policy for a period of time. But the final guarantee of any word is the fact that the people of the country accept the promise and the policy as their own.

This does not mean that all governments can be representative democracies in the sense that we understand the term in the United States. Peru and Bolivia, for example, are countries in which some five or ten per cent of Europeans of Spanish extraction overlie populations ninety or ninety-five per cent Andean Indian—the population, in fact, of the old Inca Empire which Pizarro overthrew. These Indians speak their own language, not Spanish; their customs stem from Indian tradition, not European; they have had no experience of modern institutions and have little more contact with them now than they did in the days of the Spanish conquest. It adds little to the discussion to say that this is a failure of the government of the Spanish Empire or of the governments which sprang up when the Spanish Empire fell in 1820. The fact is that any government in either of those countries can only represent the indefensibly tiny minority of their respective peoples capable of understanding modern political issues. In international relations you have to take situations as they are. Liberal American thought, for example, sometimes insists that in some of these countries the United States should insist on a free election, without taking into account that no electoral system devised can reflect the real sentiment of a population most of which have no ideas corresponding to any such process. The criticism is more justified when the United States accepts as representative of a people capable of expressing opinions a government which has imposed itself by force.

The line up of the hemisphere is constantly changing but at present it is approximately this. There are two classic, convinced and capable democracies: the small countries, respectively, of Uruguay and Costa Rica. Both have representative institutions; both have liberated policies; both have governments which have endeavored to represent and serve their peoples as faithfully as governments ever do.

Two other countries have long histories of representative government—Argentina and Brazil. In both, democratic institutions were interrupted by dictatorships—the fall of Peron probably ending the interruption in Argentina, and the end of the Vargas dictatorship in 1945 probably closing the dictatorial chapter of Brazil. In Argentina the historical cycle suggests that she will slowly redevelop her democratic institutions and maintain them for a considerable period of time as she did after the fall of her other famous dictator, Rozas, in 1852. In Brazil which had never had a dictatorship until the advent of Getulio Vargas in 1930, the forecast is rather more optimistic. The Vargas dictatorship was by no means as repressive as that of Peron in Argentina: it was ended without struggle or bloodshed in 1945; subsequent to that time free and honest elections have developed governments and Congresses representative of the popular will. The disturbances in Brazil at the end of 1955 were more apparent than real: in effect they amounted to insistence by the Brazilian Army that the result of the election in which Juscelino Kubitchek was chosen President be respected.

These two re-emergent democracies have changed the current of South American politics. The two countries of Venezuela and Colombia both are governed by military dictators and in both the element of force prevails. Yet, especially in Colombia, there is a strong feeling that the dictatorship is not successful and that it will not last. As to Venezuela, the fantastic oil revenue derived by that country from the exploitation of its oil resources has created a prosperity which dulls the edge of political agitation. Even there, the government of General Perez Jimenez has had to resort to a degree of force and police methods which suggests that like all dictatorships it will end in time. Unlike Colombia, Venezuela does have a long dictatorship tradition in recent generations; but even more than Colombia she has been developing a rapidly growing middle class, and a growing group of educated men who will not be satisfied forever with a police state.

Below the developments in any particular country is the outline
of a struggle for all Latin America.

Divisions of opinion in Latin American countries closely re-
semble divisions in American states. Conservatives in Indiana, Wis-
consin or Utah tend to gather into a national party. Conservatives
in Venezuela, Colombia and Argentina tend to gather into a continental movement. Liberals in American states find themselves a
common denominator and reflect themselves in a national party;
liberals in Latin America correspond with each other, work together,
have informal and sometimes formal contacts, and react to the same
stimuli.

Thus, the liberal bloc in South America thinks about the same on
most questions. This bloc has elected its Presidents and Congresses
in Costa Rica, Uruguay, Bolivia and until recently in Ecuador.
But its sympathizers are found all over the hemisphere. Equally, the
Venezuelan government of Perez Jimenez and the group which supports it works quite happily with the governments of Somoza in
Nicaragua, of Trujillo in the Dominican Republic and did work with
Peron until his fall in the closing weeks of 1955. They have friends
and parties who support their point of view in Chile, in Brazil, in
Cuba, and so forth. Beneath the welter of personalities, the multiplicity of national parties within each country, the multiplicity of
local moves, there is slowly emerging the equivalent of a two-party
system in Latin America—a continent-wide liberal party and a
continent-wide center conservative party. At each edge there is—as
there is in the United States—an extremist fringe of Communists
on the extreme left and of Peronist or fascist groups on the extreme
right. As always—a point not well understood in the United States
—the extreme left and the extreme right work together. The Communists supported the Peronista dictatorship in Argentina; they
have worked with the dictatorial adherents in Brazil. Communists
supported the attempt of the extreme reactionary dictator, Somoza,
to push out the liberal government of Jose Figuéres in Costa Rica.
The common ground between extremists is that neither of them believes in democracy; both believe in dictatorial force; both prefer
dictatorship to popular government and both would rather take their

chances in a struggle for power within a dictatorship than in a struggle for popular sentiment in an election or free press.

To this writer, the policy of the United States seems obvious. We can only maintain permanently satisfactory relationship with governments which believe in the rights of the individual, which will maintain so far as possible the freedom of the press, will seek to promote the welfare of the people by methods which continuously and increasingly educate their people in self-government. Relations can be temporarily pleasant and even cooperative with a dictatorship. In fact, a sane Latin American dictator will cooperate to the fullest extent with the United States government in international and military matters—provided the United States does not interrupt his internal policy of seeking and maintaining power. A cynical dictator made this observation to the writer on one occasion, adding, "Criticism passes but money and power stays in your palace—that is what is important." Their case is that they gave public order to countries where public order is easily interrupted. There is something in the argument. But it is bought at the price of intervals of grave disorder. A still greater price is the strangulation of the abilities of their people to develop higher standards of political capacity and conduct; they inhibit more stable political organization and the growth of successive groups of men fitted by experience for the tasks of statesmen. In the long pull the United States must not merely cooperate with governments. It must cooperate in organizing peoples for their highest development, economic, social and cultural.

Diplomacy, as a result of this situation, differs radically in the American hemisphere from that which prevails in others. By classic standards, a diplomatist must never interfere in the politics of the country to which he is accredited. But within the Organization of American States there is a continental politics in which every diplomat is engaged by hypothesis. Intervention is barred; not a soldier may be moved, no economic reprisals may be made; either would be bitterly resented by everyone. On the other hand, failure or refusal to interpret American ideas, even giving them application to specific situations, is no less resented. A Latin American diplomat in Washington has a perfect right to state that he thinks that some policy proposed by an American political party will be disastrous and the more ably he does it, the better is his political record. An American Ambassador south of the Rio Grande is in the same position: on issues affecting the international life of the hemisphere he is expected to state a point of view. There are times in which such a statement may mean that the diplomat must be "expendable," that is, he may be called on to make an American point of view clear under circumstances which may be disliked by the government to which he is accredited. In such cases—they are comparatively rare—the diplomat enjoys a higher standing if he sticks by his principles and says what he thinks than if he merely observes diplomatic convention and quietly separates himself from the scene. Ambassador Spruille Braden vigorously fought a fight for democracy as Peron was slowly seizing dictatorial power in Argentina. Necessarily it cost him his Embassy; but Braden stands for something in Latin America, whereas the diplomats who observed without stating a point of view are regarded as merely gilded carriers of international notes. The Department of State, which is well informed on Latin American affairs, has to determine when the time has come to state —without the slightest hint of compulsion—the American view on the local political situation.

The reason is obvious. The American family of nations is not a group of disparate, entirely separate, countries. It is in a singularly amorphous way a community of nations coming into being, vaguely attempting to forge a common body of ideas, a common body of political practice, and a common mechanism of cooperation. If world conflict ever breaks out, the United States is dependent on the rest of the hemisphere for supplies, raw materials, geography and all materials of common effort. The rest of the hemisphere without the economic military organization of the United States is at the mercy of any power which is able to master control of the sea and the air. So the attempt to forge a common bond must continue, and few are as insistent in demanding this of the United States as the Latin American politicians themselves.

7

Here is a strictly personal interlude. The writer, with nearly forty years' intermittent experience in Latin America, has a picture of that region quite different than that held by many Americans; it may be worth setting down.

For Latin America, though in one sense it does not exist but is a congeries of different cultures and civilization, in another sense is a golden unity. Your polite companion on a ship or a plane may be Paraguayan or Panamanian. But his estimate of you transmits itself by an instantaneous invisible grape-vine. You are honest, friendly, sympathetic, straightforward, courteous; you find doors open to you from the Straits of Magellan to the Rio Grande. You are ill-mannered, equivocal, dubious, an adventurer; you find that in every transaction the men you meet take their time. And, as Kipling observed, under those circumstances in that part of the world they have lots of time. The writer remembers taking refuge in a Dominican peasant hut after hostages had been shot by orders of an American Marine officer. The hut belonged to the family of one of the dead men; but the right of guest-friendship was so powerful that safety was greatest by the charcoal fire of the mourners for an American victim. An upset in another country displaced a friend who fled from his country; it was considered right by his enemies for me to greet him and take care of him though his politics were not mine. His enemies would have been the first to condemn desertion by a friend of his and of theirs.

There have been business conferences in which Latin American businessmen considered it quite appropriate to cite Descartes or Hegel (an American businessman would consider such references bad form if not positive bad manners). There have been political conferences through purple velvet tropical nights—I think of one on the loggia of an old Spanish palace by the sea—which ended in discussions of Machiavelli and Toynbee, while philosophy and ideas reached to the brilliant stars. There is the passionate search for wisdom which goes on in all circles, and the fact that almost pathetic recognition is given to an American who comes with the title of pro-

fessor, or with the authorship of a substantial book behind him. In
its strange, tortured, twisted way, Latin America is seeking not cash,
but culture; not economics, but education; not development, but de-
liverance. Politics, economics, industrialization, financial stability,
are essentially used to an end, and the end is assumed to be spiritual
—if one can only find the wisdom of the spirit.

This is not to deny the brutality which exists there as it does in
parts of the United States; nor the terrible indifference of some
Latin American upper class strata to the sub-proletarian misery
which exists around them. It is not to suggest that Latin American
civilizations have not committed all of the sins and cruelties which
have disfigured history in other parts of the world. It is to suggest
that in a curious way they have never abandoned a type of faith
which Anglo-Saxon countries barely apprehend and rarely understand. This is the reason why Latin American diplomacy, politics,
statesmanship, business, is inherently personal; the reason is, of
course, that development of personality is the chief end of Latin
American faith.

None the less, a principal pressing and urgent problem is that of
bringing up the condition of the working masses south of the Rio
Grande. Save in the industrialist centers and not infrequently there,
a laborer and his family will get up hungry, go through the day
half-fed, and sleep without knowing the sensation of a full stomach.
Though the ravages of yellow fever are under control, and of malaria on the way to being so, few escape some attack, and many have
chronic illness from amoebic dysentery or other forms of parasites.
There is the birth of a far higher degree of productivity in Latin
America but it has not yet reached the point at which the masses of
agrarian laborers or the less favored workers in cities have really
benefited. We are verging on the point at which most of Latin America will wear shoes; and that is all. Men with hungry families are
not finicky about philosophy: their physical problems demand solution first.

It is a poignant fact that the mass aspirations of the Latin American proletariat think of the United States as a focal point of hope.
Disappointed, these masses, unless they find swift solution in their

own countries will turn to other leadership. In a sense, the United States must be a powerful factor in raising the standard of living throughout the whole region, or stand in danger of losing the very base of her outstanding position in the twentieth century world. Rarely has an issue been presented in such obvious terms.

Considerable effort has been made indeed towards that end. American loans, and some American technical assistance, have been made available to most American countries—sometimes with outstanding results. Thanks to a very able career diplomat, Ambassador Edward J. Sparks, the United States moved into the Bolivian revolutionary situation three years ago, making it possible for the newly enfranchised Indians to satisfy some tiny measure of their desire for a more adequate life, and illustrations could be multiplied. These, however, have been largely uncoordinated operations, wide-spread though they are. Eventually the problem of integrating the economic life of the hemisphere, and assuring that a fair proportion of the benefits of rising production and rising economic competence reach the actual masses, must be squarely faced. Judging from the course of events, it would seem clear that the sooner it is faced and accomplished the safer the position of the United States will be.

CHAPTER Three

MID-CENTURY DILEMMA OF EUROPE

1

"It (Christendom) is a body without a head; a republic without laws or magistrates. The Pope and Emperor may shine as lofty titles, as splendid images: but they are unable to command, and none are willing to obey: every State has a separate prince, and every prince has a separate interest. What eloquence could unite so many discordant and hostile powers under the same standard? Could they be assembled in arms, who would dare to assume the office of General? What order could be maintained? What military discipline? Who would undertake to feed such an enormous multitude? Who could understand their various languages, or direct their stranger and incompatible manners? What mortal could reconcile the British with the French, Genoa with Aragon, the Germans with the natives of Hungary and Bohemia?" (Aeneas Sylvius [Pope Pius II] about 1460 A.D. Gibbon: "Decline and Fall of the Roman Empire," Chapter LXVIII)

THE STATEMENT quoted above was written by a Secretary of the Holy Roman Empire (his real name was Piccolomini) shortly after the Turks had captured Constantinople. The Byzantine Empire, last survivor of great Rome, had disappeared from the map of foreign relations. The East had erupted once more, had crossed the Bosphorus, and was engaged in a sweep which would take it to the shores of the Adriatic and to the gates of Vienna in the ensuing century. Indeed, when the writer was in school large parts of what is now Yugoslavia (the then provinces of Bosnia and Herzegovina) as well as much of the territory now comprised in modern Greece and Bulgaria was still under actual or nominal Turkish sovereignty.

One constant of European affairs has been the historic antagonism between Western Europe and Asia.

Dr. Arnold Toynbee stated the conflict in a little volume, "The World Against the West." He chooses to regard "the world" as the Asiatic world—possibly because it comprises a majority of the world's population, and "the West" as a peripheral outside force. There is solid argument for this—less solid than his argument that the West is always the aggressor. Toynbee comes by his argument with good classical precedent. The "father of history" Herodotus, writing of the Greek-Persian Wars about 446 B.C., starts with the proposition that the emergent and turbulent Greek cities had a bad habit of raiding their Asiatic neighbors for women and plunder: Jason carried off Medea, daughter of the king of a Black Sea city. Paris, son of Priam of Troy, from the Asiatic side, seduced Helen, wife of Menelaus, king of Sparta, following which the Greek cities combined in an expedition against Asian Troy. All this is far away and long ago. A much better case could be made now for the proposition that Asia has steadily been erupting into Europe since the dawn of recorded history. Certainly this has been true for the last millennium or so. Asian Huns, Goths, Vandals, pushed westward and southward in the fourth and fifth centuries, driving into the Roman Empire. The last act in the drama was a duel between Stilicho, a Vandal who had risen to be General of the Roman Armies, defending the West against Alaric, a Goth seeking to seize and plunder the Roman Empire of the East and the Roman Empire of the West as well. In the end, the Roman Emperor, Honorius, had Stilicho murdered—after which Alaric promptly captured and sacked Rome in 410 A.D.

Later, the Mohammedan invasions sliced across the Mediterranean and South Europe; they were only stopped by Charles Martel at Poitiers in 732 A.D.—but the Mohammedans held great parts of western Europe until just before Columbus discovered America. Southern Spain remained in uninterrupted Mohammedan possession for roughly eight centuries.

The Mohammedans attacked Europe from the Mediterranean; but greater peril came later. In the year 1200, a teen-age Mongol prince, Temushin, commenced a career which made him despot of an empire unrivaled in history (his only real competitor being, incidentally, the late Josef Stalin). He is known to history as Genghis Khan. He died in 1227 A.D. but the push of his movement continued. In 1243 A.D., his grandson, Kublai Khan, whose capital was in Peking or Peiping, China, controlled substantially the Chinese Empire of today plus most of the Russian and Siberian areas comprised in the Soviet Union and the satellite states. At the extremity of the movement, Mongolian armies held a north-south line through Germany not very far from the division line between East Germany (controlled by the Russians) and West Germany at date of writing.

A century and a half later a new push came out of what is now Russian Central Asia. This was another Mongol chieftain, Timur (known to history as Tamerlane or "Timur the Lame," a nickname he is said to have considered insulting). For some reason he stopped on the Asiatic side of the Sea of Marmara. In retrospect one wonders why: there was little to stop him. His advance agents, however, controlled a good deal of what is now the Balkan peninsula. He did not cancel out the conquests of Genghis Khan whom he claimed (probably incorrectly) as a collateral ancestor. Actually the armies of Genghis had retreated substantially to the confines of what we know today as Russia, and there they had stayed. They dissolved their dependence on the Chinese or Mongolian Empire but as the "Golden Hordes" they ruled Russia until approximately 1480. The design of their encampments is the ground plan of a number of modern Russian cities.

The greatest push against the west came in the mid-fifteenth century. The Mohammedan drive had picked up a new lease of life under the leadership of the Seljuk Turks. These redoubtable warriors were favored by fortune in having in succession five singularly able leaders. Their greatest obvious prey was the then dying Eastern Roman or Byzantine Empire whose territories on the Asian side they systematically overran. In Europe they already had a strong foothold north of Constantinople (the present Istanbul) in what is modern Bulgaria. To the south, they were able at will to enter what is now Greece. In 1453 they attacked and seized Constantinople, ending the last vestiges of the classic Roman Empire. Thence they pushed straight to the Adriatic. In 1530 we find them, under the Turkish Emperor Suleiman The Magnificent, at the very gates of Vienna. The history of their slow expulsion from Europe forms a large part of the modern history of eastern Europe. It has barely been completed. Great parts of what is today Yugoslavia were nominally Turkish territory within memory of middle-aged men now living, since the Austrian Empire only terminated the nominal Turkish sovereignty over the Yugoslav provinces of Bosnia and Herzegovina in 1907. Toynbee to the contrary, one could make a fairly good case for the proposition that West Europe, brought from primitive life to civilization by the Empire of Rome, has during its history been pretty continuously engaged in bracing itself against eruptive invasion from the vast Asian land mass with its overwhelmingly greater population.

The beginning of the twentieth century saw the situation rather differently. From the seventeenth century on, "the West" had had distinctly the better of the east-west argument. British traders followed by British private armies and eventually by British government forces had established control over India. Disraeli's crowning triumph was to crown Victoria "Empress of India" in 1877, recognizing a factual control which had been the reality for a century before that.

Meanwhile the Dutch had made themselves masters of much of the East Indian archipelago; the Spaniards of the Philippines; the British of Australia, New Zealand, Malaya and Singapore, Burma and Egypt. France had acquired control of Indo-China,

Portugal, of some great Pacific islands. The "West," first through the Austrian Empire, and later the Balkan nations (after the defeat of Turkey in World War I) through the medium of the succession states, had not only dislodged the Turks from all save the tiny part of Europe lying just west of Istanbul but had also taken over working control of most of Arabia. Bridgeheads had been established in the nineteenth century along the coast of China by one or another European power. The nine European empires excluding Russia (namely, Great Britain, France, Netherlands, Belgium, Spain, Portugal, Germany, Austro-Hungary and Italy), were thus substantially regnant. They had also absorbed practically all of Africa and the Middle East aside from Turkey herself. Confining analysis to the eighteenth and nineteenth centuries would give Toynbee a fair basis for his theory that world history amounted to the story of an aggressive West Europe driving against a rather quiescent Asian population and land mass.

The United States, as George Kennan has pointed out, entered this classic contest by accident.

A dying Spanish Empire surrendered the Philippine archipelago in 1898 to the United States; and America, with little consciousness of what was involved, found herself a Far Eastern Power. From then out the United States increasingly found herself tangled in the world struggles which have twice precipitated global war in the twentieth century.

2

And Russia?

Neither Russia herself nor the "West" has yet really determined whether she is part of the "West" or part of the Asian world. She herself has never quite decided the point—nor has Western Europe. The Russian peoples have had little to say about it, probably have not considered the point. Russian rulers have exhibited varying tendencies. Peter the Great (1682–1725) almost neurotically sought Western techniques for his country, but his Court exhibited many oriental characteristics. In 1762, a German Princess, Catharine, disposed of her rather ineffective Czar husband (or perhaps the group around her did—her guilt or innocence is disputed by historians) and thereupon as Empress set up a western-oriented Court. A successor, the Romanoff Emperor Alexander II, after hesitation made alliance with Napoleon but later drew away from it and became one of the constellation of princes who, after Napoleon's defeat, dictated peace at the Congress of Vienna in 1815. In alliance with Austria-Hungary, Spain, Portugal and others, he was one member of the "Concert of Powers" with its companion, the so-called "Holy Alliance," which virtually governed Europe in the early nineteenth century. This was in the main a western orientation. When World War I broke out in 1914, the Russian Empire was in firm alliance with Britain and France as a member of the "Triple Entente," and indeed a decade earlier Russia had been attacked and defeated by Japan in the Russo-Japanese War wherein Japan sought Asian dominion over the weakly held Chinese area of Manchuria where Russia was rapidly establishing imperial control in approved western style.

Her defeat in World War I, followed by the Communist Revolution of 1917, took Russia out of the western world at least for a time. European policy (in which Woodrow Wilson concurred) at the Versailles Peace Conference in 1918–1919 was, first, to try to overthrow the Soviet government and by direct military invasion to set up a government of Russia responsive to Allied ideas. This failed entirely. Secondarily, an attempt was made to erect a quarantine belt of countries (the famous "Cordon Sanitaire" of M. Clemenceau, then French Prime Minister), beginning at the north with Finland, Estonia, Latvia and Lithuania, carried southward by Poland, Czechoslovakia, Hungary, Roumania, Yugoslavia, and Bulgaria isolating the western world from contagion of Bolshevik revolution. Being a naval power, the British had primacy in Finland and the Baltic republics. France, the then dominant land power in Europe, erected an alliance with the southern mid-European states which came to be known as the "Little Entente" of the 20s.

Russian isolation actually did take place; and the Soviet rulers

appeared content to have it so. Despite that fact, Lenin exhibited
some of the characteristics of Peter the Great in seeking western
technicians and organization. He was following and adopting the
theories of Karl Marx, a German-trained Jew, much of whose life
was spent in England. Lenin himself had western experience and
in exile had operated out of Switzerland. Indeed, his Russian
emergence in the closing months of World War I was the result
of a desperate piece of western political warfare thought out by
the German General Staff. They sent him into Russia calculating
that he would disrupt the Czarist armies—as indeed he did,
thereby making certain German victory in the east. But Lenin was
not seeking western ideas and concepts, and Russia continued to
develop her own patterns. Lenin's successor, Josef Stalin, was a
Georgian whose background was certainly not western.

Endless studies have been made of the personality of Josef
Stalin. He was unquestionably the most powerful dictator of our
time. Definitive interpretation will be made only in historical per-
spective. Though he was content to enter the transitory alliance
with Europe in World War II, nothing suggests that he considered
the Soviet Union part of Europe. Or, for that matter, part of
Asia either though he emphasized to the fullest degree the Soviet
Union's Asian interests and ambitions, and erected a kind of loose
partnership between the Soviet Union and Communist China before his death.

Three possibilities are now open to the Soviet Union. She may
become a part of the west. She may become a part of the Asian
land and population mass. She may become—perhaps she already
is—the largest "buffer state" known to history, holding apart two
great groups of populations, western in Europe, oriental in Asia.
She has manifested great suspicion and fear of western Europe
because she was attacked and defeated by Germany in 1914–
1918; because the Allied Powers attempted to intervene by armed
action in her affairs in 1919–1921; because she was attacked again
by Hitler's Germany in 1941; and because she maintains that all
non-communist civilizations are necessarily her enemies. Mani-
festly it would not be in the psychology of any Russian government,

let alone a Soviet government, to concede that Czarist Russia was quite as anxious for war in 1914 as was Germany; or that the Soviet government bears a large part of the responsibility for World War II by signing the Hitler-Stalin pact in 1939 and conceding to Nazi Germany a free hand to act in Poland, or that "capitalist" countries did their best to make friends with her in the years preceding that pact. Even after World War II was over the Soviet government succeeded in seizing the government of Czechoslovakia and attempted to do the same thing in Greece.

But she has also consistently been in opposition to Japan. Though she has announced no similar suspicion of her great Far Eastern neighbor, China, the possibility of conflict of interest between herself and a strong Chinese Communist government must be in the consciousness both of the Soviet and the Chinese Foreign Office. It is not at all difficult to envisage a Chinese push northward and eastward into Asian land masses now dominated by the Soviet Union, or Chinese jealousy of growing Soviet influence in India. Of the three possibilities—a western orientation, Eastern orientation, or a buffer state—the third alternative is at least as likely to come about for Russia as either of the other two.

This brings our brief background sketch to present problems.

Following five years of "cold war" (not always so cool), the Soviet Union under the "new" policy of Bulganin and Khrushchev announced a desire to relieve "tensions" in the west. The result was the so-called "Summit Conference of Geneva" in the Summer of 1955. Since no specific matters were offered for discussion, the sole diplomatic purpose of the Soviet statesmen must have been an attempt to secure acceptance of the *status quo* by the west: the Soviet Union on her side creating the impression at least that for the time being she would not attempt to alter it to her advantage.

This, obviously, was merely a prelude to the opening of a mainline operation, conducted this time less with insult, subterranean guerrilla fighting and "cold war" techniques than with old style European diplomacy and economic weapons.

3

Western Europe merits a little contemplation at this point. It is a fascinating picture.

The Migration of Peoples which in the Fourth Century A.D. broke the old Roman lines, swirled across Europe and into Africa. It eventually came to rest leaving Europe a mosaic of peoples differing in race, language, tradition, custom and law. Even the national entities we know as France, Germany, Italy, Poland, and so forth, are themselves composed of entirely diverse strains. In Brittany, for example, Celtic is still spoken; in Alsace-Lorraine, a dialect German is as frequently found as French. In Germany there are still pockets of Wends. The Magyar Hungarians are perhaps distant cousins of the Finns. Mid-Europe is a huge scrambled pattern of different races commonly Slavic, though not uniformly so, and certainly not alike even when they are. Croats in Yugoslavia have marked differences from Serbs and Slovenes, Poles from Ukrainians, Czechs from both, and so forth.

Political organization was achieved in considerable part by the struggles for sovereign power in the feudal period. Great Houses like those of Anjou, Lorraine, Burgundy, Hapsburg, Aragon, Savoy and others, not to mention a host of lesser imitators, developed duchies, kingdoms and empires. These combinations were not based on race or language or common customs. They were assorted properties acquired by conquest or inheritance of individual rulers. These territories later finally crystallized (if they have) into the present political map of Europe. Rather less than half the land mass of Europe (counting the Ural Mountains and the Ural River as substantially Europe's eastern border) divided into some twenty-five independent countries—(counting Great Britain and Ireland as two and not counting some tiny historical mementos such as Monaco, Liechtenstein, Andorre and San Marino). The total population of this West European region is approximately 250 millions; the total area about that of the United States. The historical frame of reference of each of these units is amazingly different. Thus a Greek still thinks back to the days of Pericles; indeed, after World War I Greeks solemnly claimed at the Versailles Peace Conference sovereignty over the whole Turkish Black Sea Coast as far east as Trebizond. This was based on Greek colonization which had flourished—and had been conquered—more than 1,500 years before. A Netherlander on the other hand, will think back only to the emergence of his cities 1,000 years ago, of his lands wrested from the North Sea and redeemed from Spain four centuries ago, and will say with pride "God made other people's countries, but we made our own." A Dane will think of Viking ancestry and of a time when Danish kings controlled much of England; and so forth.

To speak of "unity" of western Europe is thus to project the conception of a kind of miracle. And yet, it is the kind of miracle that in some measure has occasionally taken place, and may—to this writer it seems, must—occur again.

The Romans accomplished it, in the days of Caesar Augustus about the time of the birth of Christ. For three centuries they held most of this area together under a Roman scepter with Roman Legions and under Roman law. Obviously the Roman Empire took over when the area was largely in the hands of primitive peoples, so that the precedent lacks weight. Or would, were it not for one fact. As the Eastern tides pushed into Rome's empire —a gradual process—they absorbed on their way and in their victory a large measure of Roman thought and Roman idealism. Eventually this brought them into the Christian religion. It is of interest that the earlier invasions were not so much rebellions or expeditions for the purpose of overthrowing Rome as for the purpose of becoming Rome. At the close of the period—let us say with the Emperor Charlemagne 800 A.D.—that monarch assumed the title of Roman Emperor and adopted the doctrine of the institution which most nearly represented Roman universality—the Catholic Church. He certainly thought of one Europe; not as one nation but certainly as one empire. For that matter, the Slavic and eastern rulers consciously believed they were joining their nations to the West when about the year 1000 A.D. Hungary, Poland and much of Czechoslovakia accepted the Catholic faith, drew bishops from Rome and sought princes and daughters of great western feudal houses for their kings and queens. If there was no unifying political organism, there was for that time a surprisingly high degree of unifying ideology.

Roughly speaking, the line parting east from west can still be traced as the line of influence of the Roman Catholic Church; it approximately divides Europe at the present western boundary of the Soviet Union, running from the Gulf of Finland south along the eastern boundaries of Poland and Roumania to the Black Sea. This is not a definitive boundary; you can move it 200 or 300 miles westward if you choose, and make all kinds of indents in it (for example, Bulgaria). But, substantially west of this line, the dominant religion was and now is Christian; the dominant thinking was or purported to be, and now is rational; the dominant law and legal institutions stem chiefly from Roman law; the dominant culture claims descent from classic Greece and Rome through Catholic and Christian-Protestant philosophy. The great centers of thought were the abbeys and universities of Italy, France and later England and Germany. Their daughter institutions are still the intellectual dynamos of the Western world.

So it comes about that, today, an intellectual of Poland or Germany is quite at home in a discussion at the University of Strasbourg in France. A British scholar is perhaps closer to his colleagues in Paris than to scholars elsewhere in the world. An impulse given to thought in any European center reflects itself rapidly in all other European thought centers. Politically divided, western Europe certainly is. Yet each part of it has, in the main, more in common with each of the other parts than it has with the Orient, or with Russia, or until recently, with the United States. "United Europe" has been only a politician's dream so far as political organization goes. It nevertheless has been in considerable measure an intellectual and philosophical reality.

And Europe has made the most of this. Scientifically and technically, Europe gave the impetus to the entire world until the latter part of the nineteenth century when the United States picked up the challenge and took it forward. Scientific thought emerged chiefly from the European nexus; out of it came the dynamic technical development which has been the outstanding feature of the twentieth century. Today, even after five years of war and ten years of anxious reconstruction, Europe is at least abreast and perhaps ahead of the United States in pure research. It is not an accident that the outstanding twentieth century discovery—atomic fission—occurred in the United States as a result of the speculations of a German Jewish refugee, Einstein, the explorations of an Italian, Fermi, and of a Danish scientist, Nils Bohr, working in the United States with a second-generation American, Robert Oppenheimer. For that matter, translation of atomic fission into hydrogen fusion was accomplished upon the foundation they laid by a Hungarian, Teller. Neither is it accident that these men were not only European, but came from widely divergent parts of Europe. The illustration could be duplicated over and over again.

Then why, in the name of sanity in foreign relations, has Europe been unable to unify herself into enough political organization to maintain her defenses and forward her economic and cultural life? The experiment has surely been tried. As we noted, in 962 A.D. Otto of Saxony tried it and did bring a great deal of Europe into a loose political combination known as "The Empire" which continued in existence for more than 800 years.

This was not so bad for a piece of political warfare based primarily on ideology; not so bad, when one recalls that in 1550 the "Holy Roman Emperor" of the day, Charles V, of Austria, succeeded in bringing most of Europe under his sway except France, and arranged a marriage between his son, Philip II, and Mary Tudor, Queen of England; not so bad when one remembers that during most of this period, Europe subscribed to the doctrine that it theoretically was, or at least should be, one "universal empire" though no one agreed who should have what in its vast domain. Yet a unified Europe never emerged.

The passionate tragedy of twentieth century Europe stems directly from this ideal of spiritual and intellectual unity set against the drama of bloody struggles between its component units. We shall not know for years—if we ever can know—the profoundest

meaning of Pan-European wars from the time of Napoleon to that
of Hitler. They are easily construed as wars of France driven by
the personal ambition of Napoleon, of Germany under Kaiser
Wilhelm II and again under Hitler, to conquer their European
neighbors. It is at least arguable that their deeper motivation was
to create a united Europe, as the great Napoleon almost did by
force of arms, and as Metternich and Talleyrand very nearly accomplished by diplomacy after 1815. A strong current of diplomacy after World War I looked toward this end. Woodrow Wilson
hoped, and Aristide Briand labored, to make the League of Nations at least in part a nucleus of common European action. But
the politics of international affairs prevented consummation of the
dreams of intellectuals; and the struggle still continues.

In result, Europe remains 25 nations comprising an area more
literate, more sentient, intellectually more productive than any
area in the world, great parts of which fear the other parts while
realizing that they are all locked by history, geography, economics,
necessity, into a single mass. The second half of the twentieth century is dominated, essentially, by the growth of American and
eastern forces whose emergence has been permitted, if not actually compelled, by European disunity.

4

World War II ended badly for Western Europe and badly for the
United States. Badly, despite the fact that American and British
arms were triumphant, that American economy had emerged so
strong that it could supply and reconstruct most of the world;
badly, despite the fact that President Franklin Roosevelt's "Four
Freedoms" (Freedom from Fear; Freedom from Want; Freedom
of Information; Religious Freedom) had become the battle-cry of
the world.

In terms of policy, an error of judgment had been made. The
Soviet Union, hanging between east and west, had attempted to
safeguard herself from Nazi aggression by entering an alliance with
Hitler in 1939. Probably this was considered "real-politik" though
other pretexts were given. Soviet propaganda asserted that impor-

tant elements in Britain (loosely called the Cliveden clique) had intrigued with Hitler to buy immunity for Western Europe, leaving Hitler to attack and destroy an unaided Soviet Union. Only the flimsiest evidence was ever presented to substantiate the charge. No doubt the idea had occurred to some Englishmen. It had also occurred to Stalin and Molotov that a Soviet-Nazi alliance might allow Hitler to destroy the capitalist west. The project of a Nazi alliance never reached serious consideration on the side of the west. It did receive serious consideration in Moscow. While British and French Ambassadors were waiting in the anterooms, Stalin and Molotov concluded an arrangement with Hitler and Ribbentrop which the Soviet Union hoped would prevent a German attack on her, with cynical indifference to the results of a Nazi attack on France. German and Russian propaganda thereafter worked together, stridently denouncing Britain, France and their allies as "imperialists" and "war-mongers."

In the early fall of 1940, the government of the United States received a strange piece of information. It was, in substance, that the German General Staff had recommended to Hitler (perhaps at his insistence) an attack on the Soviet Union. The rough plan was that German armies should be grouped in the east so as to attack on or about the 15th of June, 1941. In the ensuing campaign it was hoped to reach and capture Moscow in early fall of 1941, ending the Russian side of the war. Prior to this, of course, all sorts of arrangements had to be made virtually placing Nazi Germany in control (where she did not already have it) of the mid-European states. This phase looked, and indeed proved, relatively easy. Nazi troops had already conquered Poland in a brief campaign called "a bloody promenade" by one of the German generals. Italian armies were already attacking Greece. It was considered that, by diplomacy or by direct military action, the governments of Yugoslavia, Hungary, Roumania, Bulgaria, could easily be brought into line.

Mr. Sumner Welles, then Undersecretary of State, on behalf of the American State Department, informed the Russian Ambassador in Washington of the information thus received, as a friendly gesture. The Soviet government seems to have hesitated in acting on it. Very probably they considered it was a maneuver by the United States (known to be strongly sympathetic to Great Britain and France) to break up the happy German-Soviet co-operative relationship. But by the spring of 1941 German operations must have made it plain that Hitler's armies no longer confined their ambitions to attacking the West; indeed, the fall of France in June, 1940 had removed the last major allied fighting force from the European mainland. Agonized negotiations then began between Moscow and Berlin.

Apparently the Soviet government was prepared to buy its peace with Hitler almost at any price. German demands however, went beyond requests for aid, and even beyond prior economic rights in certain areas (notably the Ukraine) and for close co-operation between the governments. The German government demanded conditions which would have given it virtual control of the Soviet government and the Soviet armies. Probably they had no intention at any time of making any real arrangement: outright surrender of the Soviet Union to Hitler was the objective underlying the various proposals which were discussed. Delayed slightly by Yugoslav resistance and by the fact that the Greeks had shown themselves more than a match for the Italians, the German armies moved eastward. They actually invaded Russia on June 22, 1941, scarcely a week off schedule.

At this point the alliance between the Soviet Union and the west began. Mr. Winston Churchill awoke on Sunday, June 22, to receive news of the invasion. He had discussed the probability the night before with American Ambassador John G. Winant and Anthony Eden and had remarked:

"If Hitler invaded hell, I would make at least a favorable reference to the Devil in the House of Commons."

He at once broadcast a declaration:

"We shall give whatever help we can to Russia and the Russian people. We shall appeal to all our friends and allies in every part of the world to take the same course and pursue it."

Privately, he was delighted to have an ally.

The diplomatic history of World War II is becoming fairly complete and well-documented, though history has not yet revealed the secrets of the Soviet Foreign Office. It is sufficiently clear now that the Grand Alliance, despite efforts to give it a more constructive quality was, so far as the Soviet Union was concerned, a transitory policy based on the old Oriental proverb, "The enemy of your enemy is your friend." After Pearl Harbor the German government declared war on the United States (December 11, 1941), pursuant to its treaty with Japan. Churchill immediately scheduled a trip to Washington. On January 1, 1942, a document constituting the Grand Alliance, headed by the United States, Great Britain, the Soviet Union and China, and entitled by President Franklin Roosevelt "Declaration by United Nations," was signed at the White House.

War engenders close working relationships. Endeavor was made, as part of the war effort, to cultivate the closest connection with the Soviet Union. There was a powerful desire to create relationships at least between the major Allied Powers which would survive the period of war, and would lay a foundation for constructing an eventual permanent peace. This was the posture of affairs up to the summer of 1944.

In that summer, the balance changed. France had been successfully invaded by the American Expedition under General Dwight Eisenhower. The German armies had been driven back. The Rhine had been reached. The German armies, defeated and stopped in the East at Stalingrad in January, 1943 were now entirely unable to handle a two-front war and were almost expelled from Soviet territory. American and British planes were systematically pounding German cities to rubble. Ultimate defeat of Germany was fairly certain. (The British General Staff estimated it would be complete by the end of 1944, though their time calculation was thrown off by the German counterattack resulting in the Battle of the Bulge.)

Such evidence as is available strongly suggests that the Soviet Union thereupon reviewed its foreign policy; probably in June or

July of 1944 though possibly somewhat later. Decision seems to have been taken at that time to close out the relationship of war cooperation and to play a lone hand against the field. The decision was secret, and much of the evidence rests on the fact that the Soviet Union quietly withdrew from a number of the negotiations then proceeding to organize post-war Europe. The irregular forces, or "undergrounds," in various parts of Europe cleft sharply; those dominated by Communists were primarily seeking to seize the governments of the countries in which they operated. It became increasingly clear that whatever the nominal relationships at the summit, on the operating and fighting levels the Soviet alliance had been replaced by her overt or covert hostility.

What was really going on here was a struggle to be the dominant force in the governments of the countries formerly occupied by German armies and now coming out of the shadow. The "governments in exile," the old political parties and institutions still surviving German occupation, the old forms of government, were to be superseded by Communist governments resting on the forces of armed Communist guerrillas constituting the pro-Russian undergrounds. Wherever Russian armies entered, they succeeded in eliminating all pro-Western forces and promptly installed pro-Communist groups by fair means—or by foul.

Mounting evidence that the era of cooperation ended as soon as Germany was no longer a threat did not deter western Allied statesmen from seeking an understanding. Both Churchill and Roosevelt were resolved to find common ground and to effect a working and friendly understanding with the Soviet Union if it could possibly be done. This fact, which led to the Yalta meeting in February, 1945 (to which the writer was opposed), has been the subject of most violent political controversy. From all the welter of charges and countercharges, however, it is reasonably clear that the attempt to continue the wartime alliance for peace-making cooperation was based on two motives:

1. President Roosevelt and, importantly, though less warmly, Winston Churchill, believed that real peace in the West could only be made by common action of Great Britain, United

States and the Soviet Union. They envisaged the three Powers, together with emergent France, as a group which, working together, would reconstruct Europe.

2. They were anxious to have the cooperation of the Soviet Union in attacking and defeating Japan immediately after the defeat of Germany. In doing this, they were acting on the advice, indeed at the urgence of the senior officers responsible for conducting the war. A majority at least of the Joint Chiefs of Staff considered that without a Russian attack on Japanese armies then in north China, the task of conquering Japan would involve extremely great loss of life.

In the light of hindsight, it is clear that the Allied statesmen were right in their first objective. European peace could only have been solidly constructed on the basis of cooperation with the Soviet Union. But, as has been noted above, the masters of the Soviet Union had decided not to cooperate.

As to the second, the Allied statesmen were simply mistaken. Though it was perhaps impossible for them to have known it, Russian aid in the Far East was completely unnecessary. The Japanese Imperial government was already convinced of impending defeat and was attempting to negotiate a settlement. Also, a few weeks later the atomic bomb was successfully exploded at White Sands, New Mexico. As we know now, the problem was not one of getting the Soviet Union into the war against Japan but rather in keeping her out of northern China.

In retrospect also, a moral can be drawn.

Military strategists for years had agreed that the first and chief task of an army in the field was to destroy the enemy's forces in being. This is a straight military approach. Today, with more experience, we should modify this. We should say that, as victory approaches, an army has to combine its military objective—destroying the enemy's forces in being—with a second, political objective. It must establish political control and conditions which will serve as a base for the intended peace.

The Soviet armies, being politically directed, understood this. The Allied armies, or at least the American armies did not. It was entirely in the American tradition that General Eisenhower, who might have captured Berlin, chose instead to pursue and destroy the remnants of the German armies in the Erzgebirge. Military logic here crosses political logic; today most General Staffs accept that fact. In 1945, the fact that as victory draws near military, political and diplomatic action must coalesce had not been thoroughly absorbed.

At all events, the western forces accepted the Soviet Union as full partner in the reconstruction of western Europe and delimited "zones of occupation," not for political purposes but merely to assure each army an administrative area in which it was expected to keep order, maintain peace and so forth. Government and reconstruction were to be worked out and carried on by committees representing the three, or rather the four governments (for France had emerged). These, sitting together, were to recreate Europe.

The Soviet Union, of course, had no such idea. Stipulating for a large "zone of occupation" to the east of the area—virtually a line from Stettin in Germany due south through Austria to Trieste on the Adriatic—she immediately made of it a boundary. Behind it, Soviet generals and politicians undertook to create governments, states and economic systems, responsive to Moscow dictatorship. The single enclave within that area was Berlin, capital of Germany, surrounded entirely by Soviet-occupied territory. On the eastern side of the armistice line (which, augmented by Czechoslovakia, is the line of the Iron Curtain today) the Soviet Union indulged no nonsense whatever about cooperation with her erstwhile allies.

The effect, naturally, was to give the Soviet Union military control over the huge mid-Europe area with a population of roughly 90 million people; with most of the strategic roads through which west Europe can be invaded; with a stranglehold on some of Europe's richest natural resources. She wasted no time in imposing her Communist system on this area, conscripting its population to her economic needs and into satellite armies.

The Soviet Union had thus occupied the same territory as that taken by the armies of Kublai Khan in 1243. She had moved the physical, and now attempted to move the intellectual frontier of Europe from the old line of the eastern boundary of Poland to a new line eight hundred miles or so west. On the north—at Stettin, on the Baltic—this is only three hundred miles from the border of the Netherlands. Western Europe, from having been nearly half a continent, became merely a great peninsula, sealed off from the Eurasian land mass. So it remains in 1957.

5

Russian foreign policy has always been flexible, and the same is true of the foreign policy of the Soviet Union. Its outstanding quality is tenacity; objectives once determined on remain the same for decades if not centuries. The unvarying aim is to build up a position giving the Russian government power to take advantage of available opportunities and, if possible, to manufacture opportunities.

Soviet diplomacy from this point of view has been excellent— uncomfortably so for the west.

The Soviet Union had made the most of her position as the war ended. Her statesmen had promised participation with the United States and the western allies in the war against Japan to commence shortly after the defeat of Germany. In return for this, she sought wide advantages in Europe—the Stettin-Trieste line, and recognition of her position in North China. Briefly, the result of the conferences at Yalta in February in 1945 and Potsdam in July, 1945 gave her control of East Germany and the Baltic Sea, of Central Europe and the Balkans (excluding Greece) and a promise that the position and influence in China which she had lost when defeated by Japan in the Russo-Japanese War in 1904 would be returned to her. In return she gave promises that the mid-European countries should have "governments of their own choosing" and other guarantees. As Russian armies were in control these promises could not be enforced and thus far have meant little or nothing.

Political controversy still rages in the United States about the

Yalta and Potsdam agreements. No attempt is made here to pass final judgment, but one point needs to be noted. As the Western statesmen saw the situation at Yalta, even though Germany approached defeat Japan remained a potentially formidable opponent. Her defeat was probably certain, but as military estimates then ran it would require most of the American strength to accomplish it, and the price in American life might have been very great. The American plan was to redeploy the bulk of the American forces which had been used against Hitler and direct them towards crushing Japan. Necessarily (since the British forces were far smaller than the American, and other forces comparatively insignificant), this would leave the Russian armies overwhelmingly supreme in Europe.

American statesmanship might, perhaps, have avoided this. The American command might have adjourned the final attack on Japan, might have kept American forces standing in western Europe, might have pushed farther eastward in Germany, perhaps into Poland, holding the Russians more nearly on their own frontier. This, of course, is pure hindsight. If in 1945 an American President or politician had advocated postponing defeat of Japan, with consequent prolongation of the war, for the purpose of "containing" Russia, he probably would have been immediately eliminated from public life, both on the ground that he was prolonging the war and also on the ground that he was favoring the then extremely unpopular Japanese. American public opinion had not forgotten Pearl Harbor, or the Death March of Bataan.

At all events, this was not done. Redeployment of American forces from Europe to the Pacific began; attempt was made to work out with the Soviet Union a joint Allied government of Europe. It never got off the ground. The Soviet Union promptly set up Communist puppet governments within her zone of occupation and warned the western representatives off the premises. The western powers were forced to reorganize the west Europe we know today as best they could.

Soviet diplomacy apparently considered this a golden opportunity for further expansion in western Europe. In any event it

promptly blazed away. A Communist "revolution" in Greece began almost at once. It was carefully masked as a "spontaneous"
uprising of Greeks for "democratic government"; nothing was said
about the fact that there was a steady flow of arms from Russian
centers of occupation in adjacent Bulgaria, or that there were
training camps for guerrillas within the Russian lines in nearby
Yugoslavia. The then Stalinist Tito became Communist leader of
Yugoslavia and promptly joined it to the Soviet system. In 1948,
three years after the defeat of Germany, with threatening Russian
armies on three sides of Czechoslovakia, a Communist revolution
was fomented there.

The Greek civil war (to give it a more respectable name than a
fomented revolution really deserves) from 1945 to 1947 went
badly for everyone. The Greek guerrillas even with Communist
help had not quite force enough to take over, chiefly because
Greece had been assigned to the British army as an occupation
zone and British troops forthrightly resisted Communist efforts. To
fellow-travellers and confused idealists who insisted the revolu-
tionists merely wanted "democratic government," Winston Churchill scornfully replied that democracy could not be picked up off the
street by a mob armed with tommy guns. But the burden bore
so heavily on the British that in February, 1947 they made repre-
sentations in Washington. The British government said in substance that it no longer had the money to pay for Greek defense
in view of its own impoverished post-war state, and squarely
dumped the question in the lap of President Harry S. Truman. He
settled it by stating (March 10, 1947) to the Congress that "It
must be the policy of the United States to support free peoples who
are resisting attempted subjugation by armed minorities or by outside pressures" and accordingly that the United States would provide economic and military assistance to Greece. This was the
so-called "Truman Doctrine," and it opened a new phase of affairs.

We only know the western side of what followed next. Soviet
armies along the whole Iron Curtain line from Stettin to Trieste
and notably in Austria deployed in a fashion suggesting that they
planned to cross the border assigned to them by Yalta and Pots-

dam arrangements, and to march westward. Certainly there was insufficient western force to prevent them from doing so had they moved forward. By that time the American army, having ended the Japanese War in the Pacific, had been (too hastily) demobilized. American occupation forces in Germany had been almost reduced to the "token" stage. The writer has seen unconfirmed reports that the Soviet General Staff recommended to Moscow an immediate westward movement. Soviet sources are not yet available to check these reports. At all events the Kremlin finally decided against overt war, but instead began the "cold war" which has exacerbated Europe ever since.

A last major attempt to cooperate with the Soviet Union was made by the United States and West European countries by initiation of the so-called "Marshall Plan" shortly after the United States had assumed the defense of Greece. This plan envisaged vast economic aid to Europe. It was proposed that the United States, Great Britain, France and the Soviet Union should jointly participate in its administration with the objective of rebuilding a prosperous unified Europe including both sides of the Iron Curtain. A conference was called in Paris to work out a plan. The Soviet Union, flirting with the idea, sent a large delegation of diplomats and experts to work on it. But, in the course of the conference the Soviet government decided on a contrary policy. Her delegation abruptly announced that the Marshall Plan was nothing more than a plan of economic imperialism designed to reduce Europe to the status of an economic vassal of the United States. Western European governments did not agree with this and the Soviet delegation left Paris in a cloud of denunciation.

Organization of the Marshall Plan thereupon went forward, with Communist propaganda opposing it at every turn. In November and December of 1947, apparently, Soviet diplomacy plus subversion attempted a major thrust. Communist organizations and Communist-dominated labor unions in both France and Italy were directed to call general strikes. These were really aimed at the overthrow of the pro-western governments of these countries. Presumably the plan was to develop them into full-fledged, Communist, pro-Russian revolutions, bringing two principal countries of western Europe into the Soviet sphere. If so, the Soviet statesmen had overestimated the capacity of their propaganda and Communist organizations—a mistake they have sometimes made in other operations. At all events, by Christmas 1947 first the Italian and then the French general strikes failed; disorder did not develop; revolution did not happen; pro-western governments remained in power, and the Marshall Plan went forward.

The only remaining action which might have changed the situation would have been direct invasion by the Russian armies standing on the border of the east German zone. They did not march. The Soviet Union probably considered the risk too great. That might have precipitated a new world war; at all events, the Soviet Union, angrily, accepted the *status quo.*

More accurately, she accepted for a time only. There was an isolated enclave of pro-western power in Berlin. This was a single city, surrounded entirely by Russian-held territory and by Russian troops. But it was also an outward, visible symbol of a possible reunited Germany. There were some material and many psychological advantages if it could be seized. In March of 1948, the Soviet troops in effect blockaded Berlin by the simple process of refusing to allow railroad trains, trucks and other transport to enter the city. This meant, of course, that the population of roughly 3,000,000, administered by a Commission composed of American, British, French and Russian officers, was deprived of fuel, light, and food. Whether the Soviet Union would have persisted in the blockade had Americans undertaken to send trains from West Germany into Berlin under armed guard and risked the ensuing fighting no one can now tell. The actual American answer was to supply Berlin by air, using army transport planes to carry coal, oil, food and supplies—an improvised, unheard of operation whose possibility had not occurred to the Soviet policy makers. Or, probably, to anyone else either. For some months the blockade continued, and likewise the airlift.

In terms of propaganda this was an enormous demonstration of what American aircraft could do, and it eventually became clear that for Russia, too, the game was not worth the candle. After some months, at a meeting of the United Nations in New York, a Russian diplomat suggested to an American diplomat that the matter might be settled. After some typically exasperating negotiations, the blockade was finally discontinued. For practical purposes, this was to be the last attempt of the Russians to use power politics against western Europe up to the date of writing, though the possibility of future attempts of course continues.

The situation thus created, as Americans undertook to prevent revolutionary seizure of Greece and as the Soviet Union attempted to make acceptance of the Marshall Plan cause for civil war, forcibly compelled the entire west to face frankly the problem of its own defense. General George C. Marshall, then Secretary of State, and Robert Lovett, his brilliant Undersecretary, undertook negotiation of a European defense pact, modeled along the lines of the inter-American defense pact worked out between the United States and the other American nations at Chapultepec in 1945. The result was creation of NATO—the North Atlantic Treaty Organization—by treaty signed in Washington on April 4, 1949. This provided for collective defense of the area. It contemplated creation and maintenance in Europe of armies capable of defending the area against attack. The NATO forces gradually came into existence. At date of writing, they are still Europe's chief defense against armed action from the east. Combined with the economic arrangements worked out under the Marshall Plan (they had been put into the form of a "Convention for European Economic Cooperation," signed at Paris on April 16, 1948), there was thus established a measure of military defense and economic underpinning for Western Europe.

Western Europe and with it, the United States, meanwhile had a bit of luck. Yugoslavia occupies a singularly strategic piece of real estate, since, among other things, it commands access to the Adriatic and so to the Mediterranean Sea. When added to the zone of Russian occupation, including Hungary, it gives to the Soviet group of nations the possibility of operating in the Adriatic and Mediterranean—a long coveted opening for the Russian empire. Yugoslavia had, as noted, been one of the breeding grounds for the attack on Greece. But apparently the Communist dictator, Josef Broz, better known as Marshal Tito, had ambitions of his own. Also, the Soviet Union overplayed its hand in demanding economic concessions and exacting supplies from Yugoslavia. Tito in 1948 seceded from the Soviet group, maintaining that Yugoslavia was sole exponent of true Communism, and that the Soviet Union had now deviated from the true faith. He proposed accordingly to maintain himself equipoised between the Soviet east and Western Europe. He was prepared, among other things, to accept arms from the west and indicated that if the Soviet Union tried to depose his government by force, he would meet it with arms.

The Soviet Union made no effective reply, but merely turned its propaganda guns with their customary abuse upon Tito. This affected him relatively little. For the time being at least, Yugoslavia was lost to the Soviet complex; lost also as a further stamping ground from which Communist guerrillas could continue to raid Greece. As a result, the Soviet system lost not only its land access to the Mediterranean but also the chief base for its attack on Greece, so that the Greek "civil war" presently collapsed.

Thereafter the Soviet Union adjourned its western push. Instead, it turned its efforts eastward where it had strong interest in China, and some lively package-revolutions exported or in process of export to French Indo-China, British Malaya, Burma and the Philippines. Hunting was apparently better on the Pacific side. The result was an interlude of comparatively static cold warfare on the west front. It lasted from 1949 until Stalin's death in March 1953.

6

Though the progress of Soviet foreign operations in the Pacific theater is not our preoccupation here, one aspect of it has to be noted to comprehend the western events of 1954–1955.

Communist triumph in China became complete in 1950 and with it came recovery of the dominant Soviet position in Manchuria and China lost by Czarist Russia to the Japanese in 1904. On the face of it, Soviet diplomacy had secured a smashing victory. Her four-day costless participation in the war against Japan in 1945 had gained for her the Kurile Islands screening the Asian mainland to the north of Japan, had gained also the southern half of the Island of Sakhalin; had yielded her the possible occupation of the port of Darien; had given her substantial control of the Chinese eastern railroad which connects the Trans-Siberian Railroad with the Pacific; and a number of other, perhaps even more important, advantages. For practical purposes she now controlled the industrial plants of Manchuria; this, added to the economic developments just north of Korea, gave her a powerful position. The Communist government of Mao Tse-tung appeared to be a huge addition to the Moscow system.

But there was a price to pay. China, described as a "sleeping giant" by Napoleon (and he strongly advised against waking the giant), had been energized. The Chinese Communist organization proved dynamic enough to accomplish some measure of the important task: it pulled together a government of a more or less unified China and enabled that government to use Chinese manpower and resources for foreign as well as domestic adventure. Whether the awakening is permanent and continuing can not now be estimated. Unquestionably it is still going on.

It was sufficient to effect powerful intervention in favor of North Korea in 1950; it may perhaps have been the cause of the attempt of North Korean Communists to seize South Korea though more probably that was sparked by the Soviet Union.

It was sufficient to effect one development which changes the entire history of our time: the organization of a powerful Chinese land army. It was this army that forced General MacArthur back from the Yalu River to the 38° parallel in Korea; it is this army which has organized air bases on the Chinese mainland, capable of threatening Japan as well as Formosa; it is a formidable force. With its growth, China emerged as a power in being.

A great power, in fact, capable of asserting equality with the Soviet Union; and this almost necessarily must have played a part in the calculations of Foreign Minister Molotov and his extremely able staff in Moscow. China did not emerge as a Soviet satellite. It emerged as a comparable, though weaker, power.

Now it is clear that this emerged China posed a square problem for the Russian diplomats and politicians. The resources of a captive power such as Poland or Czechoslovakia could be used by Soviet Russia for its own ends. The resources of China would be used primarily for Chinese ends. Expansion of the Soviet Union at Chinese expense would set up a clash of interests between the two powers in which, over the long run, the Soviet Union would be at a disadvantage. Soviet-held Siberia is sparsely settled, empty territory; Communist China claims a population of 600,000,000 (the real figure is probably in the vicinity of 480,000,000). There are no sufficient barriers to that population should it decide to seep northward and westward into Soviet-held territory. Emergent China not unnaturally is attracted by the idea of achieving a hegemony in Asia. But much of the area which would interest her lies along Russian frontiers and probably has been ticketed by Soviet expansionists for future Soviet conquest. Common sense would suggest to any Soviet policy-maker that the conflict be avoided, certainly for the present.

Actually it was at the insistence of the Soviet government that armistice ending the Korean war was finally achieved. Equally, the Soviet Union went far towards satisfying Chinese ambitions by relinquishing to the Chinese Communist government the ports and transportation concessions and so forth she had secured in Manchuria. On the other hand she became obviously sensitive in respect of certain areas where Chinese influence tended to grow,—for example, the hazy state of Outer Mongolia, recently proposed as a full member of the United Nations but for practical purposes a Soviet satellite. And Soviet statesmen became still more sensitive when the Chinese Communist statesmen indicated a warm interest in developing close ties with the government of India.

What appears to have happened at date of writing is development of a typical oriental alliance of somewhat uneasy friendship. The Soviet Union was and is heavily involved with the success of China. On the other hand she does not wish her partner—at pres-

ent her junior and rather weaker partner—to commit the Soviet
Union in a world war, or to engage Russian strength in struggles
which would primarily redound to the benefit of Peking rather than
Moscow. Since the Chinese, for all their manpower and resources,
are not organized sufficiently to maintain large conflicts or use their
newly organized armies without assurance of Russian supplies of
munitions and matériel, the Soviet diplomats are in a position to
exercise a degree of control over China.

To do so, that is, so long as some headstrong or violent move by
the Chinese government does not precipitate a struggle between the
East and West. The Soviet Union quite rightly has reason to wonder
whether if Chinese ambition precipitated a full-scale war in the Pacific, the West would not immediately consider the Soviet Union as
an enemy. To have circumscribed the Korean conflict as a "limited
war" was something of a minor miracle. No one would care to base
policy on an estimate that the miracle would occur again. The United
Nations and American resistance in Korea made it sufficiently plain
that attempts to occupy further Asian territory, however disguised
as "spontaneous popular revolutions" (unaccountably equipped
with Russian airplanes and ordnance manufactured in Czechoslovakia) would probably encounter violent armed resistance.

Adding up the score, the Soviet Union was approaching the immediate limit of her expansion in the Pacific. The time had obviously come, one surmises, when the Soviet Foreign Office decided
to hold the line for the time being and attempt no more major invasion in that area until better opportunity offered. So, it would seem,
the situation may have appeared to cool-headed, cynical Soviet
policy-makers at the close of the year 1953. They had made all
that they conveniently could for the time being on the Pacific side.
The moment had come to re-examine the situation in Europe and
in the Near East.

7

We may safely assume, I think, that in their re-examination which
may have taken place shortly after the death of Stalin, Soviet policy-
makers saw the situation somewhat as follows:

Western Europe, up to the Iron Curtain line (now interrupted at the Yugoslav border instead of going all the way to Trieste) was defended by the now substantial forces of the North Atlantic Treaty Organization—the NATO Powers. These were in process of being reinforced. Western Germany had now recovered economically and it was clear that she would in part cease to be an "occupied" country in the near future. Her former enemies in the west were actively aiding her recovery, and they were likewise proposing that she should rearm and join her projected army with the NATO forces. Force politics in this direction, therefore, meant trouble—quite possibly World War III. There is every reason to believe the Soviet Union, like the United States and practically all the world, premised its policy on the theory that World War III would have wholly unpredictable results, and that substantial risk of it was not worth taking. Literally no one understands the implications of air (and by 1958, rocket) warfare with hydrogen bomb warheads. No effective defense has really been worked out and reprisal however successful is not the same as victory.

On the other hand there was, and still is, a soft under-belly south and east. This comprises Yugoslavia and Greece in the Balkans, Turkey, Iran, Afghanistan, Pakistan, and possibly, India; and south of that a whole group of weak and quarrelling countries around the eastern and southern Mediterranean. Now this happens to be an area in respect of which Russia both under the Czars and under the Soviets has long had great ambitions and concerning which it has long made some rather surprising claims.

The ambitions are logical enough. The Soviet-Siberian land mass has no real safe outlet to the ocean. The Baltic Sea, with the disappearance of Germany as a naval power, has become virtually a Russian lake, but it can be blocked at its narrow entrance between the coasts of Denmark and Sweden. The Arctic from Archangel on the far side of the Finnish peninsula, across the top of Europe and Asia to Bering Strait is frozen much of the time. The Soviet Union has manfully struggled with ice-breaking arrangements to open a northern sea lane there, but it is no substitute for warm water transport. One warm water port, Murmansk, at the

very top of the Finnish peninsula (by "warm" we mean that the
water does not freeze: it is usually 33° Fahrenheit) is far away and
unhandy. Her Pacific port of Vladivostok is frozen in winter and a
long way from Russian production centers. Her real outlet is to the
Black Sea—but the neck of that bottle is the narrow Bosphorus
and the Straits of the Dardanelles across which Turkey has sat
since 1453. Controlling the outlet from the Black Sea—taking
Constantinople in the old days (Istanbul today)—has been the
dream of Russian diplomacy for at least 200 years.

Unfortunately the outlet from the Black Sea is not to an ocean,
but to the Mediterranean—another closed sea. One end of the Mediterranean, of course, opens through the Suez Canal, the Red Sea
and the Strait of Aden into the Indian Ocean. The other, to the
Atlantic through the Straits of Gibraltar. Getting out of the Black
Sea and into the Mediterranean is merely the first move, the second
being to get out of the Mediterranean either to the east or west.

The Czarist empire moved in this direction nearly a century ago
and was blocked by Prime Minister Benjamin Disraeli of Great Britain at the Conference of Berlin in 1878. He landed a contingent of
British troops in Constantinople; then the Czarist Ministers backed
down, and Disraeli returned to England saying proudly and truth-
fully that he had brought about "peace with honor." In World War
I the Western Allies had promised Constantinople (as it then was)
to Russia as part of the division of spoils when Kaiser Wilhelm's
Germany should be defeated; but these promises were cancelled
when United States entered the war in 1917—and in any case Czarist Russia was defeated in that war. Finally, the Soviet diplomats
had put in a stiff claim for control of the Bosphorus and the Dardanelles at the close of World War II. Their driving support of the
Communist revolution (or, if you choose, invasion) of Greece after
the war was probably one of the moves looking toward this end. It
was also one of the reasons why Turkey, though not predominantly
European, had nevertheless joined NATO, and why as the Greek
crisis developed the United States dispatched a fleet to the eastern
Mediterranean which is maintained there now (1957).

And, to this writer, it is clear that the Soviet design did not end with control of the Dardanelles and access to the Mediterranean. In the course of some negotiations in 1944, the Soviet representatives proposed to the writer that an American airline should meet, end to end, with a Soviet airline in Cairo, Egypt. The implication was reasonably plain that the Soviet sphere of influence was to include Cairo; presumably also that the Soviet Union would control the intervening territory. This is a substantial contract: Iran, possibly Turkey, the Arabian States, presumably Israel, would have to be in the controlled area, which would thus include Suez. But the Greek revolution, or invasion, had been stopped, partly by the British and partly by the Americans. The Turks had declined to admit any Communist influence at all. The Soviet Union, blocked for the time being, waited her opportunity, leaving the question open while her diplomats, propagandists, underground agents, and other forces pursued their adventures, first against Western Europe and later in the Far East. By 1954, matters had taken a different turn and the weather looked more propitious for a Near Eastern operation.

Soviet Foreign Office specialists, surveying the picture, would have found something like this.

The Arab world was in considerable conflict. They had resented the creation of the State of Israel in 1948, and had made war to prevent its establishment. Israel had beaten off the attackers, but this did not end the problem. Israel, after all, is a small state with a population of about a million and three quarters, dependent for defense and for economic existence on help from the outside. The western Powers and notably the United States had assisted in the creation of the State of Israel and indeed Zionist sentiment in these countries has not unnaturally exerted such influence as it could in favor of the Zionist country. As a result, much of Arabian sentiment had come to regard the western Powers and the United States as against it in this controversy.

The Arab States are not one among themselves. The Saudi-Arabian dynasty has always feared the dynasty of old Emir Hussein (the Hashemites, so-called) which have the thrones of Transjordania and Iraq; there are endless disputes which can be easily nurtured in these undeveloped countries. Egypt is a member of the

Arab group (though much of its population is not Arab but Copt);
it is no less violent than the others in its dislike of Israel, and has
had trouble in establishing a well settled government. Egypt had a
side quarrel with Britain whose troops had guarded the Suez Canal
for many decades.

Then there were the Turks and the Greeks. These two peoples
have fought each other from the beginning. The Greeks have never
forgotten that half the Roman Empire in its later stages was ruled
from Byzantium (later, Constantinople and Istanbul) and regard the
Turks who only held it for 500 years as interlopers; Greece only
emerged from Turkish bondage in 1829. Even in our time the history has been ferocious. Considerable progress had been made towards establishing peaceful and indeed friendly relations between
the two countries; it has been a major objective of both British and
American diplomacy since World War II. But the deep fires still
burn; and Cyprus presently emerged to fan their flames.

Cyprus, at one time Turkish, had become a part of the British
Empire in the nineteenth century. Much of the population is Greek
in language and origin and has been since ancient times. The island
has never in modern history been under the Greek flag but the Greek-
speaking population has increasingly developed a desire to join
Cyprus to the homeland. For the past ten years great agitation has
been built up by this group against the British whose garrisons
occupy the Cypriot base and whose flag flies in the Mediterranean
breeze over the island. From 1952 on, this nationalist sentiment
grew steadily in strength. It will surprise no one to discover that the
Communist Party in Cyprus, well organized though relatively small,
merrily supported the agitation. In 1954 and early 1955, it reached
the eruptive stage, with violent demonstrations, terrorism, counter
measures, and so forth. This was matched by a powerful agitation
in Greece itself for recovery of this Greek territory and naturally
British-Greek relations suffered. By the beginning of 1955, it was
clear that the problem demanded attention; voices were raised asking that the British turn the island over to Greece and withdraw—
and at this point the Turks came into the picture.

For Turkey, remembering that the island was part of the Turkish

Empire, has maintained a sort of shadow claim to its return. The Turks had grown philosophical about British possession of it; the British over the years had proved friends of the Turks (despite the fact that Turkey was on the wrong side of World War I). So long as the island remained under the British flag, Turks were content to accept the situation phlegmatically. But its possible take-over by Greece was another story altogether. There were and still are considerable Greek populations in the Turkish cities all the way from Istanbul south and east. Greeks had attempted, unwisely, to take Turkish territory by force after World War I and had been defeated. Cyprus would be one more link in a chain of islands surrounding Turkey; anyway the Turks did not like the idea. They took the position that if Cyprus stayed where it was, all would be well. But if it was to be released by the British Empire, they wished to enter their own claim. This brought a Turkish-Greek dispute to the fore.

Finally, there were the States of Iran (Persia) and Afghanistan. Russians and British competed for ascendancy in these two countries through much of the nineteenth century. At one time they had worked out a division of spheres of influence whereby the Czarist Empire was to have the northern half and the British the southern half of Iran. One of the proudest British campaigns in her "little imperial wars" was that when Roberts marched a force from the then British India to Afghan Kabul and Kandahar; indeed, his title in the British Peerage was Earl "Roberts of Kandahar." Iran is a large, difficult piece of territory in which there are a number of semi-autonomous tribes, including a substantial group of Kurds who claim that they should be free, and who, however primitive themselves, have a Harvard-educated Kurd as chieftain. The Afghans on their side are a mountain people who have resisted western infiltration and who are quite capable of developing their own private disputes with their eastern neighbors in Pakistan which, incidentally, takes in the geography of the famous Khyber Pass, one of the few land routes by which an army can pass from the Soviet Union into Pakistan and India.

In great-power diplomacy there is usually good fishing in troubled waters. The waters here were troubled enough for anyone.

To cap it all, there was a significant diplomatic date coming up, the expiration of the so-called "Montreux Convention" in November 1956. This is the European treaty which regulates control of the Bosphorus and Dardanelles. In specific diplomacy, the Soviet Union had sought, in 1945 and 1946, to have a new arrangement made under which the Soviet Union rather than the Western European states should "guarantee" or (in plain English) control this waterway, and by which the Soviet Union should have the right to establish fortified bases along the line, and so forth. This had been turned down as we have seen; the provisions of the Montreux Convention had, with some revisions, been extended for a period of ten years to expire in 1956; the Russian claims could then be reasserted. In power-diplomacy when plans are made to assert a claim, the claimant will take all practicable measures to create a situation on the ground making it as nearly impossible as can be to refuse to grant the claim. (Perfect power-diplomacy consists of taking the property first, and then inviting the world through appropriate diplomatic action to recognize your title.)

All in all, a promising area. There is the plain, historic target: exit from the Black Sea necessarily implies exit from the Mediterranean. There is a sparsely populated, weakly held, undeveloped area, divided into a number of weak nations, quarrelling among themselves—and quarrelling too with western Powers which do not support their respective claims. There was (at date of writing, still is) an unsettled Israel-Arab-Egyptian war, never ended: merely quieted by an armistice. The paper relations between the States, such as the alliance between Yugoslavia, Greece and Turkey, the common membership of Turkey and Greece in NATO, might be reduced to unimportance if the parties themselves pushed their quarrels.

Factually, the Soviet Union took prudent and pragmatic measures to exploit, if not actually to produce, a useful crisis: the Suez crisis of 1956. At date of writing this crisis is undetermined; in any case, the historic facts are not yet known. The Soviet Union apparently decided on an activist policy in the year 1955, and implemented that position by building up arms supplies in at least two countries: Syria and Egypt. The munitions cached contemplated force beyond that available certainly to Egypt, probably to Syria. In other words, they were intended to be used by Russian-directed force, probably masquerading as "volunteers." Powerful encouragement was given to the extreme nationalist claims of Nasser in Egypt. When he seized the shares of the Suez Canal Company (and also operation of the Canal itself), the scenery was already set; all that was needed was for the actors to move on the stage. This they promptly did, in a drama not yet finished. After futile negotiations with the United States (which somehow failed to realize that the supply of commerce and oil from the Middle East to the West European countries meant life and death for the latter), British and French forces moved into Port Said. They synchronized their advance with an Israeli invasion of the Sinai peninsula.

It would have been perfect diplomacy for the nineteenth century; but the twentieth works differently. The United States, no party to the invasion, was outraged and demanded that the United Nations require withdrawal of the British and French and Israeli forces. The Soviet Union issued a thinly veiled threat of atomic warfare against Paris and London. Syria destroyed most of the pipelines conveying oil to the Mediterranean; some other Arab states imposed a boycott on shipments to Britain and France; the Egyptians blocked the Suez Canal with sunken ships. The combination of pressures halted the British-French advance. The United States angrily insisted on their immediate retirement. As combined threat and bait, it offered to supply oil for Europe's needs, replacing the Near Eastern supplies which no longer flowed when (but only when) the British and French had agreed to withdraw; and the United Nations organized a small international force which was to take over as the British and French troops left.

The Soviet diplomats might well consider this a good day's work for the Communist empire, despite the fact that they had probably not foreseen the dispatch of the British and French forces, nor the destruction of a substantial part of the arms they had carefully deposited for future use. They had reason to assume that British and French force would be excluded from the region. Russian force, of course, would move in by manipulating Egyptian and Arab arms, by playing on the Arab hatred of Israel, and by steadily infiltrating volunteers (Soviet-directed troops in other people's uniforms). Also, a very pretty quarrel had been induced between the United States and her NATO allies of Britain and France; with luck, NATO might cease to be a substantial element. With skill, time and good fortune, the Soviet Union might become master of the Middle East as well as of the mid-European strip.

We do not yet know what answer the west will forge.

8

The dilemma of Europe is thus extreme.

No single European Power is capable of coping with the Soviet Empire; in combination, they are more than a match for it. Yet the European countries thus far have been as unable to unify themselves in the twentieth century as they were when the Mohammedans seized Constantinople. Combined, they have greater population, more developed industrial capacity, higher technical skill than the Russians. Divided, unable to take common action, they can be cut to pieces.

As in the eighth, thirteenth and sixteenth centuries, a Power professedly hostile to their philosophy, their religion, their culture and their social organization has established itself in the crucial area of mid-Europe and has challenged for the Middle East. The Soviet Union's control of the mid-European strip corresponds roughly to the Turkish control of the Balkans before the fall of Constantinople; the Russian campaign to control Suez and the eastern Mediterranean corresponds substantially to the Turkish intent to end the Byzantine Empire. By all the old rules of the game western Europe (unless it acts quickly) is looking down the gunbarrels of cultural extinction as it has done at least three times earlier in the Christian era. It could be that the long day of west European dominance in thought and in affairs is nearing its end.

Unless, of course, something happens. New forces might arise, changing the entire picture.

For one thing, western Europe might abandon its rivalries and unite, militarily and economically, as it is already more or less united culturally. A new, tremendously powerful entity would then emerge, dominating the world scene.

Or the instrument we know as the United Nations might develop strength capable of preventing further imperialist development by Communist or by any other Powers.

Or the reach of Soviet imperial Communism may touch—indeed may nearly have reached—its limit. In the pressure of the Soviet imperial sweep, the Communist Revolution has increasingly lost the dynamic of its idealism. Soviet arms today maintain a Russian Empire not a Social Republic in mid-Europe and elsewhere. When their force is absent, the fabric dissolves. There is some indication even now that the military empire of the Soviet Union may not, much longer, have any great measure of force for export.

Or there may be World War III. Should this happen, the ensuing period would be terrible, but the probability is that in it the Communist empire would fall apart. Most revolution-built empires do collapse when they become involved in general wars, as both Napoleon and Hitler discovered. It would be Russia against the world, and Russia would probably lose. But whether eventual Russian loss would save Europe is anything but certain.

The dilemma of Europe is also the dilemma of the United States. If western Europe were to fall permanently under eastern sway, the United States would be a lonely country indeed.

CHAPTER Four

CRISIS AREAS: MID-EUROPE

1

ANY SERIOUS STUDENT of foreign affairs can forecast with tolerable success the parts of the world in which crises are likely to occur. An amateur, indeed, can do that without too much difficulty if he cares to put in a little time.

The simplest way of doing this is to watch a map. A large globe, preferably with a light inside it, is the most useful. A fairly big wall map comes next, but in that case the Mercator projections common on many schoolroom walls may give a false picture, since they do not show the narrowing lines and diminishing size of areas as one approaches the North and South Poles. A Mercator world map, for example, shows Greenland as large as South America—which, of course, it is not. A Mercator projection can be used if one acquires the mental habit of correcting for its distortions.

To those interested in carrying the process a little farther, other maps can be studied, notably those used by the airmen. To fliers the world is really round or at least substantially so. They do not feel under any necessity to consider the North or South Poles as centers. They can place their world-center in Kansas, Alaska or Moscow with equal ease. As they can go or come in all directions, they can choose any axis they please, and they make maps accord-

128

ingly. From that kind of map distance relations are apparent which you would not have in mind. It becomes immediately clear (it can be worked out on a globe, too) for instance, that if you are in the Azores Islands lying well off the coast of Portugal in the Atlantic Ocean, the nearest American land is not the United States but Labrador. ("Labrador" is a Portuguese word meaning "farmer"; the name comes from a Portuguese farmer in the Azores who backed the expedition which explored Labrador more than three centuries ago—precisely because it was the nearest Western Hemisphere mainland.)

Watching the map is not a one-day affair. A good foreign affairs student will look at it while he scans the headlines in his daily newspaper or if he is in the State Department, while he is reading his daily grist of cablegrams. Or perhaps after he has read a book about any area or has listened to an impassioned campaign speech on foreign matters. He will do it a few minutes daily. Presently his information begins to build up around various points on the map; after awhile, the map seems almost to be a living thing. In time, it almost speaks back to its observer as though trying to tell him that some things *must* happen, and that attempt to block them spells trouble.

Look, for instance, at a map of the Far East. You will see Japan, a relatively small group of islands populated with 90 million people crowded into an area which means that they must trade and exchange with other areas or literally risk starvation. Immediately across the Japan Sea is the mainland of Asia, chiefly occupied by Communist China—a natural field of exchange. You know, without being told, that sooner or later Japan must be part of some economic group arrangement which includes China, or be an international waif begging, borrowing or stealing to eke out an existence. The newspapers report a strong policy of which the United States is a leading protagonist, against permitting trade between free world countries, including Japan, and Communist countries. There is a strong move to discontinue aid to Japan. The map tells you that if the move succeeds, Japan will be almost forced to seek trade relations with

Communist China and that if there is opposition, some sort of crisis must ensue.

Geography, actually, goes far deeper than merely locating places on the map: that is merely the starting point. In and about the places and countries, the coasts, rivers and mountain ranges are peoples with varying characteristics there or arriving there; and natural resources of varying kinds. The two together result in production. There are means of transport, railroads, roads, waterways, shipping lanes. There may be a few people in a high productivity area (as in the case of the Middle East oil countries) with a production which must be transported elsewhere else it is useless. There are crowded areas to which production must flow. And so forth. Geography is really the science of relationship, not merely of parts of the surface of the earth to other parts, but also of people in relation to the earth's surface and to each other.

Continuous map reading in the light of current happenings can become one of the most passionately absorbing indoor sports (not to say vices) in the world. In a surprisingly short space of time each scrap of information coming your way attaches itself to the map.

Relationships of that particular area and people to the rest of the world become increasingly plain. Each new piece of news fits into a living picture; the story framed by the map comes alive.

It would be impossible in any brief study to cover all the problem areas of the world, or even to do more than to look at the surface of a few principal ones. It is here sought to take three such areas: mid-Europe in this chapter, the Middle East in the next chapter, and the Asian coast in the following chapter. This review makes no pretense in any area of exhausting any of these on each of which whole libraries have been written. It should outline the areas which will perhaps offer most of the major crises in the next few years, and indicate a few adjacent areas which are also unhappily likely to come into vivid news.

Mid-Europe is here taken to mean that belt running almost due north and south from the Baltic Sea to the head of the Adriatic on the west and to the head of the Aegean Sea on the east. This is, all things considered, the most tragic zone in the Western world. It lies between the Slavic empire of Soviet Russia and the Germanic countries (Germany, Austria, much of Switzerland). Both the Russian and the German peoples are powerful. Both have had, and probably still have, dreams of expansion. Both have been competitors for European or world leadership and actual rule or conquest, and are constantly grinding against each other.

The strip itself is composed of twelve countries running roughly from north to south: Estonia, Latvia, Lithuania, Poland, Czechoslovakia, Austria, Hungary, Roumania, Yugoslavia, Bulgaria, Albania and Greece. As the East is driven against the West—or from time to time, the West against the East, the peoples composing these States have been squarely in the line of march of invading or retreating armies. This alone would have guaranteed them a stormy history and infinite suffering; it is the reason why some European observers call the mid-European strip the "Devil's Girdle."

Worse still, the peoples within the area itself are in the main different in characteristics, and have had an evil heritage of hatred of each other as well as of fear of their powerful neighbors. The Estonians and the Latvians, like the Finns, were probably descended from the earliest races in Europe, but were driven by tides of history steadily northward until there was no other place to go. They are commonly fair-skinned and gray eyed. The Poles are Slavs, cousins to the Russians, without the Russian admixture of Mongolian blood, probably with some mixture from the Germanic side. Czechs and Slovaks again are Slavs, each, however, with a somewhat different race mixture, somewhat different habits of language and somewhat different habits of thought and action.

In the next tier south, Austria is a small German enclave flung eastward several centuries ago. (Vienna is actually east of Prague, though few people realize that fact, just as Czechoslovakia is the westernmost Slavic wedge driven into the West.) Due east of Austria lies the great mountain-encircled plain of Hungary, once a principal granary of Europe. But Hungarians probably are a branch of the Turkish race, though they also have some blood relationship to the far-away Finns; their language is Magyar, which is not directly connected with any of the other languages of the region. The eastern State in that tier, Roumania, is predominantly Latin though with much admixture, and the language they speak stems from Rome. One wonders how many descendants of Roman legions stationed there sired that population, giving it a gaiety and charm one associates with Italians.

Just south of these three non-Slavic countries lie Yugoslavia and Bulgaria, again predominantly Slav but infinitely tangled. Yugoslavia is itself a combination of three more or less distinct branches of Slav races—Serbs, Croats and Slovenes. Historically, Serbs and Croats have not got on together. Bulgaria is Slavic, its people probably have closer affinity with Russians than most other Slavic groups.

Lying across parts of both Yugoslavia and Bulgaria and sticking down towards Greece is an area which has a small though relatively distinct population—Macedonians. They may be descendant, as their name implies, from warlike Macedonia of old which produced Alexander the Great, though so many migrations have passed through that area that the claim would be hard to establish. Macedonia is little more than a geographic expression now, though there are attempts to set up a "Macedonia" from time to time, often as diplomatic moves by one Power or another which desires to invade or weaken a neighbor. The Soviet army which occupied Bulgaria at the close of World War II made moves in this direction; probably the Russian general and his political directors hoped thereby to tear pieces out of Greece. The local "Macedonian" port would be nearby Salonika which is Greek, and in Greece at the head of the Aegean Sea—a fact the Greeks never forget.

On the western side of this tier is Albania. This is predominantly Mohammedan, a remnant of the old Turkish Empire in Europe, an unstable country with a bloody history. Its Islamic population spills northward into Yugoslavia, just as a Greek population spills northward out of Greece into southern Albania. It will be noticed that the coast of Albania lies over against the heel of the boot of Italy, being separated from it only by the narrow Otranto Strait. It will not therefore surprise any student of foreign affairs to find that its naval port, Vlöri, is one of the minor prizes in the power politics game; indeed there probably is a Russian submarine base there at date of writing.

Greece is clearly in this area but, in several senses, lies apart from it. On the north, she neighbors Albania, Yugoslavia and Bulgaria. But her main contact with the world is by sea, so that she figures more largely as a part of the Mediterranean problem than as a part of east Europe. There is a high factor of race unity in Greece; her language and magnificent history would almost draw even a disparate population together in any case. Greece is perhaps the true birthplace of western culture, and Greeks do not forget that fact.

This mid-Europe has an aggregate population of more than 80 million, and aggregate natural resources which, under peaceful, orderly development could make it one of the great productive areas of the world. It holds, really, the geopolitical balance of power in Europe. The European land Power lying either to the east or to the west which possesses and dominates this strip is materially and strategically superior to, and therefore threatens, the opposite land Power which does not.

Such a threat exists at date of writing. The Soviet Union at the close of World War II took, held and now controls the entire area from the Baltic to the Adriatic (with distinct reservations in the case of Yugoslavia) down to the Greek border. Added to the 200 millions of Soviet population and the Soviet resources, the 80-odd million population of mid-Europe and its resources give to present-day Moscow clear preponderance on the European mainland—especially because, as we have observed, west Europe has not achieved unity.

In fact the Soviet Union has rather more because in her post-war westward sweep she also seized nearly one-third of Germany (the "East Germany" of today), and riveted on that area a Communist government and a military army of occupation. This last puts her within striking distance (two hundred plus miles) of the Atlantic coast via Hamburg or Denmark, and of the Rhine River with the great Ruhr Basin on which West Europe depends for coal and iron, not to mention Vienna and the Alpine passes into Italy. If Soviet control were complete, it would also permit her (from

Communist Albania) to block the entrance to the Adriatic Sea, making it virtually a Russian lake, and to gain entrance to the Mediterranean through the Aegean Sea by driving south through the narrow Greek strip and taking the port of Salonika and the coast of Thrace. France and Germany combined—possibly even France, Germany and England combined with Italian and Spanish help—would hardly have resources and manpower sufficient to stand off a determined attack by the Soviet Union so long as this situation endures—provided the Soviet Union can attain the political support of, as well as military domination over the peoples of this mid-European region.

In fairness to Soviet Russia it should be noted that when the West European Powers controlled this region, Soviet Russia herself was in considerable danger. For practical purposes Germany and Austria did control most of it in 1914; on the outbreak of World War I (though Czarist Russia cannot be absolved of war guilt), Russia was immediately exposed to invasion and devastation, as she was later when Hitler controlled it in 1940 and attacked in 1941. Consequently, whenever mid-Europe is decisively in the hands either of a strong eastern Power (Russia), or of a strong western Power (say, Germany), the other side is frightened, uneasy, and endlessly seeking a change in the situation. If there were nothing in the situation but that, mid-Europe would be a problem area.

Actually there is much more in the situation. 80-plus million people are themselves a substantial percentage of the European population. They have languages, history, national desires, ambitions and hopes of their own; and they have their own lives to lead. In other words, they want freedom presumably within national groupings which correspond approximately to the linguistic, cultural and social framework they know and love. They also have a desire to become greater and to grow.

The area is thus unstable. Trebly so, because it presents at one and the same time three groups of problems. The first is the problem of the imbalance of power in Europe, because at present the strip is, for practical purposes, under control of the Soviet

Union, a single very great power. Second, because each component unit within the area is struggling for a greater measure of independence, and self-determination. Third, because even between these component nationalities no really successful or settled modern framework of peace and cooperation has been worked out, perhaps because the great powers never wished to work one out. Superimpose these three conditions on the fact we observed earlier, namely, that the line of "Western" culture was flung out and established on the eastern side of this strip, adjacent to non-Roman-Catholic Russia—and the elements of instability become apparent. A key region, unstable in itself but in the main within the intellectual and spiritual framework of the West, is held under military and police domination by the Soviet Union which, nevertheless, has been unable to conquer either the inherent nationalisms or the independent minds of the population.

It is a situation which is bound to change in some direction.

2

The nineteenth century considered the mid-European problem substantially solved. The area in the late eighteenth century had been more or less satisfactorily (in the view of all but its inhabitants divided among four empires—the Hohenzollern Empire of Germany, the Hapsburg Empire of Austria-Hungary, and the Russian Empire of the Romanoffs; for practical purposes, the old Turkish Empire.

Most of this had been done by direct annexation. Germany had absorbed western Poland; Russia held Estonia, Latvia, Lithuania and eastern Poland: a substantial balance, happily for everyone, except of course Estonians, Latvians, Lithuanians and Poles. With Poland went a racial wedge, the West Ukrainian salient which in later times formed the southern tier of Poland, but was then chiefly in Austrian hands. To the south, Austria-Hungary held under one device or another Hungary, Czechoslovakia, most of Yugoslavia, and substantial parts of present-day Poland and Roumania.

There were recurrent struggles as the dying Turkish Empire

was forced first out of Greece (1830), later, by stages and after many struggles, out of Bulgaria (1875), Roumania (1877), Yugoslavia—then Serbia—(1878). Greece emerged first after the Napoleonic Wars and promptly fell into the sphere of influence of Great Britain—a tribute to British naval power, to British interest in the Mediterranean lifeline, and to the solid support which British intellectuals and liberals had given the Greek Independence movement from 1820 on. (That movement gave us Byron's famous poem, "Isles of Greece"; Byron himself died in an attempt to lead a Greek independence rising against Turkey.) The other three Balkan countries eventually attained or regained independence as a result of a diplomatic scramble (1875–1876) followed by a brief war (1877–1878) by Czarist Russia to conquer Turkey and seize Constantinople. Russian armies were successful in defeating Turkey; but all West Europe gathered to prevent Russia from seizing the Bosphorus and the Dardanelles, and from becoming too powerful in the mid-European strip; and the Balkan States emerged from the ruins of Turkey's Western Empire as the Russian Empire was balked of its prey.

The ensuing equilibrium was unstable, but the area was small enough and West Europe unified enough so that it did not immediately produce serious trouble (later it did). Thus mid-Europe, for practical purposes, navigated its serious nineteenth century crisis and reposed (for that region) in comparative quiet. There was substantial balance of power.

But there was not any serious satisfaction of the desires of the local peoples. Though the Austrian Empire gave to its States a high and effective degree of economic development (they have never been as well off since that Empire fell) and the Germans provided a tremendous dynamic advance for the parts of Poland they had annexed, and though Russia probably governed the territories she dominated no worse than she governed her own, sleeping fires of unfilled nationalist aspiration continued.

The great Powers on both the eastern and western sides had by no means relinquished their ambitions to end the balance and take a dominant world position. The rivalries and weaknesses of the region offered a golden opportunity for intrigue and imperialist dreams.

In 1911, the equilibrium ended. In that year, Italy decided to seize the weakly held Turkish African province of Tripoli (Libya of today), declared war, marched her armies in, and annexed the territory. The Turkish State was in no condition to resist. Thereon Greece, Serbia and Bulgaria took advantage of the situation in the mid-European strip. For once in a way they temporarily sank their differences, formed the "Balkan League," and (without blessing of the European Powers) marched into the remaining Turkish-held area in Europe—chiefly the region called Macedonia. They found justification in the need (which was real enough) of protecting the Christian population in Macedonia against oppression and massacre by the Turks. Their military victory was swift. The end was that the Balkan League seized Thrace (lying just north of Greece), taking away from Turkey most of her remaining holdings in the Balkan peninsula. In the ensuing scramble among the three Balkan Allies to divide the conquered territory all gained, though Bulgaria probably came out best. This would not of itself have created unmanageable crisis. But the context was that of growing Russian ambition to dominate the area, conflicting with growing desires of the Austrian Empire in the same direction, and with the powerful ambitions of Hohenzollern Germany to become a leading world power by dominating the Middle East. The powder keg was laid open for any spark. The result was World War I.

All manner of explanation has been offered for the end of the peaceful Victorian century, and most of them have some degree of validity. The immediate fact was that Germany and Austria, in alliance with Italy, were seeking to move eastward, desiring to extend their influence through Turkey and beyond to Arabia, Persia and the whole Middle East. But Russia had an ancient and exactly similar interest; she was grinding nationalist or Pan-Slavic axes in the Balkan countries and in mid-European areas annexed to the Austrian Empire. That grinding, plus a nationalist movement in Serbia, eventually produced the incident which sparked the war—the murder in 1914 of an Austrian Archduke at Sarajevo by a Serbian nationalist. Both the Austrian-German and the Russian combinations were prepared to appeal to arms.

The end, in 1918, was the defeat of the German Empire and complete dissolution of the Austrian and Turkish Empires. A century earlier the victorious Powers would have moved in and annexed the territory. But a new force, or more accurately, a new recognition of an old force, had come into the world. This was Woodrow Wilson's principle of "self-determination of nations," which meant recognition of the smoldering nationalist yearnings everywhere for independence. Acceptance of this principle was part of the price of America's entry into World War I; and Wilson was specifically talking about the nations of the mid-European strip. While the principle electrified minority groups all over the world its impact was greatest on the mid-European areas occupied by the German, Russian and Austrian Empires.

3

When at the close of World War I the Allied Powers met at the Paris Peace Conference, general agreement had been reached between the American Delegation and the British that independent nations should be established throughout the entire area. The French concurred; the Italians who hoped to inherit a promised strip of Yugoslavia across the Adriatic Sea had distinct reservations. Russia, an ally of the West, had faded from the picture, since Lenin after taking power in 1917 had made a separate peace with the Germans. This was assumed to cancel Allied promises to give Russia control of Constantinople. In any case, Russia was in full throes of revolution and civil war. Out of the Versailles peace there came into existence Finland, Estonia, Latvia, Lithuania (carved out of Russia), Poland (taken from Russia, Austria and Germany alike). From Austria emerged Czechoslovakia and Hungary, Roumania taking and eventually holding a slice of Hungary known as Transylvania on the way. From Austria were also taken certain Slavic areas which were added to Serbia as was the small kingdom of Montenegro; the bloc was combined into the "Kingdom of Serbs, Croats and Slovenes" known as Yugoslavia today. The largely Mohammedan population south of Yugoslavia was constituted as the kingdom of Albania.

Alas for illusion. Theoretically self-determination necessarily produced an atmosphere of peace. In actual event, each of the new States as it emerged made large claims of territory, necessarily at the expense of its mid-European neighbors. The southern tier of Poland claimed independent existence as West Ukraine; whereupon Polish troops seized it. Czechoslovakia and Poland quarrelled over the valuable coal and steel basin of Teschen, Lithuania and Poland quarrelled over a strip which, ironically was at least 40 per cent Jewish in population. An American delegate to the Versailles Peace Conference, General Tasker H. Bliss, wrote sadly to his wife that these infant nations appeared to be born with fangs and claws and in their cradles cried out for weapons with which to attack their neighbors. Old peoples could be reestablished as nations; but unhappily disputes of still older history emerged with them.

Yet allowance has to be made for pains of rebirth, and in the ensuing decade a degree of peaceful coexistence was achieved, though not without military adventure and bloodshed. A Russian attempt to retake Poland not merely for Communism but unquestionably for Russia took place in 1921, the Russian Red Army being accompanied by an obscure political commissar later famous as Josef Stalin. It was defeated by a Polish Army aided by French divisions. (It may be that memory of that defeat played a part in impelling Stalin later to dicker for Poland with Hitler in 1939 and to seize Poland at the close of World War II.)

The Great Powers moved to stabilize. As principal proprietor of military land power in Europe at the time, France held the senior interest. Her policy was to maintain these countries as a barrier to the spread of a Communist Russia which France especially feared. She made alliance with Bulgaria, Roumania and Yugoslavia, and a more or less separate alliance with Poland. Britain undertook to support the countries bordering on the Baltic Sea: Finland, Estonia, Latvia, Lithuania. The Italians seized and held a part of Yugoslavia, including the port of Fiume, by supporting an "unofficial" expedition headed by the Italian poet Gabriele D'Annunzio; and eventually made the seizure good. Greece continued primarily in the British orbit. Matters jogged uneasily along until the rise of Hitler in Nazi Germany augmented the earlier rise of Benito Mussolini in Fascist Italy, and the great and hideous game of world power began anew.

In retrospect, it is fairly plain that Hitler's Germany was, essentially, following the foreign policy of the Germany of Kaiser Wilhelm II. It proposed to push eastward, seizing territory as it went, with the concealed intention of taking into its orbit the mid-European strip and promptly using the area as a take-off from which to conquer Soviet Russia and strike southward into the Middle East. Fascist Italy was willing to go along, hoping to become lord over Yugoslavia, Albania and Greece—this despite the fact that Mussolini feared Hitler would seize Austria (which he did in 1938), plant himself firmly astride the Alpine passes which lead into Italy and put himself in position to double-deal with his Fascist partner (as Hitler also did in the later stages of World War II). Factually the first step in the procedure was precisely that seizure of Austria in 1938; it was followed by a threat to Czechoslovakia and by Europe's shuddering agreement at Munich to give crucial areas of Czechoslovakia to him under threat of war (again in 1938); and by his seizure of the remainder in 1939. Hitler's plans for capture of Poland were, even then, well advanced. (When the German armies entered Prague in early 1939 a Nazi propaganda squad, having got the wrong case of printed material by mistake, stuck up posters in Polish addressed by the German army to the residents of Warsaw.) The eastward grind of a new Germanic combination was under way. Events moved swiftly after that.

A fascinating but predictable element in world affairs is the quality of the British nation. Its yearning for peace is so great that it tends to compromise in every crisis—up to the last one. Then, when much of the world has (unjustifiably) written off British will to resist, London suddenly announces that in case of further aggression Britain will fight. So it was in 1939. A singularly obtuse British Government under Neville Chamberlain had retreated, even compromising the Munich crisis by giving Hitler the keys to Prague and with them the strategic eastward routes. Now the British Government said, "No Further," and backed it by an agreement with Poland guaranteeing her frontiers and pledging to fight if they were crossed.

Hitler believed this was mere "diplomacy." If he could assure that the Soviet Union would stay out of things, would not resist when he entered Poland, would therefore not be dangerous should Britain be called on to make good her guarantee, he took for granted that the British would not keep their pledge. Accordingly his Foreign Minister, von Ribbentrop, negotiated a treaty with his opposite number Molotov (the same Molotov who is active today). He wished Russian benevolent neutrality or at least inaction when he made his next move into the mid-European strip. He was prepared to pay a high price for it. As usual in power bargains between territorial empires, each bought the assent of the other by giving away countries and peoples which were not theirs. Hitler agreed that the Soviet Union might take over Finland, Estonia, Latvia, Lithuania and the eastern marches of Poland. Stalin agreed that he would not oppose Hitler's seizure of the western half of Poland and, probably, of dominion over Hungary. Thereupon, after some negotiations for form's sake, on September 1, 1939, Hitler's armies marched into Poland. German forces were once more dividing the mid-European strip with the Russians, though probably neither power intended the division to be permanent.

Both Hitler and Stalin in this instance made a major error in the career of each. Stalin assumed that he had met Hitler's price and could contain him within the agreed zone. He was entirely wrong. Hitler probably had, even then, a more or less settled design of attacking Russia as soon as he had mastered most of the mid-European strip. Less than a year later (that is, in the Summer of 1940) his General Staff actually began working up the plans for invasion of Russia. Hitler's mistake was that he assumed as a matter of course that far-away Britain would not try to keep its pledge to fight. He was completely in error. The same Neville Chamberlain who had made an ignoble compromise about Czechoslovakia immediately asked Parliament to declare war; it did so on September 3, 1939. France, ally of Great Britain, followed suit at once. For the second time in a generation, the struggle to dominate the mid-European strip had precipitated a world war.

4

In the writer's view (the evidence is not open and shut), the foregoing chain of events explains the odd situation prevailing through the Fall and Winter of 1939–1940. A couple of weeks, of course, sufficed to defeat the Polish army and establish German forces all over that country. But this swift victory did not dispose of the war in the West where the classic enemies, Germany and France, backed by Britain, faced each other across the Maginot Line. But Hitler did not attack. Rather, his propaganda suggested that there was no need of this; that these were not his real enemies, and so forth. The period has been called the time of the "phony war." Probably Hitler hoped to work out a truce of some kind with the British and the French, leaving him free to attack Russia without being engaged in a two-front war. "After all, why die for Danzig?" cried the peace party in France. "Should we not get together with Hitler and defeat the Communists?" said some reactionaries in Great Britain and even a few in the United States.

Hitler's efforts in this direction had no avail. Something else besides the mid-European strip itself was now involved. Possession of it would clearly leave Hitler with preponderance of power in Europe. Everyone had come to fear Hitler's violence and his armies—and to distrust his word. They had come, still more, to hate the Nazi doctrine which maintained that Germans were the Master Race, that Jews should be massacred, and that other races should be assigned to varying conditions of servitude. By Spring of 1940, Hitler concluded that his best chance lay in crushing the

West while the Soviet Union was still inert. He made a fast northward flanking movement around the Maginot Line, through Denmark, Holland and Belgium, knocking France out of the war.

In the Fall of 1940, Mr. Sam Woods, a singularly able American commercial attaché in Germany (the United States was neutral at the time) received and sent to Washington a plan of
campaign against the Soviet Union drawn up by the German
General Staff. It contemplated taking over by diplomacy (if possible) or by arms (if necessary) the balance of the mid-European
strip so that Nazi Germany should have full control of Hungary,
Roumania, Yugoslavia and Bulgaria. This Germany could easily do.
By June 15, 1941, they should be in shape to invade the Soviet
Union. If fully successful, they expected to capture Moscow in
the Autumn of 1941, eliminating the Soviet Union as a factor.
Failing that, the General Staff prophetically observed by way of
warning, Germany might lose the war.

The information was passed on by Mr. Sumner Welles to the
Soviet Embassy in Washington. There is no evidence that Stalin,
if he got it, took it seriously. Perhaps he thought it was an American intrigue to break up the friendship between Hitler and Stalin.

The projected political steps followed with great rapidity. The
governments of the remaining mid-European countries were either
intimidated into cooperation or subverted by Nazi fifth columns.
In the case of Yugoslavia, an army revolt under General (then
Colonel) Mikhailovitch brought about armed opposition to the
eastward march of the German Legions through Yugoslav territory. Further delay was caused by the fact that Mussolini, anxious
to get in on the kill, had expanded an attack he was carrying on
against Albania into a full-scale attack on Greece; but the Greek
armies first held and then soundly drove him back, so he was
forced to ask Hitler for assistance. Complainingly, Hitler detached
sufficient divisions to overcome the Greek resistance. But as noted
in the previous chapter, this only delayed the schedule; actual
invasion of Soviet Russia by German armies took place on June
22, 1941. In fairness to the bravery of the Greek and Yugoslav
patriots it should be added that their resistance pinned down some

German divisions, weakening to that extent the thrust of the almost successful German invasion of the Soviet Union.

5

We do not here follow the history of World War II. Enough to note that three years later, that is, in the Summer of 1944, the tide had changed and was flowing strongly against Germany. British and American armies had now reconquered France and had crossed the Rhine. Russian armies after retreating to Stalingrad had held, had come back and were steadily pushing the long German line back westward through Poland. Irregular troops in Yugoslavia harried Italian and German forces of occupation. An American force was driving up the Italian peninsula. By the fall of 1944 it was obvious to everyone that the German bolt was shot.

Now there is a rule in warfare that never received adequate attention from American students. As a war approaches its end, strictly military objectives tend to wane in importance; political and territorial objectives increase in importance. The German army in defeat was desperately struggling to create conditions from which they could negotiate some sort of a peace which did not mean political destruction: this was their political objective. The Western Allies—Britain, United States and a reconstituted French force with added forces recruited from the troops of the other occupied countries—were struggling primarily to reconstitute the nations overrun by Hitler and to concert a form of world organization which emerges today as the United Nations. The Soviet Union meanwhile was grimly concentrating on seizing territory she expected to hold and dominate after the war, irrespective of whether her allies liked it or not. Her primary objective was precisely the mid-European belt of countries. In retrospect it is perfectly clear the Stalin government knew exactly what it was doing and why. This explains, perhaps, the bloodiest and most tragic closing phase of the war in the West—and sets the scene for the crisis area of today.

Wherever Russian armies moved into the mid-European strip,

they promptly wiped out the resistance groups which had survived from the pre-war governments or were acting under orders
of the governments in exile or of the Western Powers. Members
of these Western-oriented undergrounds were treated as brutally,
perhaps more brutally, than captured German soldiers. They were
shot out of hand, relegated to distant Russian prison camps from
whence few emerged or, in fighting zones, were betrayed to any
superior German force in the area.

One particularly cynical case occurred in Warsaw in the fall of
1944. There, a very considerable Polish underground resistance
existed; it was supplied from Great Britain and from the American
forces. It was directed to follow radio instructions from the Russian
side and to coordinate its operations with the slowly advancing
Russian armies. One day it got instructions to come into the open
and attempt to seize Warsaw against a superior German force. In
theory this was to be a rising within the Polish capital against German forces, timed to coincide with a Russian attack against the
German occupation army from just outside. The rising took place
—but the Russian army halted. The Germans, naturally, threw in
force enough to crush the revolt and massacre the resisters. The
Soviet forces stood still and philosophically watched. After all, this
was a Western, not a Communist, underground. On liberation it
would want to assume control of Poland; whereas Soviet Russia
proposed to dominate Poland with a Communist government,
guarded by Russian guns. The Russian halt was, in the writer's
opinion, not an accident, since the Russians even refused to allow
use of their airfields by American bombers dispatched for the purpose of aiding the beleaguered Poles. In the end it all worked out
nicely—for Stalin. The Germans slaughtered the Western underground; after which the Russian army moved into Warsaw and
promptly installed its own Communist underground as the government of Poland.

So in one way or another it went throughout the whole mid-
European strip. A committee of Communist Poles organized in
Moscow became the foundation of the present Polish Communist
government. Similar undergrounds, also under protection of the

Russian armies, emerged as governing groups in Hungary, Roumania and Bulgaria, while Tito's Communist irregulars installed him in Yugoslavia. Estonia, Latvia and Lithuania had long since been wiped out by the Russian armies following the Hitler-Stalin Pact of 1939; they simply continued as Russian territory. The Communist "revolution" boiled merrily in Greece, aided from now Communist Bulgaria and Yugoslavia, and a like "revolution" achieved power in Albania.

Upon surrender of the German armies in May, 1945, the Soviet rulers wasted no time. In international matters, possession is not merely nine points of the law; it is, if you act decisively enough and with enough force behind you, all the law there is. Stalin immediately treated the occupation lines not as defining a provisional administrative zone for military purposes, but as a territorial limit of the Soviet system. The Yalta Agreements, it is true, had pledged him to give the countries occupied by his armies governments of their own choosing determined by free election; but who was to enforce it with Russian armies on the spot? For that matter, an effective army-and-police system was quite capable of settling that no vote would be cast in any election except at Stalinist dictation. For practical purposes consolidation of the mid-European strip into a Soviet Empire went immediately forward. With it went assumption by the Soviet Union of a preponderant territorial and military position threatening all Europe, firmly held in Soviet Russian hands. Europe has not really been at peace with the Soviet Union since.

By 1946, the mid-European strip except for Czechoslovakia and Greece was firmly in the hands of Soviet armies. These had installed Communist governments which almost insultingly warned any Western representative off the premises. A vigorous Communist party was being financed in Czechoslovakia, later helped by threat of Russian military action to take power as a Moscow satellite in 1948. A revolution was exhausting Greece, to be checked, and then stopped, only by President Truman's intervention in 1947.

The old Western cultural line had been crossed. The balance

of power in Europe had been effectively upset. The national and cultural desires of the mid-European peoples for self-determination had been ruthlessly overridden. Any patriot who had stood for his country with the aid of the West was relegated to a felon's grave, a slave camp, or exile—if he were lucky enough to escape.

The Iron Curtain was erected lest information from the East reach the West or ideas from the West reach the East. So far as Soviet power could impose the fact, the boundary of the Soviet Empire had been extended deep into Western Europe. There the Soviet imperialists proposed it should stay until it could be moved still further westward.

6

Men of experience in foreign affairs learn not to accept any condition they see as necessarily eternal or irreparable. Some accordingly did not accept as permanent the Soviet possession of mid-Europe.

There was a possibility, of course, that it could be consolidated and held for Communist civilization. But that assumed Soviet capacity to do two things: to wipe out or reduce nationalist sentiment in these nations, and also to convert them en masse to Communist thinking with resulting Communist control. Soviet statesmen knew this too, and promptly set about it in approved Soviet fashion. Dissenters were eliminated. Schools educated children to be loyal little Communists. Private ownership and other vestiges of capitalism were wiped out. Attempts were made to collectivize farms.

Mid-Europe is in general more highly developed than is Communist Russia; consequently, the production of Czechoslovakia factories, of the rich lands of Hungary and Roumania, and of the Western Polish cities was channeled into the Soviet Union. Definite plans were made to integrate the economies of these fiercely nationalist countries—this last, on the whole, the chief really useful thing done by the Soviet rulers.

But, as Czarist Russia, Hapsburg Austria and Hohenzollern

Germany had found, as Napoleon had learned, as nineteenth-century Europe had discovered, these are tenacious countries. Conversion did not take place. Communication with the West is going on, through radio stations, balloon communications, and a difficult but constant passage from one side or other of the Iron Curtain border. (It is actually a barbed wire curtain, guarded with machine guns, alongside of which usually runs a strip sown with land mines.) Somehow or other, Hungarians have remained Hungarians; Poles are still Poles; Bulgarians still wish to be Bulgarian; and so forth. Youth grew up in Communist schools but developed a surprising reluctance to swallow Communist doctrine whole. Farmers resisted collectivization of their farms; when collectivized the farms failed to produce. Factory production continued and still does: Czechoslovakia supplies arms for the Communist world, but the going continues tough. Every once in awhile the smoldering fire leaps to the surface in some fashion. It may be as limited as a slow-down strike in a Czech factory, or as overt as the food riots in Poznania in June of 1956, or as explosive as the blazing rebellion of Hungary in November, 1956. The weakening restraint on free expression after Khrushchev's denunciation of Stalin let loose a flood of discussion, little of which is complimentary to present Communist regimes. It is true that life has gone on, and that certain achievements have been reached, such as the rebuilding of Warsaw. It is true that the Communist occupation has powerfully affected institutions. But it appears not to be true that acquiescence in the Communist imperial system is due to conviction; rather it is due merely to the fact that the Soviet armies have overmastering force. In a word, at the first weakening of Soviet power, the whole situation can explode. And from explosion behind the Iron Curtain will follow repercussions throughout all Western Europe which likewise does not acquiesce in Soviet holding of the mid-European strip though it is not ready to fight a war to change the balance.

Such an explosion is perhaps gathering as this manuscript goes to press. In the writer's view the Hungarian massacres of November, 1956 probably announce the beginning of the end of the

Soviet imperial system, though many years may pass before their significance is evident.

Actually, in the Summer of 1956, the Soviet Union undertook reorganization of its relations with the captive mid-European countries. The proposal was to grant them a wider range of autonomy, and, while recognizing their "independence," to unite them into a "commonwealth" of Communist States. Probably a controlling motive in doing this was the desire to bring Yugoslavia, which had pursued its independent Communist career under Marshal Tito, back into working alliance with Moscow.

The "commonwealth" was organized, or at least proclaimed. Marshal Tito's adherence was secured. At least formal recognition of the increased autonomy of the mid-European countries was given. Then came the convulsion.

Riots in Poznan, Poland, in June, 1956, were not repressed by Polish Communist troops and the movement assumed revolutionary proportions. A Polish "Titoist" leader, Gomulka, eventually achieved at least a temporary angle of rest. The Polish government was to be "independent" but it agreed to continuing occupation by Soviet troops. The intellectual and thought controls imposed by Moscow were, for the time being, relaxed; the Gomulka government's substitutes for them had been relatively ineffective. That government claimed to desire more contact with the West, and is presently urging an American loan, using its singularly unpopular representative in the United States, Dr. Katz-Suchy, as its chief protagonist.

In Hungary a like revolution broke out, and did not reach this angle of rest. Beginning with a demonstration on October 23, unorganized but practically universal demand for real freedom swept the country. Its "Titoist" leader, Imre Nagy, promised wide reforms, almost amounting to democracy, and promised an end of occupying Soviet troops. But this over-passed the limits which the Soviet Union considered permissible; also it interrupted their very useful military line which they were apparently constructing through Hungary and Yugoslavia to the Adriatic. After five days in which the revolution was successful, Soviet troops in early November, 1956 entered Hungary, and massacred many thousands of Hungarian workers, students, women and children. A bloody quiet was imposed on Budapest. Nagy, who had sought asylum in the Yugoslav Embassy, was given promise of safe conduct for purposes of negotiating, and was promptly kidnapped as he came forth. Russian troops now occupy the principal cities and lines of communication. The rest of Hungary is in a state of passive, non-cooperative resistance; it is, in fact, a country occupied by the troops of an enemy. Of interest is the fact that some of the élite Russian troops defected on discovering that they were shooting down not Fascists, or capitalists, or even Americans (as they had been told) but Hungarian students and workmen.

The situation will probably be brought to at least outward calm somehow. Russia has force enough for that. But in the bloody days of November, the Soviet Union lost one of its major assets.

Prior to this convulsion, the Soviet Union had represented a set of ideas, or, if you like, ideals, assumed to be capable of commanding the loyalty, cooperation and assent of the peoples of mid-Europe. This meant that they could use most of their force for other purposes—say, invading the Middle East—since they could count on the use of the geography, the resources, the manpower, of mid-Europe. After the convulsion few, if any, mid-Europeans had the slightest interest in cooperating with the Soviet Union or granting to it use of their geography, their resources or their manpower—save where a Soviet gun was present to compel such action. From being the chief State in a great revolution commanding loyalties beyond its borders, the Soviet Union became a military empire whose influence was limited to the ambit of its force.

A problem area is thus developing its crisis, and a new chapter in a long story is about to begin.

CHAPTER Five

CRISIS AREAS: MIDDLE EAST

1

THE MIDDLE EAST, properly considered, is merely an extension of the mid-European strip. A European diplomat once observed that the key to the possession of Istanbul and the Dardanelles lay on the Baltic coast; there is more truth in the observation than one would think.

Experts have never agreed on a boundary for the Middle East. The Department of State which has a Division to attend to the affairs of this region has in recent years changed the geography on a number of occasions. Some consider all the Mohammedan world as in the Middle East but in that case the area would take in all of Northern Africa including the Moroccan coast, and ought to include Indonesia as well. Arbitrarily, perhaps, for this discussion, we here limit the area so that our western boundary runs down the western boundary of Turkey through the Aegean and across the Mediterranean Sea, down the western border of Egypt, across the Sudan to Ethiopia and down the southwestern border of Ethiopia to Somaliland and the Indian Ocean. This western boundary in Africa thus runs roughly parallel to the Red Sea about 600 miles to the West.

The northern boundary of the area runs eastward along the

Black Sea coast of Turkey to the Caucasus and Iran, then follows
the northern borders of Iran and Afghanistan. Our eastern border
begins at the sharp corner where Afghanistan and Pakistan touch
Kashmir, running southerly along the Pakistan-Indian frontier
until it reaches the Indian Ocean near Karachi. The Indian Ocean
does the rest of the boundary work for us. The region is thus
a huge triangle with all sorts of explosive problems inside it. The
list of countries are these: northern tier: Turkey, Iran, Afghanistan, eastern Pakistan. The middle, or Arabian, tier: Syria, Lebanon, Iraq, Israel, Jordan, Saudi Arabia (this last including most
of the Arabian desert) and a collection of small, oil rich principalities or sheikdoms, some of indefinite character but including
Kuwait, Bahrein (a Persian Gulf island), Qatar, the two Omans,
the British Protectorate of Aden, and Yemen. (All these are comprised in the quadrilateral-shaped peninsula, largest in the world,
that is Arabia, lying between the Mediterranean Sea, the Suez
Canal and the Red Sea on the west; the Indian Ocean on the southeast; the Persian Gulf and the Tigris-Euphrates Valley on the
northeast, with Turkey accounting for the northern boundary.)
The western tier: Egypt, Sudan and Ethiopia (which now includes
the former Italian colony of Eritrea on the Red Sea).

No short study could, even remotely, do more than suggest
the tangle of local problems within this area. We shall be rather
heavily emphasizing those of the northern tier, and those of the
Suez and Red Sea area. To go beyond this would take us far afield
into problems of the Far East and of continental Africa. Those
problems are certainly real enough and they are by no means
disconnected; but to make the story manageable, some line has
to be drawn.

The statement, surprising at first reading, was just made that this
was in effect a prolongation of the mid-European problem strip.
Geographically, Turkey is, of course, the southern neighbor of that
strip since in Europe it adjoins Bulgaria. If you follow the northern
tier you will see that straight across to Kashmir, it borders on the
Soviet empire until it reaches India. The grinding of the great
northern Russian force against this area is therefore one common

element. Also since Africa is largely held at date of writing by the West European Powers (British Commonwealth, France, Belgium, Portugal), the other side of the triangle is thus presently controlled by what is left of the old West European imperial system. This is precisely the system that the Soviet Union is attacking; it is also the system Asian nationalism challenges; and at the moment Asian nationalism and the Soviet empire march together though this may not be more than a passing phase.

Through this area pass two of the great waterway trade routes of the world. One of them is the outlet to the Black Sea through the Bosphorus, the Sea of Marmara and the Straits of the Dardanelles. This same waterway, if you like, may be called the mouth of the Danube River which carries traffic clear into Austria. (It is literally possible to sail a boat through Holland up the Rhine, take it over the Rhine-Main-Danube Canal and sail it down the Danube, across the Black Sea and into the Mediterranean. An American newspaperman, Negley Farson, once did it; at least he got as far as the Black Sea.) For that matter it is also the mouth of the great Russian rivers Don and Dniester. Old Russia, like the Soviet Union today, has always wanted to get out of the Black Sea as well as to get into it. She has, therefore, coveted the Turkish position astride the Bosphorus and the Dardanelles and her imperial policy has steadily driven towards Istanbul from earliest times.

To get into the Mediterranean, valuable as that is, is not access to the open sea; you also have to get out either by Gibraltar or by Suez. Russian policy-makers have not overlooked this fact; they therefore want ultimately to control one or other or preferably both of these waterways.

When you are through Suez you still have to get out of the Red Sea on the other end; hence the importance of the Strait of Aden and the importance that the British government who control it now attach to that area.

The Persian Gulf, of course, does not go through but inside, giving the bordering countries, notably Iran and Iraq, access to the ocean. It is also the means of transport for oil from the bordering fields. It is literally possible to pump crude oil from a well in the Persian Gulf to a ship lying within pumping distance. Some of this oil is, therefore, cheapest to produce in the entire world. By any commercial reckoning the area is of first importance. It is one of the great links between the European West and the Asian East.

Economically, the region is no less important. For some reason which only Providence can explain, oil is liberally distributed under great parts of the surface of this area. As a result, roughly 80% of the oil which turns the wheels of Western Europe moves from the Arabian or Persian coasts either through Aden, the Red Sea and Suez, or through pipelines crossing Arabia to the Mediterranean coast. There are other resources besides oil, though they have hardly been scratched; even without them, the real estate as international real estate goes probably ranks as one of the richest tracts presently known. Unhappily, the area has not been well enough governed and organized in modern times so that the natural resources could be developed by the local countries. Especially in the case of these nations life in the economic layer of development has been quite distinct from life on the sociocultural layer. The developers of the oil were primarily great British, Dutch and American companies which drilled the wells from which the riches of the area are drawn. Perhaps unhappily also, the oil when brought to the surface finds little market in the sadly underdeveloped countries of the region. The markets for it are in Britain, France, Germany, Spain, Italy, the United States and elsewhere. A country like Saudi Arabia, for example, can say, "This oil is ours." But this leaves other countries free to say, "True, but our markets for oil are ours. We will fill them from somewhere else: say, Texas or South America."

Oil obviously does not constitute the only Near Eastern economic asset or its only economic problem. Three fourths of all Egypt lives on cotton-producing, storing, marketing, and so forth. But Egypt must sell its cotton elsewhere. In every phase in the Middle East, the conflict between the conception of nationalist sovereignty and the fact that economics is international is apparent. It is less obvious in the northern tier countries: Iran, Afghanistan, Pakistan, but this is simply because those countries are still in a semi-primitive stage. The first stirrings of progress, of which now there are many, bring them also squarely into the conflict between nationalist sovereignty and factual internationalist economics.

This area likewise carries the highest freight of cultural and religious sentiment on earth.

The Jewish religion was born and flourished there. Spread now all over the world, it nevertheless has maintained for three thousand years an unlimitedly intense interest in the city of Jerusalem and the land of Israel. If you are familiar with the Book of Psalms (try the 48th and the 137th), you will understand why.

Nearly two thousand years ago from that same area came Christ, from whose teaching stems the civilization of the West. Across the sea in Greece, and from the old Greek cities including Byzantium (Constantinople—later Istanbul), comes the Greek culture, foundation of much, perhaps most, of our present learning. A Greek philosopher, Aristotle, accompanied Alexander the Great when he made himself master of the region about which we are writing. Mohammed was born in Arabia in the year 570, and established his new faith there about 622. Today Mohammedanism is also a world religion and the prevailing religion of this region. The key city to which good Mohammedans make a pilgrimage if they can is Mecca in Saudi Arabia. Finally, one of the great ecclesiastical organizations of Christianity, the so-called "Greek Catholic" or "Greek Orthodox" Church claims Istanbul as its capital—a throw-back to the days when, as Byzantium, that proud city was the religious as well as the political capital of half the "western" world. More than economics, more even than local nationalism, this religious emotion runs in the region; by events there, the deepest instincts of peoples all over the earth may be stirred.

This is why (the writer has seen both) you will find a meeting in the Bronx to support Israel or a congregation of Negro Mohammedan pilgrims taking over the airport at African Dakar en route to Mecca. Or a Greek Orthodox Patriarch or bishop claiming (in the name of a departed Byzantine Greece) a share in determining the fate of Istanbul or Cyprus. This is why Moscow, which in some fashion claims to be heir of the long-dead Byzantine Greek-Catholic Empire, insists on a sentimental as well as geopolitical right to deal with Turkey; why Moscow likewise asserts a major interest in Mecca in light of the fact that perhaps 12% of Soviet population is Mohammedan. Probably it explains why the English liberals, brought up on Greek poetry, so passionately desired the liberation of Greece in 1820.

2

The stakes in this region are virtually unlimited.

This is Asia, though detached from the big Chinese and Indian blocs. It is also the land approach between Europe, Asia and Africa; domination of it gives a strong possessor a major instrument with which to control those three continents, if not the entire world. Britain had that position during the latter part of the nineteenth and the early part of the twentieth centuries. It was precisely that position that Czarist Russia sought when she attacked Turkey in 1877; and that Hohenzollern Germany and Hapsburg Austria sought as a result of World War I—an aspiration sloganized into the phrase "Berlin to Baghdad." It was this the Soviet Union intended to have when in 1946 she backed the Communist revolution in Greece, demanded the right to fortify the Dardanelles and moved an army into northern Iran. The Soviet Union controls the mid-European strip now. If she can add to that the adjacent Middle Eastern triangle, and has the strength to organize and hold both, there will be little question what empire can speak most forcefully in world affairs or most readily crush an opponent.

This fact may explain why modern world contests have commonly been determined by battles in this area. Most students have some lingering area of superstition; the writer is superstitious on this score. Boundary was put to Napoleon when he failed to become master of this region, which is why the Napoleonic Empire became only a European and not a world dictatorship. Britain, for practical purposes, reached her top position when Disraeli in 1878 threw down the gauntlet to the Russians by landing troops in Constantinople. Turning point in World War I was General Allenby's victory over the Germans and Turks on the plains outside Jerusalem. The crucial battle in World War II was, I think, not Stalingrad (important as that was) but Marshal Montgomery's defeat of Hitler's General Rommel in 1942 at the battle of El Alamein in Egypt. As long as there are contests for world power, the answer in diplomacy or battle is likely to be given in these ancient, glorious, blood-soaked, terrible mid-Eastern lands. So it has been through the ages.

3

Like the mid-European strip, this area is a tangle of races. There is a certain unifying element: the Mohammedan religion which offers a common divisor of thinking. It is, I think, a relatively weak factor. It has never been able to unify the region under a single political head. That was done—when it was done at all—by sheer force and continued only so long as force remained. Mohammedan leaders and princes have rebelled against, conspired against and fought each other with gusto practically throughout their entire history. Indeed, one great country—Iran—though Mohammedan is heavily of a different sect. A large number are Shiites and acknowledge little contact with the greater body of Mohammedans, chiefly Sunnites and others. There are some powerful separatist sects. Saudi Arabians, for example, profess a singularly Puritan form of Mohammedism; they are Wahabites. Egypt at the moment claims leadership of the Mohammedan world and a great Mohammedan university is located there; but a large part of the population of the Nile valley are Copts whose religion is an ancient form of Christianity, and racially the non-Coptic Egyptians more nearly stem from Turkish and African stock than they do from Arab.

There is, however, a solid if mixed racial group known as Turks and these, as might be expected, are the dominant race group in Turkey. But there are also solid blocks of Greeks in Istanbul and the coast regions of Asia Minor. In Iran there is a loose grouping of considerably different races which can be fairly described as

Persians or Iranians—though the differences within the country
are very great. Afghanistan is again a collection of peoples of
whom about half are "Pukhtuns" (or "Pashtuns"). We shall be
encountering them a little later. The rest are chiefly Tadjik.
"Pakistan," newly carved out of the late Indian Empire of Britain,
is not at all one people racially—it has the Mohammedan or Islamic faith instead as its unifying principle, and among them are
a great many Pukhtuns (which suggests ideas of aggrandizement
to Afghanistan at Pakistan's expense.) You will find Persians,
Arabs, a few Greeks, ten million or so Hindus, even some Mongolians, within its borders.

The second tier, lying south of the countries mentioned above,
is somewhat more unified racially—though not much. The inhabitants of the Arabian quadrilateral are chiefly Arab, which is to
say that they are a Semitic race, first cousins to the Jews, though
with all kinds of separate and subordinate mixtures. But much of
Lebanon like the Egyptian Copts professes Nestorian Christianity
and obviously comprises a mixture of many races.

Israel is now solidly Jewish (the Jews themselves are a mixture
of several race streams at least); but in order to achieve this
nearly a million Arabs had to be expelled in 1948 from present-
day Israel. They are now "displaced populations" living in Arab
States near Israel's borders.

One racial group offers rich possibilities for power-politics intrigue: these are the Kurds, which inhabit a diagonal strip, one
end of which is in Iran and which stretches southwest across a
corner of Turkey and through the northern part of Iraq into the
eastern part of Syria. Incidentally, this race bloc cuts across most
of the pipelines from which some of the Near Eastern oil crosses
the Arabian peninsula is to reach the Mediterranean Sea at the
ports of Lebanon. Not unnaturally, this situation offers attractive
bait to troublemakers. A Kurdist rebellion can occasion a maximum of disturbance with a minimum of risk to outsiders who
foment it. There used also to be a large number of Armenians in
various parts of Turkey; but the policy of Sultan Abdul Hamid's
Turkish empire in the early days of the twentieth century was to

arrange for their massacre. This was carried out so ruthlessly that most of them did not survive, though they once were dominant in the provinces of Kars and Ardahan and in Turkey's eastern sector.

The fiercest pressures (aside from the Arab-Israel conflict) are likely to occur from outside the area. In the northwest sector of Turkey, Slavs lie to the north; under Soviet influence they steadily push southward into the great mid-Eastern triangle. In the mountain region between the Black and the Caspian Seas—the Caucasus —there are many races; but Czarist and Soviet Russia alike has steadily pushed Slavic settlers south to the border. Interestingly enough, Stalin, who was a Georgian, was as active in this policy as any modern Russian ruler—though the application of it tended to absorb or wipe out the Georgian race group. Well, Marx, or at least Engels, writing with him, thought small surviving race-groups were only refuse of history, and had to be unified with greater groups.

Across the Caspian Sea the Soviet Union holds the largest Middle Eastern colonies in the world; they lie northeast of Iran and north of both Afghanistan and Pakistan. This is Russian Central Asia; the peoples there are Turcomen, Uzbek, Tadjik and so on. They are remnants of kingdoms of Genghis Khan and Tamerlane; once proud peoples whose capitals of Tashkend and Samarkand in their time were queen cities of the oriental world. Again, Russian policy has been to infiltrate Russian Slavs in these areas, breaking up the old race groupings. But perhaps it would be well not to be too condemnatory; it is the method rather than the result which inspires terror. The United States with its freedom has probably absorbed more race groups (converting them into a people we call "American") than any other great Power.

Soviet southward pressure is clear, continuous and obvious. Unlike the mid-European strip, the fate of this area is still in doubt. It lies at hazard of one of the least known and greatest diplomatic and power conflicts of the twentieth century. The Soviet Union has aimed to break it from the north. She has had no success in Turkey; she was diplomatically beaten off (1946) in her chief attempt against Iran. Smoother tactics have been em-

ployed in the half-primitive country of Afghanistan. At date of
writing it would seem as though the Soviet Union had won the
contest, since that country now has Soviet military instructors,
Soviet (probably Czechoslovak) arms, Soviet engineers, and so
forth. A major drive to extend these gains into Western Pakistan is
in progress. We noted that a majority of Afghanistans were Pukhtuns (or Pashtuns. We stick to Pukhtuns because this is what
Afghans call it). There is a large Pukhtu minority in Western
Pakistan. Since it lies along the passes of the Hindu Kush Mountains, and these passes would be a land route for an army from
the Soviet Union into India, the position is strategic. A lively
movement for Pukhtu "autonomy" (meaning, independence from
Pakistan and domination nominally by Afghanistan, really by the
Soviet Union) is being cheerfully and energetically encouraged by
the government of Moscow.

The end of that area is the Pakistan corner which encounters
Kashmir. Now Kashmir, a country where four empires meet, is a
problem of its own. We leave it here, because its ramifications
stretch deep into the very heart of the Far East. Nehru's India
has it now; Pakistan claims it; a United Nations commission seeks
to keep peace there. From Kashmir comes almost all the water
Pakistan has—the water of the Indus River. When therefore the
Soviet Union supports Afghan Pukhtuns in their drive into Pakistan and when India asserts control of Kashmir, both are really
pointing out that, if need be, one or other might have power to
break Western Pakistan by diverting or controlling its water. In the
Soviet case, that empire by breaking Pakistan would find itself able
to reach the Indian Ocean, and would have no great difficulty in
making its way into the Persian Gulf. As matters stand, the Soviet
Union is rapidly creating a situation in which she could shove a
great wedge from the plains of Soviet Turkistan and Russian Central Asia straight to the Indian Ocean and the mouth of the Persian
Gulf—just as control of the mid-European strip gives her possibility to shove a wedge through Bulgaria to the Aegean Sea and the
mouth of the Dardanelles.

In the Middle Eastern case there is no strong line of opposition (east of Turkey) in case of break-through. In the mid-European strip, the Western side is occupied by solidly organized West European peoples of high capacity, quite firmly devoted to a way of life of their own and quite opposed to having the Soviet Union (or anyone else) impose a different civilization on them. Save in the case of Turkey, it can hardly be said that countries in the northern tier, or for that matter in the Arabian Desert are equipped to offer any solid resistance. The real check is the possibility that the West, fearing to concede to the Soviet Union so striking a position in world affairs, would throw their own force into the balance. That, of course, would mean a new world war.

4

The history of this remarkable area is longer, probably, than any other recorded human history outside of China since it begins (if that was the beginning) with empires of Hittites, Egyptians, Babylonians, Assyrians, and so forth, and includes Persia, Alexander the Great, the Roman Emperors, and the Crusades. We pick it up only in its most recent phase.

As the twentieth century came in, control for practical purposes was held by the dying Turkish Empire, powerfully backstopped by the British Empire, then senior power in the world. Russia had made her unsuccessful bid in that direction when she drove towards Constantinople in 1878 while Bismarck and Disraeli mobilized the Western Powers to give her check. At about the same time, a talented French engineer, De Lesseps, was dickering for a franchise to build the Suez Canal, in Egyptian territory. Egypt was nominally a province of Turkey, but actually its rulers—they were called "Khedives"—were absolute monarchs, paying only lip-service to the Turkish Sultans in Constantinople. De Lesseps got his concession; he built and opened his canal, selling stock partly to the Khedive and partly to French and other investors to pay the cost of construction. Thereafter, in 1887, the Khedive being badly in debt, the British government bought his shares, giving Britain "working" control of the Suez corporation. In 1887, also, the British intervened heavily in Egyptian affairs, in time reducing the Egyptian government to the status of a British protectorate. For the rest, all Arabia (including present day Israel) was a collection of Turkish provinces. Eastward, the weak Persian Empire was divided into spheres of influence: British in the south, Russian in the north. A kind of tacit stand-still agreement had been reached.

No one particularly liked the brand of government put up by the old Turkish Empire. However, it had one merit: its weakness prevented it from using its unparalleled geographic position in a power play against the other empires. So long as the Dardanelles, the Persian Gulf, the eastern Mediterranean coast and the striking-distance position towards Suez were in Turkish hands, no one was afraid; no one was afraid, that is, so long as none of the other great Powers moved in. In effect there was a kind of general understanding that no one would move in. The British, it is true, were firmly ensconced in Egypt. This, together with their working control of the Suez Canal Company and of the Aden Protectorate at the other end of the Red Sea gave her solid control of the waterway. But then, Britain was a moderate Power whose word (given by treaty in 1888) that the waterway would be open to all nations was good. The Russians did not then have control of the bulk of the mid-European strip as they do today; they were in no position to risk a major war by a push either towards Constantinople, the Aegean Sea and the Dardanelles, or towards the Persian Gulf. Russian statesmen were probably not satisfied, but they were halted. In any case, the Siberian Far East offered them easier possibility of expansion. Thus the balance of power established about 1880 remained without serious threat.

The real danger to the situation lay in the fact that this area with its then population of about 75 million was worse governed perhaps than any area in the world. The condition could not be expected to last, especially since areas of it were in contact with more effective civilizations and more effective government. Constantinople, however badly administered (it was not renamed "Istanbul" until after World War I), was nevertheless a cosmopolitan city with a first-rate American school, Roberts College, which was steadily educating most of the leaders of the Middle East. Lebanon was a trading country and its capital, Beirut, also had an American mission school, Beirut University. The Jewish world was slowly becoming interested in a new incarnation of Zion in Jerusalem. The Egyptians had contact with the British. The Germans were active in disseminating propaganda, in organizing research, scientific teaching, and so forth. Ideas were being absorbed throughout the area: notable among them were two. One was that the Turkish Empire was due for a thorough overhaul. The second, spreading through the provinces, was that the nominal allegiance of Egypt and the Arabian and other areas of the Turkish throne need not last forever. Both movements suddenly flowered.

In Turkey what happened was the "Young Turk" revolution of 1908. The Young Turks may not, in historical hindsight, have turned out a much better brand of government than did the court coterie of Abdul Hamid whom they displaced. But they effectively disposed of the decaying remains of the ancient caliphate. By 1910, the beginnings of a Turkish democracy emerged. There were stirrings throughout other parts of the Turkish Empire, put down with a heavy though inefficient hand. In 1911, as we have seen, the balance was tipped when Italy declared war on Turkey, seizing Tripoli (now Libya). As this was in the main a rather unattractive and empty desert, the other European Powers were philosophical about it, and Italy took over.

But if one province could thus be detached, so could others. Note has already been made of the seizure of Macedonia and the Turkish-Balkan area by Greece, Bulgaria and Serbia in 1912. A lively Egyptian nationalist movement started. There was no possible point in keeping up the fiction that Egypt was under the suzerainty of Turkey. For that matter, to Egyptian nationalists there was no particular reason why it should be a protectorate of Britain either. In Arabia, though nominal Turkish suzerainty existed, the fact was (the fact is now) that the interior desert is independent by fiat of God. No one has ever solved the problem of bringing nomadic Bedouin tribes under fixed rule. They can merely be kept under a sort of loose, sporadic control. The ferment was well on in 1914 when the Sarajevo incident in the mid-European strip started World War I.

While the Hohenzollern-German and Hapsburg-Austrian combination immediately wanted control of the remaining portions of the mid-European strip, their larger object was domination over just this Middle Eastern area. They used diplomatic pressure to bring the dying Turkish Empire into war on their side. In this they succeeded; it perhaps was partly intimidation, because two powerful German cruisers, the *Goeben* and the *Breslau*, took refuge from the British fleet in the then neutral harbor of Constantinople. Though interned, they trained their guns on the city. The combination of reasons finally brought Turkey into war against the Western Powers, a notable consideration being that Britain and France were then acting in alliance with Turkey's historic enemy, Russia. It was perhaps the greatest mistake the Turks could have made. One of their defenses, of course, is that they feared a Russian seizure had they not allied with the opposite Powers.

The result of the Allied victory in 1918 was the end of Turkey as an empire and the rebirth of Turkey as a nation. The British political warfare people, with Colonel Lawrence of Arabia (T. E. Shaw) heading their Commandos, incited the Arab sheiks to revolt. The British regular army under Allenby finally cleared Turkish troops out of the Arabian quadrilateral. Throughout the war Egypt was for all intents and purposes a British garrison. The Italians wobbled and finally came down on the side of the Western Allies. They kept control of Libya and took a slice of the Red Sea coast at Eritrea. The Turks crumbled in total defeat; Allied forces were completely victorious in the area. In that posture the Powers met at Versailles in 1918.

Clearly the Middle East was one of the great affairs of that conference; clearly, too, the Western Powers were, for once, in a position to dictate. Russia was in the throes of a Bolshevik revolution, therefore for the time being out of great power politics as the Turkish Empire dissolved. Equally clearly, Great Britain and France were not in full agreement. Nationalist tides were running strongly in the lands formerly under Turkish rule. The United States was in no mood to share responsibility for the area. An embarrassing circumstance—the Allied promise to give Constantinople to Russia in case of victory—was solved by simply forgetting it. The theory was that it had been canceled by Lenin's surrender to and separate peace with Kaiser Wilhelm's Germany and, in any case, President Wilson and the United States were no party to it.

Now began one of the strange adventures in which great powers occasionally indulge.

British Prime Minister Lloyd George considered not only that the Turkish Empire had outlived its time but that Turkey itself should cease to exist for all practical purposes. Even while the Paris Peace Conference was sitting, the British government encouraged an all too willing Greek army and government to seize great parts of Turkey proper. Greek troops invaded from the West towards Constantinople, and also landed at Smyrna and moved into western Anatolia. A puppet Turkish Sultan was installed by the British forces occupying Constantinople; he was to have an insignificant portion of Turkey. Constantinople itself and the Straits of the Dardanelles were to be under international rule, presumably dominated by Great Britain, working with her Greek allies. An Armenian State was to be set up south of the Caucasus. The arrangement actually was embodied in a treaty (the Treaty of Sèvres) signed by the puppet Turkish government in Constantinople; but, by this time, national forces had reasserted themselves.

Mustapha Kemal, later known as "Ataturk," a Turkish army officer, rallied a remnant of the Turkish army in Anatolia, and called a national assembly which laid the foundation for a true national Turkish movement. In April, 1920, its successor assembly named Kemal head of the government. His forces checked the Greeks, broke up the nascent Armenian State, negotiated for the withdrawal of the sulky French and Italian troops which had joined the British raid into Turkey, got supplies from Bolshevik Russia and at length, after a year's campaign, drove the Greek armies into the sea in 1922.

By now the British had had enough of the ill-fated venture. Under political pressure at home, they withdrew their support from the Greek armies threatening Constantinople from the European side. The game was clearly up: it was time to settle, for nationalist Turkey was now in control substantially of the present territories of Turkey, and nothing short of a full-scale war would change the situation. Settlement was eventually made by the Treaty of Lausanne in 1923. Turkey got back Constantinople, and a tiny European strip around it along with the boundaries of Turkey in Asia about as we know them today. With it went control of the Bosphorus and the Dardanelles, subject to certain international rights of peaceful transit.

The non-Turkish territories of the former Turkish Empire, got their independence though under "mandates" of the League of Nations. The League of Nations granted "mandates" to supervising Powers over newly emerged countries thought not to be ready for complete independence and in the Middle East, Great Britain drew the lion's share. There were created under her "mandate" the countries known today as Iraq, Lebanon, Syria and Transjordania. France had been promised a "position" in this area; she eventually got the mandate for Syria and Lebanon. The largest of the new countries, Hedjaz (now Saudi Arabia) was carved out by military seizure of a great part of Arabia by the tough Wahabite chieftain, Ibn Saud, who took it by arms without much benefit from Allied politics.

The area comprising present-day Israel was held and governed under a separate arrangement by Great Britain. It was known as "Palestine" and the British declared their intention to make of it a national homeland for Jews. Not, it will be noted, a separate Jewish State—merely an area in which Jews had special rights of entry and dwelling. A local movement to take Egypt out of British control meanwhile went vigorously forward; but Turkey, not Britain, had been defeated in World War I, so that it gained no great recognition until later. The theory of League of Nations mandates in Arabia was that the countries under them should be developed toward full independence as rapidly as practical. All Arabian

States were, one by one, freed from mandate status in the ensuing twenty years, becoming as completely independent as small undeveloped nations usually are in the twentieth-century world.

It is a mistake to regard the Arabian peninsula as united. Indeed it probably is a mistake to think of Arab nationalism in the same sense that we think of most other nationalisms. Loyalty in much of that area has historically been rather to a tribe or family than to a precise geographical area. Ibn Saud, for instance, in constructing Saudi Arabia displaced another great Arab prince, Hussein, whose sons later took over, respectively, the kingdoms of Iraq and Transjordania. There is no love lost between the sons of Ibn Saud (now ruling Saudi Arabia) and the grandsons of Emir Hussein today. Syria again has within itself several conflicting elements and the government has not really been stable either before or after the French mandate was terminated. It is heavily infiltrated with Soviet technicians. The sheikdoms of Kuwait, Oman, Bahrein, Yemen and Muskat, and a dozen or more shadowy tribal groups for practical purposes are independent, while the Aden protectorate is under British rule.

World War II found the area in an uneasy pattern of emerging nations. In broadest respects it reflected the historic drives of World War I, though with sharp differences. Turkey this time had the good sense to remain neutral. Vigorously pressed to join the war against Hitler (Hitler's intentions against Turkey were certainly hostile enough), old President Inonü, who had succeeded the powerful dictator, Kemal Ataturk, estimated the hand. He calculated that entering the alliance against Hitler would mean that he would be "allied" with the Soviet Union; that the Soviet Union would promptly put a Russian army into Turkey to "protect" the country and that the Russian army would never leave. In that case, Turkey would be defeated either way. So he kept out. As events proved, he was everlastingly right. At the beginning of World War II, a French army dominated one part of the Arabian peninsula, but when France surrendered to Germany in 1940, it was left hanging in mid-air. British military control was fairly well established in Egypt and the remaining portions of the Arabian

peninsula from the beginning; whereas in World War I she had
had to conquer the territory.

Hitler nevertheless played boldly for the mid-Eastern stake. He
already had the whole mid-European strip. Through Italy he sent
one of his best generals, Rommel, with an army (the famous
Afrika Korps) which presently took over the North African coast
from Tunis to the Libyan desert west of Egypt. His objective was
to seize Suez and dominate Arabia. The British under Marshal
Montgomery set up headquarters in Egypt and counterattacked.
The tide of battle ebbed and flowed, but finally reached a climax
on October 23, 1942 at El Alamein—near the Mediterranean
coast and deeply inside Egypt (it is not far from Alexandria at
the mouth of the Nile). American help by this time had begun to
flow to Britain; Montgomery defeated Rommel and the Germans
were obliged to retreat. Fortunately by this time the Western part
of North Africa was firmly in Allied hands, thanks to a British-
American expedition headed by General Eisenhower; in the end,
the Germans were driven out of all Africa. The entire Middle East
—and with it the balance of power in World War II—remained in
the hands of the anti-Fascist coalition.

This included not control of, but powerful influence in, Turkey
as well. For, with the Germans defeated, the chief Turkish fear
was of Russia, and it became an evident Turkish interest to establish the closest possible relations with the Western Powers. In
this instance, the Western Powers were, quite clearly, Great Britain and the United States. Such was the approximate condition of
affairs when World War II ended in 1945.

5

Then the mid-Eastern pot really began to boil. Behind it was the
fantastic development of the Persian Gulf and Arabian oil fields.
This, of course, released commercial rivalries. But, as noted, the
world had made some progress in adjusting economic disputes.
The great oil companies in 1928 worked out a sort of world truce
or world alliance—a world cartel agreement, if you like—and the

evolution of that alliance accomplished a more or less friendly division of oil, supply, transport, markets and so forth. Of even more importance was the fact that Western Europe increasingly came to depend on precisely that oil—80% of Western European oil supplies now moves from the Persian Gulf and Arabia by tankers through Suez or through the several pipelines that find their way to the Mediterranean coast. Cut the supply, and Europe has no oil: unless, of course, oil is supplied from the Western Hemisphere. Now the Western Hemisphere has or can have oil enough and probably could supply European needs even though the Arabian oil wells were shut down—though a good many oil companies would suffer substantial financial losses. What Europe could not readily do, however, is pay the Western Hemisphere for that oil: the Western Hemisphere, though it buys about 25% of its import needs from Western Europe does not buy enough, now, to give it American dollars sufficient to pay for sudden shift in oil imports from Near Eastern suppliers to American and South American suppliers.

To Near Eastern politicians this dependence of Europe on Near Eastern oil seemed like an excellent diplomatic card to play. In the early stages, each of the countries with oil fields increased their demand for a share of the oil profits. These demands were gradually acceded to. The revenues on which the States of Iraq, Bahrein, Kuweit, Oman, Yemen and Saudi Arabia are operated are chiefly the royalties they receive from the concessions they have granted to the foreign companies. But it presently dawned on some politicians, notably in Egypt, that the position might be used for political as well as financial advantage. One of these politicians was a young army officer, Colonel Gamal Abdul Nasser, a rising power in the Egyptian nationalist movement. Egypt, of course, by now was fully independent, a kingdom with a rather unattractive ruler, Farouk, wearing the crown.

At the same time, the growing Jewish concentration on establishing the Jewish homeland as a sovereign country began to exert influence in the Western world. Jews went to Palestine, taking refuge from Hitler before his defeat or seeking asylum after the war from blood-soaked border areas in which their brethren had been ruthlessly massacred. The young Arab States reacted intensely to this. They insisted, first, that Jewish immigration into Palestine would merely begin a Jewish move to take over increasingly great parts of Arabia into this national Jewish homeland; second, that in any case Jewish occupation of Palestine would result in driving out the million or so Arabs who had been there for fifteen centuries or so; third, that they were opposed to the Jewish religion and to forced Westernization anyway. They identified the emergence of Israel as an act of "Western imperialism."

Zionists on their part asserted their ancient historic preoccupation with Zion, and added, quite accurately, that for some centuries, neither under the Turks nor under Arabian governments had there been any substantial improvement of the condition of the people of the region. They were, of course, bringing their highly developed Western civilization into Palestine, and into direct contact with a substantially medieval Arab culture and civilization which at the time was quite unable to cope with twentieth century technique. The clashing rivalries of the Arab world were, for the time being at least, more or less submerged. At the close of World War II, in 1945, a loose Arab League (Egypt, Iraq, Jordan, Saudi Arabia, Syria, Lebanon, Yemen and the nascent State of Libya) was formed for the purpose of maintaining Arab "solidarity." They resisted Zionist claims as these finally came to the point of realization.

In 1947, the General Assembly of the United Nations divided Palestine, apportioning part of it to a new Arab State and another part to an Israel later to be set up. The Arab League threatened boycott and war—the latter threat was thought by some Zionist advocates to be a bluff. On May 14, 1948, the Republic of Israel was proclaimed; it promptly took over the territory assigned to it by the United Nations and claimed Jerusalem which had not been so assigned.

The Arab League immediately attacked; claims were made that the Israelite forces had already pushed beyond the United Nations frontiers. In the ensuing war, the Jewish armies prevailed. They

not only defended the territories granted them by the United Nations but occupied the entire Palestine territory. Ironically, their
final push was powerfully assisted by purchases of arms from the
Communist-held mid-European strip, that is, from Czechoslovakia. In 1949, a United Nations team headed first by Folke
Bernadotte and after his assassination by America's Ralph Bunche
negotiated the present armistice lines.

Since then armistice—by no means peace—has prevailed between Israel and the neighboring Arab States—including Egypt as
an "Arab State" because Egypt includes itself in the Arab League.

One at least of the Arab fears was justified. Through stress of
war and pressure of incoming Jewish immigration, the new State
of Israel thought it necessary to expel nearly a million Arab inhabitants from her now militarily established borders. By grim
historic jest, this was about the number of European Jews who
had taken refuge in Israel. These refugees settled just outside the
Israelite borders and there they remain. They wish to go back.
Proposals to finance their repatriation have found little sympathy
from the Arab States: they do not much want the refugees, and
they do want the issue against Israel.

The tiny Israelite State flourished, due partly to the unparalleled industry and devotion of its population, partly to continuous
help from outside. Its very progress may have contributed to the
counter-development: the dream of Arab empire which rapidly
took form. This deserves a word: we may hear a good deal of it
in years to come. Surprisingly, the center of the movement is in
the non-Arabic but Mohammedan State of Egypt, perhaps owing
to the fact that a great Mohammedan university is located in
Cairo and is a recognized center of Mohammedan thought. Also
Egypt has had the most continuous contact with the twentieth
century West, it is the largest population bloc (22½ million
people) and has need for expansion.

The reactionary and corrupt government of the Egyptian kingdom which emerged after World War I broke up in 1952. An
army revolt under General Mohammed Naguib seized Cairo and
expelled King Farouk. Two years later the young Colonel Gamal

Abdul Nasser succeeded him and became dictator of Egypt. He promptly began a vigorous reform movement, perhaps the first serious attempt to aid the poverty-stricken Egyptian masses; but he also picked up the banner of Egyptian and Arab nationalism, and the cause of "liberation" from Western "imperialism" of which Israel and British control of the Suez Canal were considered the great symbols. He considered that control of oil in the Middle East could be a powerful card in the game; and he began to agitate the dream of an Arab-Mohammedan empire which should include the whole Arabian peninsula and all North Africa as well. After all, if the Zionists could revive and make real a kingdom of Israel which had passed into history 2,000 years ago, why could not Arabs revive and make real an Islamic empire which had reigned and had broken up a mere five centuries or so ago?

The difficulty is not with the dream. Arabic is the language of this vast territorial bloc running from the Persian Gulf to the Atlantic Coast of Morocco. There is substantially a common religion. There were in days past great Mohammedan emperors and caliphs. There is at present a common desire to shake off the supremacy of the Western European countries, notably that of France in Tunisia, Algiers and Morocco. There is a common cause, as Arabs see it, against Israel. But the days of Arabian empires were days when empires did not depend on modern economics, and even the history of the old caliphates is a chronicle of internal revolts, divisions and internecine warfare. Princely leader after princely leader refused to acknowledge imperial power, while family struggled with family to seize local thrones, great and small. Brother murdered brother to remove rival candidates for power. It may have been very naughty for the Western European powers to seize control of the Barbary (North Africa) States and to attempt control of the Arabian peninsula. But the Barbary States were hell-holes of slave trading and oppression, supporting some Pasha, Bey, Emir or Prince reigning in Oriental splendor by despotism and cruelty amid indescribable misery. The Western seizure of the area was in part a direct result of centuries of misgovernment, plus a continuous propensity of these States to practice piracy in the Mediterranean.

Another difficulty lay in the fact that Egypt, separately, has her own troubles. She is dependent entirely on the Nile for water; to increase in any degree the habitable land of the country something must be done. One improvement was made when the Aswan Dam was constructed. The other possibly feasible improvement (some experts disapprove of it) is the "high dam" south of that—a dam which will be perhaps the second largest in the world and might cost today a billion dollars to construct. A third difficulty is that Egypt (and indeed all Arab countries) must depend on other countries for the arms essential in realizing any part of the dream of empire.

Now the dream begins to march. While the Western Powers and notably the United States in an endeavor to reduce tension were talking "foreign aid" to Egypt (including financing the "high dam"), conflict between the Arab League and Israel was rising. The Egyptians were seeking arms; late in 1955 they bought them from the Soviet bloc, that is to say, again ironically, from Czechoslovakia. This was admittedly a Russian job—Moscow was taking a hand in the Great Game.

The Soviet Union was really answering a piece of Western diplomacy. Wishing to defend the northern tier of our Mideastern triangle against Russian aggression, Britain, with United States approval, had stimulated the formation of a sort of little NATO—Turkey, Iran, Pakistan and Iraq, and both had likewise stimulated a pact between Turkey, Greece and Yugoslavia on the Western side. The Soviet Union was now jumping this tier and opening relations with Egypt. Nobody would accuse the Soviet Foreign Office of not knowing that the Suez Canal went through Egyptian territory. In July, 1956, the United States abruptly broke off negotiations with Egypt looking towards American financing of the "high dam." Equally abruptly, Nasser countered by "expropriating" (that is, taking by eminent domain) the shares of the Suez Canal Company—and asserting Egypt's sovereign right to operate the Canal itself. He insisted that he would allow free use of the Canal to all hands but there was little confidence in his word; in any case, the Suez seizure was intended to be, and was, a gesture of defiance to the Great Powers. There was at least surface evidence that the step had been taken in consultation with the Soviet Union; possibly though not certainly with the acquiescence of the Indian government under Nehru, and with the obvious sympathy of Communist China. The vortex of the Near East whirlpool was slowly drawing in all the powers, just as Czarist Russia's attempt to seize Constantinople in 1878 had involved every power in Europe.

It is too early to suggest the implications of the Near Eastern crisis of October and November, 1956. Quite literally it has shaken the world. The writer believes the facts will turn out to be these:

At some time in 1955, the Kremlin decided on a main line Near Eastern move. It was planned to achieve control over the Suez-Red Sea area and possibly also (we do not know) over the Dardanelles. To do this, the Kremlin took advantage of a favorable opportunity and supplied arms to two countries, Egypt and Syria. Possibly to others: we do not yet know. These were not arms merely for use of the local Egyptian and Syrian soldiers. They were dumps designated to supply a considerably greater body of troops, presumably "volunteers" supplied from the Soviet Union and possibly from Communist China.

A glance at the map will show that there is not an open landline from the Soviet Union either to Egypt or Syria. An open line was necessary and the obvious one was the line running through the mid-European strip. The Albanian port of Vlöri is already substantially a Russian base. From it, arms and men could be sent very handily to Egypt. But as Yugoslavia was at the moment not within the Soviet orbit, the line had to be built.

In the Summer of 1956, accordingly, the Soviet Union worked out a plan (noted in the preceding chapter) to create a "commonwealth" of Communist States including Yugoslavia. One surmises that an article of the agreement with Tito permitted sending volunteers through Yugoslavia in transit to Egypt. Probably in small contingents; Tito would hardly allow great bodies of Russian troops in his own country. One also surmises that the push was scheduled for the Summer of 1957, though this is only a guess.

But, in the Summer of 1956, Nasser precipitated matters by seizing the shares of the Suez Canal Company and attempting to take over operation of the Canal. This frightened and angered Western Europe. Britain and France proposed to use force to maintain their control of the Canal—not unnaturally since their vital oil supplies came through it and no one had much faith in Nasser's naked promises not to close the waterway. The British and French conferred with the United States, gradually learning that the United States would not countenance the use of force, but obtaining a false notion that the United States would support them. Elaborate negotiations with Nasser broke down, and Britain and France came wholly to distrust American assurances that somehow or other the Canal would remain under international control. They then, with Israel, secretly planned a move to occupy the Suez area with British and French troops, Israel agreeing to occupy the Egyptian territory (Sinai peninsula) east of the Canal and of the Red Sea. This was done in late October, 1956.

So it came about that simultaneously Russian policy encountered two blows. The first was the revolution in Poland and Hungary elsewhere described. The latter cut the chief railway lines leading from Soviet Russia and Poland into Yugoslavia and Vlöri: the western line was thus jeopardized. Though the Russian armies stamped out the Hungarian revolution in blood and thereby restored Russian control over the Hungarian part of the line, the effect of their violent action frightened Tito and probably made Yugoslav cooperation undependable.

At exactly the same time, the British and French expedition moved towards Suez, and Israel moved into the Sinai peninsula. This did not touch the cache of arms built up in Syria, but it unquestionably destroyed a considerable part of the ammunition dumps built up by the Soviet Union in Egypt. So far the Soviet Union was having the worst of the power play.

Then came a serious turn for the Western Powers. The United States, angered by the British and French move, took the Arab-

Egyptian side in the ensuing debates in the United Nations. They
demanded, and got, a cease-fire order, and occupation of Suez by
a token force of United Nations troops—a few thousand in all.
This split the United States from Britain and France: the NATO
alliance was thus endangered.

In the course of the process the Suez Canal was blocked by
sunken ships, preventing tankers from bringing oil through it from
Western Europe. Also some Arab States moved to prohibit ship-
ment by any route (tankers can also go around Cape Horn) destined for Britain or France. Syria, now under Soviet influence,
blew up most of the pipelines through which oil flows from the
Persian Gulf and Mosul area to the Mediterranean Sea. In result,
Western Europe as this book goes to press does not have adequate
oil supplies.

The United States, having joined in demanding the recall of
French and British troops, added to the general confusion by
declining to offer oil supplies to Britain and France until their
troops were withdrawn, though probably the talk was rather
more serious than the ultimate intention. In this condition the
matter is under present debate in the United Nations.

Both sides emerged damaged in this affair. The Soviet Union
has lost part of the resources for its intended mid-East push
and has no very effective line to introduce an army (masquerading
as "volunteers") though she can unquestionably infiltrate some
guerrilla troops. Whether her military and political people consider that the power position is enough to start again remains to be
seen. But the West is equally damaged. The cornerstone of the
free world had been united action between the United States and
West Europe. The United States did not support Western Europe
in the matter of an interest vital to its life—the oil transport line
—and as Britain and France moved to protect their position in-
dependently, the United States temporarily appeared to have helped
to impede receipt of supplies from any route. Allies do not easily
forget this kind of division.

The Near East, by consequence, is a crisis area now. It will remain a crisis area (though the crises will take different forms) for a considerable time to come.

This brings us up to date of writing. It emphasizes, however, one point referred to above.

Egypt asserts "sovereignty" in the eighteenth century sense of the term. So, for that matter, did the petty Rhine barons in the Middle Ages when they levied tribute on every vessel navigating the great German river. Now while Egypt is unquestionably "sovereign" over the geography of the country and under international law can take over Suez shares (it is an Egyptian company), the canal itself is an international waterway for the world, and control of it powerfully affects the balance between East and West. "Sovereignty" is no answer to this situation. The case is dead ripe for an assertion of "world sovereignty" or, if you choose, world restriction of national sovereignty, ultimate control being actually exercised by some non-national or supra-national force such as the United Nations.

But in this case would not the same considerations apply, let us say, to the Panama Canal? Probably, yes; there are rumbles to this effect in Panama and Latin America. A problem is thus presented to the United States as well as to Britain and France. Some day, unquestionably, the Peace of Nations, with clear rules of conduct, backed with some international peace-keeping force will resolve these situations. The twentieth century is driving us to just this sort of solution.

6

To call the East a crisis area is, if anything, an understatement. It has geographic problems like that of Suez, economic problems like those resulting from oil, sentimental problems like the conflict between the old dream of Arab empire and the older dream of Israel and Zion. It has an almost wholly unsolved social problem: hardly anywhere in the world are the masses more depressed, the governments less responsible, the rich less willing to aid the poor, the kings, princes and dictators less able to give the standard of living and justice accorded, for example, by the British in British-held areas. Arab aspirations obviously were not created by Communist propaganda, but they obviously represent a golden field for Soviet intrigue, in time to be followed by Soviet Power politics looking toward eventual incorporation of the area into the Soviet imperial system. When the Germans attempted like maneuver first in 1914, later in 1939 (though in each case they began in the mid-European strip), the result was world war.

Yet failure to challenge might mean, should the Communist system establish itself, a situation in which the Communist world could make war upon the free world with every strategic chance of victory. The Soviet Empire now does possess the mid-European strip. If it possesses the Middle East as well, for practical purposes the free world would be limited to the Western countries of Europe and the two American continents, together with some scattered geography in distant parts, instead of being the far wider world we know today. This could happen. Wherefore, Western statesmen, understanding the implications, watch over the mid-Eastern problem with anxiety.

There are, to be sure, qualifying considerations. The Communist Empire, like other empires, is encountering the grim rule of mathematics that the area of a circle increases by the square of its radius. Has the Communist complex the resources, the men, the ability, to integrate control over this area as well as over the vast colonial empire it already dominates? Would Communist China and Communist Russia stay together? Would the loose Arab unity prevailing over the issue of Suez and Israel continue, or would Mohammedan history repeat itself as chieftains of various Arab countries struggle against any central power and with each other? Thus problems are presented to statesmen at Moscow too. Yet it must be conceded that the problems are not of the same valence. To Western Europe, the issue is one of survival—just as it was in 743 when the Mohammedan Empire, holding North Africa, seized Spain and overran half of France; or again in 1553 when the Turkish Emperor Suleiman pushed from Constantinople to the Adriatic, seized much of the Mid-European strip, and threatened Vienna. To Moscow, it would seem, the question is whether the Soviet system can keep its own system strong and also commit time, men and resources to challenge for power over most of the world. To the West European Powers—and, let it be added, conceivably even for the United States—the problem could be one of sheer national existence.

CHAPTER Six

CRISIS AREAS: THE ASIAN COAST
AND "COLONIALISM"

1

A THIRD AREA condemned to crisis is the Asian coast. To give it manageable scope we consider it here from the Isthmus of Kamchatka (which juts from the tip of Siberia) through the Kurile Islands which shoe-string to the northern tip of Japan (and thus form the boundary of the Sea of Okhotsk) and from Japan all the way south to Indo-China and Malaya ending at Singapore and Sumatra. This is not all the area, nor can we consider all the problems. Because this book is neither a history of the world nor a geographic study of the planet, a single aspect of this area is chiefly dealt with: the theme of "colonialism." Following that theme, though geographically it seems no part of the Far East, some observations are included on the slowly developing, yet vitally important, problem of Africa—again a typical "colonialism" issue.

The Asian coast presents, in vast theater, the familiar elements of a "problem area." Behind that coast are three great countries and population blocs organized, or capable of being organized, into formidable power machines. The Asian territory of the Soviet Union is the most northerly of these blocs and occupies the largest geographic extent though much of the geography is subarctic steppe, but the population bloc is less numerous and derives its strength from the European rather than the Asian Soviet population. Immediately to the south lies the vast Chinese empire. Like the Soviet Union, China is presumably Communist. Whereas Soviet Siberia is sparsely populated, Communist China (twenty per cent larger than the United States) claims 600 millions of population, though 475 millions would probably be closer to the actual figure. (No one really knows.) Southeast lies India (one third the area of the United States), with a population approaching 375 millions.

Two of these three, the Soviet Union and Communist China, steadily grind against their frontiers in one manner or another. Both push outward into the Pacific Ocean, and the effect of that is pressure against the largest and most developed archipelago in the world, that vast line of great and small islands beginning on the north with the Kuriles, including Japan and the Ryukyus, taking in Formosa and the Philippines, and the collection of three thousand islands (great and small), we call Indonesia. On the eastern side of this archipelago is the greatest ocean in the world which absorbs some of the shock—though not as much as one would guess. The United States lies far away on the other side; but the continent of Australia is not by any means so far away.

Mainland China is still in the throes of a revolution whose length, breadth and depth probably no one can forecast. The ancient empire was overturned in 1912 by the republican revolution of Sun Yat-sen. Two years later World War I broke out, with the Japanese entering the war on the side of her then ally, Great Britain. Since World War I was fought in Europe, Japan's principal activity consisted in strengthening her position in China— despite the fact that China also had declared war against Germany. When World War I ended in 1918, Japanese troops had occupied and held the ports and railway lines in Manchuria and had occupied a slice of China coast around Shantung. (Vigorous "defense" of an ally is one of the diplomatic euphemisms for occupying a piece of its desirable territory.) That year likewise found American troops occupying the Russian port of Vladivostok, and also in

Manchuria—partly to block off supposedly pro-German activities of Lenin's new Communist government of Russia, but chiefly for the purpose of endeavoring to prevent America's Japanese associate from extending her conquests at China's expense. In the diplomatic play-off after that war's end, Japan finally was led to relinquish her Shantung seizure, but in 1931 she seized full sovereignty over Manchuria. Her imperialists, however, had ambitions; further Japanese probing expeditions were made against China, leading to the famous Japanese invasion in 1937.

The Chinese Republic thus had its difficulties from the very beginning and developed relatively little centralized strength. In 1928 a leader appeared. General Chiang Kai-shek, under whom China maintained some semblance of national unity and under whom it defended itself rather inadequately, as Japanese armies after 1937 pushed deeper into Chinese vital areas. Even the greatest admirer of Chiang Kai-shek is forced to admit that great parts of Chinese territory and Chinese force were separately held by Chinese leaders ("war lords") working perhaps as much in their own interests as in the interest of the central Chinese Republican Government.

World War II ended badly for China. Japanese armies were deep in her territory at the time of Japanese surrender in 1945. Still worse, a Russian Army was moving southward through Manchuria and into North Korea. Stalin had kept his promise to President Roosevelt and Winston Churchill that he would declare war on Japan after Germany had been defeated; he did so in August, 1945, exactly six days before Japan surrendered. But this gave adequate excuse for his pushing troops into Manchuria and North China, nominally to attack the remnants of Japanese force in that area; really to establish himself as political arbiter of China's future government. By this time, of course, he had very little to do with defeating the Japanese. On the other hand he had a great deal he wanted to do in China.

It was extremely well done. Communist organizations were armed with weapons surrendered by the departing Japanese troops. Local Communist movements were assisted by Russian organizers and in some cases protected by Russian force. Since the Chinese economy and political organization was in desperate shape after seven years of Japanese invasion, and since the Chiang Kai-shek government had proved itself far from competent, a Chinese Communist faction increasingly established mastery in the nation and rapidly put itself in position to paralyze any Chinese recovery.

In this situation the United States government attempted reconstruction of China by diplomacy. Its basic idea was to work out a coalition government between the Communists and the administration of Chiang Kai-shek. In that effort it failed. The result was civil war; the Chinese Nationalist troops did not make a determined resistance; the government of the United States did not wish to intervene militarily and could think of nothing else effective to do. In 1950, Chiang Kai-shek with the remnants of his Nationalist government took refuge on the island of Formosa (Taiwan) where he still is, claiming to be the legitimate government of China. This was logical: the United States, Great Britain and the Soviet Union had agreed with Stalin that Formosa, a Japanese conquest for more than half a century, should be returned to China after World War II. The Communist forces headed by Mao Tse-tung promptly constituted themselves the "People's Republic of China," established their capital at Peiping and set about the business of converting China into a Communist country on the model of and in close cooperation with the Soviet Union. Though the United States continues to "recognize" Chiang Kai-shek's Nationalist government as the "government of China," (whereby it still holds a seat in the United Nations and on its Security Council with the right of veto held only by great powers) the realistic fact is that Chiang's government controls only an island. The Communist government of Mao Tse-tung and his associates (the "People's Republic of China") holds the mainland, controls its 475 million population, and has done so for the past seven years. It has done more: it has thrust its armies into North Korea, establishing a puppet or satellite republic there, and it has powerfully assisted the creation of a Communist State, Viet Minh, in Indo-China.

Communist China thus claims Formosa and has intermittently threatened its forcible seizure. But to do that, Mao Tse-tung and his Secretary of Foreign Affairs, Chou En-lai, must reckon on the probable opposition of the United States Fleet in those waters. The danger of war is not as great as would seem. China wants Formosa much as France wanted Alsace-Lorraine while it was in German hands. She does not necessarily want Formosa now sufficiently to risk war, any more than France wanted Alsace-Lorraine sufficiently to make war in 1900. More immediately the Chinese People's Republic would like to eliminate Chiang Kai-shek as the chief remaining center of opposition to Communist reorganization of Chinese life. More deeply, she would some day like to break the island chain off the Asian littoral which, as yet, remains outside the Communist imperial grasp, and Formosa would be an excellent place to begin: but she is under no pressure. China has time. In result, of the three great powers on the Asian coast, the Soviet Union, the People's Republic of China, and India, two are Communist, so that the Asian coast is Communist-held from the Arctic Ocean to the Gulf of Tonking, halfway down Indo-China. In terms of geography as well as population, this is a vast frontier from which Communist pressure can be developed in the Pacific against the off-shore island chain.

Though these three great neighbors push powerfully outward against the island chain, they also grind steadily against each other. Almost the entire northern border of China—several thousand miles—marches with the southern border of Soviet Asia. The Chinese population is enormous and needs land. The Soviet population—200 millions including Europe—is relatively small and its Asian lands are comparatively empty. Almost inevitably the Chinese will one day move into that area; almost inevitably the Russian Slavs will dislike the development though the process will take a long time.

Moscow knows this; so does Peiping. Even today, while the People's Republic of China and the Soviet Union act as partners, the Chinese Communist government cautiously asserts itself. It has already pushed Russian domination out of Manchuria and is gently nudging it out of the Russian-dominated mid-continental Mongolian republics. Mao Tse-tung is quietly building up a barrier of Chinese population in the most exposed and comparatively empty Chinese province of Sinkiang, not far from Afghanistan. The interior Asian area is out of our study. But the quiet Chinese thrust to the north in Manchuria and Mongolia and westward in Sinkiang and Tibet suggests that another generation may see sudden reversal of the relative positions of the two chief Communist Powers.

But let us get back to the coast.

The Asian littoral, like the Asian continent, has only the vaguest unity. An extremely able observer, Mr. Dwight Cooke, surveyed it as correspondent for Columbia Broadcasting System, and he accurately entitled his resulting book, *There Is No Asia*. He meant that the word "Asia" or "Asian" is a geographic, not a political, expression. Only to the occidental is there an "oriental" world. The actual differences between Asians in the area are, more often than not, far deeper racially, linguistically, historically, socially, and philosophically than they are between occidental nations and groups. An American is literally closer to a Russian Communist in ideas, outlook, common experience and ability to communicate, than a North Chinese is to a Thailander, a Japanese to a Filipino, or probably an Indo-Chinese to an Indonesian. Even countries fairly well-established historically, such as Thailand or the now divided Indo-China, must absorb within their structure a series of religions, cultures and races, each one of which differs from its compatriot race at least as drastically as, say, Swedes differ from Italians.

Geographically also, the problem of definition is not as simple as it seems. From the tip of Siberia where it approaches Alaska down to the point where Siberia meets China near Vladivostok, there is one country—the Soviet Union. The control and language is Russian; but the indigenous races are by no means submerged. Again coming down the coast southwesterly, we encounter Manchuria, presently Chinese, but recently a prize of struggle between Russia and Japan. Next comes the peninsula of Korea which is neither Chinese nor Japanese, and, at present, split at the 38th

parallel (where the Korean War ended in 1953) between a North
Korean Communist republic dominated by China and a South
Korean republic fighting for its economic and political existence.

The China coast, bordering the Yellow Sea, is itself a product
of many Chinese internal struggles. It includes so many variations
of Chinese culture that no one spoken language will take you
from Tientsin to Canton or to the Indo-Chinese border. It can be
dealt with as one area now, because it has presently a centralized
control under "The People's Republic" of China. But in the Gulf
of Tongking one strikes the edge of the Indo-Chinese puzzle. That
tip of southeastern Asia includes a more or less choate northern
strip presently called Vietminh (which is Communist) and a southern strip called Vietnam comprising the rest of the Indo-Chinese
coast (which is not). Just west of these two lie two independent
countries, Laos and Cambodia—allied races, and old cognate cultures, but different. These form the eastern and southern borders
of Thailand (Siam), again a racially allied people but different
both in history and in general orientation. The southern tip of the
peninsula is Malaya, in turn a combination of several more or less
disparate countries, slowly and steadily becoming ethnically Chinese as the race push of that huge country infiltrates the population.
The Malayan Federation is a British colony; it almost bumps up
against the Indonesian island of Sumatra. Between the two passes
one of the three great waterways of the world, the Strait of Malacca, dominated by Singapore. As an international highway, this
strait ranks in importance with Suez and Panama.

The archipelago, or more accurately, the series of archipelagoes
making up the screen of islands masking the Asian coast, is no
less disparate. You will find in the Kuriles almost primitive populations somewhat similar to Eskimo; and next them Japanese, certainly one of the most sophisticated, cultivated and highly organized races in the world. The Philippine Republic is itself a
combination of races in various stages of emergence, with a Spanish overlay. The galaxy of the old Dutch East Indies is presently
distributed among a number of political divisions. New Guinea, for
example, is an Australian holding whose future status still has to

be developed; it has modern cities like Hollandia, and also areas in which primitive races pursue their courses untroubled by what we call modern civilization. It is not quite, but almost, true that the civilization of the assorted islands lying to the westward differs literally from island to island and that in the larger of them, you may find all stages from primitive and semi-primitive to highly organized and developed.

Java, the queen of the Indonesian Republic, with 53 million people on it, was overpopulated but tremendously productive as part of the Dutch Empire. It is still overpopulated though less productive and highly organized now than under Dutch rule, and consequently suffers economically. (We have seen before that the empires did have their economic uses whatever their other faults.) Yet just off the east coast of Java lies the small island of Bali, whose tender and gracious primitivism may well be wrecked by its recent contact with modernity.

Here is the second ingredient of a crisis or problem area: an aggregation of States, races and cultures, no one of which is powerful enough to maintain itself in the stress of a modern imperial struggle. In mass it is a huge area which has excited on its Asian flank the imperial interest and cupidity of the two Communist empires, Soviet Union and China. From the seaward side it has been exposed for a couple of centuries to the prehensile pressures of the eighteenth and nineteenth century Western empires. And also, of course, to the curious economic and cultural influence of the powerful, though not imperial, United States. Add the fact that the area itself is fragmented into endless race, linguistic, cultural, and political groupings in all stages of technical development, and the possibilities are plain. Change is certain. Evolution may be peaceful. It may also be violent.

2

Observers in this region are unanimous in reporting one current of emotion and thinking which at date of writing dominates the whole picture. This current is variously called "nationalism" or "anti-colonialism." It enters into political action practically everywhere from the northern tip of Japan to Singapore. Its battle-cry is "Freedom from the West," and its immediate effect is to produce a crop of movements varying from place to place but chiefly directed towards setting up national governments.

In part, this is due to the fact that, save for Japan, the entire island area was parceled out among the western powers until World War II. It was, in fact, a "colonial area," and part of it is yet. "Anti-colonialism" reflects, therefore, the emotions of men who either live in colonies (Singapore and Malaya) or whose lives were chiefly spent under the rule of empires which have receded—as in the case of Indonesia. The briefest glance at the area history proves the point. Let us work from north to south covering some of the major groupings.

Japan, always independent, had made an early leap into the twentieth century. Closed to the world since its beginning (say, 660 B.C.), its doors were forced open by America's Commodore Perry in 1853; whereupon the Japanese ruling group seriously applied itself to learning this Western system. In this period Czarist Russia was in full flush of progress towards the East, systematically pushing into the then relatively empty territory of Manchuria and Korea, and was gradually establishing herself on the Chinese coast and the Yellow Sea. In 1904, Japanese armies challenged. They defeated the Russians on the field of Mukden in Manchuria, having, incidentally, sunk a Russian fleet. President Theodore Roosevelt offered facilities for negotiating a peace which was signed at Portsmouth, New Hampshire, on January 2, 1905; its effect was (virtually) to replace the Russian penetration in Manchuria, North China, and Korea, with Japanese influence.

This was the first solid assertion by an Asian country of modern Asian military power. It broke the centuries' old current of events in which Western powers, equipped with modern arms and technical capacity, defeated supine and unprepared Asian powers working with medieval weapons.

Korea, projecting south from Manchuria, was clearly in line of fire. Japan occupied and in 1910 annexed it as a Japanese province under the name of "Chosen." This proved to be the beginning of an Asian push, since the chain of islands to the south, the Ryukyus (of which Okinawa is best known to Americans) was also Japanese. They run in a long string to the island of Formosa, or Taiwan. Now Formosa had been, historically, Chinese, but Japan had seized it from China after a brief war in 1895. The result of the Russo-Japanese War was thus the emergence of Japan as a modern Asian empire, controlling a string of islands running more than 3,000 miles along the China coast, together with the solidly held Korean peninsula and having a free hand to work in Manchuria (an area comparable in size to, say, present-day Turkey).

One might argue that this empire had been carved out largely at the expense of other Asians. This indeed was true; but the fact also was that it had been taken in fair conflict, not so much from Asians as from the octopus-reach of Russian imperialism.

South of Formosa is the great archipelago of the Philippine Islands. This fell to the United States when Spain was defeated in 1898. The formation of the Philippine Islands into a nation which is presently the Philippine Republic is, on the whole, one of the more inspiring dramas of twentieth century history. Before the American conquest, the archipelago had been a collection of unregarded islands and civilizations (to some extent it still is), running all the way from primitive Igorrotes to the highly developed city of Manila. When America replaced Spain, Filipino leaders (one remembers Aguinaldo for his tenacity and courage) promptly emerged claiming freedom for the Philippines; for a time they were in open rebellion against American occupation and administration. During half a century the steady influence of American health services, American schools, increasing communication and economic development of the region, bore fruit. Today it can be fairly said that there is a nation.

The American conquest precipitated a decision in the United States which has turned out to be of first importance. Briefly, the question was whether the United States would now accumulate an empire as the European Powers had done—or whether it would attempt to act as midwife for nations being born. A group of American liberals formed an organization—the "Anti-Imperialist League"—in which the leader of the Massachusetts Bar, Moorfield Storey, and the writer's father were active. Their purpose was to exact a pledge, eventually given by the United States Congress, that the islands which had fallen under American rule by reason of arms would be set free. In 1934 the American Congress set a date for the consummation of Philippine independence; the year set was 1945. When 1945 rolled around, the United States was at war and the Philippines were under Japanese occupation. There was talk of postponement; President Franklin Roosevelt ruled against it. Honorably, the United States fulfilled its obligation, organized a Philippine government "in exile" which took over when the Japanese were expelled in 1945. The independence of the Republic of the Philippines was proclaimed on July 4, 1946—by which time the Japanese war was over, and the Philippine people became master in their own house.

At this point we must pick up an influence which remains to plague much of the area though it is least formidable in the Philippine Republic.

The sweep of Japanese conquest at the beginning of World War II had led to occupation by Japan, not only of the Philippine Islands, but also of most of Indonesia (chiefly a possession of the Netherlands Empire at the outbreak of World War II), of the Indo-Chinese peninsula (then a French possession), including the present countries of Vietminh, Vietnam, Laos, Cambodia, Malaya and Singapore, and likewise of Thailand. This was naked conquest. The Japanese were imperialists, and their armies were by no means kindly masters. The West assumed as a matter of course that the populations of these countries would resent and resist an imperialism which aimed at reducing them to the status of colonies—Koreans had resisted Japanese invasion and had hated Japanese rule for forty years. This assumption turned out to be only partly true.

The Japanese although they were imperialists, conquerors, and colonialists were, nevertheless, Asians. A split emotion prevailed in many of the peoples involved. Asians were at least pushing out the white races of the West; to that extent, this seemed a step in the right direction. The Japanese armies and military politicians rather cleverly cultivated this sentiment. They sought Quisling politicians from among these peoples who would join in governing, though under Japanese influence and force. These local politicians made their propaganda and gathered their followings around the central idea that Asia was now asserting its independence from the West; was throwing off the old European empires; that the Japanese were the true friends of Asian nationalism; and so forth. In many areas this exerted a powerful appeal. It also brought into focus as potential leaders men who owed their prominence to cooperation with the Japanese invaders. When in 1945 defeat forced retirement of the Japanese armies, these Japanese-fostered political movements remained the chief organized movements in the area.

Cores of nationalism thus emerged. Such political organizations as existed were perfectly clear that they did not want their former European masters back. Such forces even challenged for power in the Philippine Republic, asserting that the Philippine government, organized partly while in refuge in America, was merely a puppet of the United States. Happily the American anti-imperialist record was clear enough and the Philippine politicians and statesmen were able enough so that the Philippine elections were won by men not compromised with the Japanese.

The retiring Japanese forces thus left behind them nationalist political forces; but these were paralleled by Communist political forces aimed at quite different results. In studying the mid-European strip we noted that the end of World War II unveiled a three-cornered conflict: Communist undergrounds struggling against the Western undergrounds for control of the emerging nationalist governments. The same thing occurred throughout the entire Asian coast. The Philippine Republic was no exception. The Communist-led movements marched under the banner of local nationalism but they were sparked by Moscow-trained men. Their real nature did not become generally apparent until later.

In the Philippines the movement took the form of the Huk-Balahap rising. Communist propaganda as usual presented this to the West as a simple desire of semi-primitive peasants and farmers to have their land, and to throw out their landlords, and to have a more just social system. But somehow, in this innocent and primitive soil, there grew caches of tommy guns and guerrilla weapons which oddly enough came from the famous Skoda munitions plant in Czechoslovakia (since 1948, under Communist control). The Philippine peasant had, and still has, plenty of grievances, but the brains and the guns behind the Huk-Balahaps were aimed not at redressing agrarian grievances but at expanding Communist empire. Had not the dodge of "spontaneous agrarian reform" worked well as a cover for preparing the civil war which conquered China for Communism in 1949? The tactics were standard: Terrorism, minor guerrilla fighting, expanding to the stage of full-scale military operation.

But in this case it did not work. The Philippine Republic, which has produced a remarkable number of wise and dedicated men, came up with a just and able political leader, Ramon Magsaysay. He combined liberal policy reform with military measures. Elected president in November, 1953, in two years he was able to bring the Huk-Balahap movement under control and reduce it to manageable proportions if indeed he has not stamped it out altogether. As commonly happens in conflicts with a Communist-inspired underground, vigorous and liberal democratic government proved far abler to cope with the problem than have military dictatorships.

The pattern, though not always the outcome, is repeated in a number of Asian coast countries.

This pattern appeared in the neighboring East Indian archipelago now emerging as "Indonesia." Most of this, as noted, had been held as a colony of The Netherlands: perhaps the richest piece of colonial real estate in the entire imperial galaxy. There too Japan, having expelled the Netherlanders, worked up a local administration; its propaganda purported to favor in some sense the nationalist aspirations of the area. When victory attended the Western armies and Japan surrendered, The Netherlands took for granted that it would reassume its old position. This would be complicated in any case since as noted Indonesia includes altogether some 3,000 islands; but the main issue revolved around five large and rich islands: Java, Sumatra, Borneo (of which The Netherlands held the southern part), Celebes, and New Guinea (of which The Netherlands held the western part). With these islands as a nucleus, something like a national framework could be spelled out.

Two men emerged who did so: Dr. Sukarno and Dr. Mohammed Hatta, and they were not in favor of renewed Netherlands control. Both had previously collaborated with the Japanese. For practical purposes, under their leadership, a state of guerrilla warfare continued between Indonesian nationalist forces and the returning Netherlands officials from 1945 (when the Japanese withdrew) to 1949. Attempts were made to work out some form of "commonwealth" cooperation under the Queen of The Netherlands. These failed, and on November 2, 1949, sovereignty over all Indonesia except Dutch New Guinea (New Guinea is uncomfortably close to Australia which holds its eastern half) was transferred to a provisional government of a new country, "The Republic of the United States of Indonesia." Dr. Sukarno was elected President of the Republic in 1949; in 1950, Indonesia was elected the sixtieth member of the United Nations. A new area left the framework of empire of the nineteenth century.

The struggle to hammer into viable organization a vast territory of endless differences and complexity has been and still is enormous. Not only are there variations of race, religion, background and so forth; there is also the economic fact that Java is the most densely populated area on the planet, requiring high organization to keep its economics in shape. Formerly this had been provided by the extremely able Netherlanders. A new organization had to be worked out—a task of many years. Add the fact that the officers and politicians of the new republic have had relatively little practical experience and the scope of the problem becomes apparent. Especially so, when one remembers that the initial push had come from Japanese officers and politicians who were in no mood to let the nationalist forces they encouraged get very far on the road to real self-government.

Nor was the factor of Communist activity omitted. The movement, save for a brief rebellion in 1948, chose to move politically rather than with arms (in 1955 it cast 20% of the total vote) and it used the familiar tactic of attempting formation of a "popular front." The event is still in doubt. Indonesian Communists have had a limited success and their strength is said to be growing. But they have not been able to take over, and they have been stiffly opposed by the Masjumi or Indonesian Moslem Council which works with the old nationalist party. The Indonesian State has not fallen into the orbit of the Chinese Communists. The writer's estimate is that it will not; but the situation is not free from danger.

The story of the Indo-Chinese and Malayan peninsula (which pushes out from the South Asian mainland) has the same plot and a stock cast of characters—but the action is bloodier. Indo-China had been a French colony, an aggregation of a number of previous, more or less independent States. These included Annam, Tongking and Cochin China, and the independent monarchies of Cambodia and Laos. France had accumulated them by conquest between 1862 and 1885.

This colony had also been overrun by Japanese forces. On Japan's surrender the general outlines of the Indonesian situation were repeated. Only, in this case, the nationalist forces which had worked in greater or less degree with the Japanese invaders got assistance from the new and powerful regime of Communist China, their northern neighbor. France put up a political as well as a military struggle to retain the area. Granting a measure of economic independence to the monarchies of Cambodia and Laos, she presently recognized as Chief of State and emperor Bao Dai, a former emperor of Annam, who unhappily had been rather better known on the French Riviera than in his own country. The play was to set up under his rule an independent "Vietnam" (including also the northern area today known as Vietminh) along with Laos and Cambodia, as "associated States" within a French Commonwealth. It was hoped in Paris that this would satisfy the nationalism of the area.

It did not. Two could play at the game of encouraging nationalism and controlling the resulting government. In point of fact, Communist China undertook to play it, unquestionably with the support of the Soviet Union. A Communist-trained leader, Ho-Chi-Minh, commenced his nationalist movement at least as early as 1945. He had probably maintained a degree of underground organization during Japanese occupation. The situation resembled in many ways that created by the Russian Communist politicians in the Mid-European strip. Ho-Chi-Minh's underground first carried on organized terrorism, underground resistance and guerrilla warfare in the North. Around Hanoi it steadily made orderly government in northern Indo-China impossible. Ho was supplied with ever increasing stores of arms and munitions. His force emerged in 1951–1952 as a full-scale belligerent with organized armies, artillery trains and adequate ammunition. French officers commanding Vietnam troops, together with French army units, fought them as they could. But, certainly in the north, there was no telling friend from foe among the Indo-Chinese. The French reinforced their troops but in 1954 were defeated in a final engagement at Dien Bienphu. An armistice was negotiated under the not very benevolent supervision of Soviet diplomats, which divided Vietnam at roughly the 17° parallel.

This was a Korean-type settlement. The Communists retained the north but not, theoretically, Laos and Cambodia. The independent State of Vietnam kept the south. Unhappily, Laos and Cambodia under these circumstances are extremely difficult to defend should the Communist State of Vietminh with support of Red China or of Russia elect to push forces, guerrilla or organized, into these States.

Vietnam immediately had its difficulties. The Communist powers clearly considered (as also did this writer) that the task of organizing it before the Communists infiltrated was almost impossible. Actually, it has come along surprisingly well. A Vietnam nationalist leader, Ngo Dinh Diem, emerged; he had first to pacify his own country, torn between semi-military religious sects; he seems to have succeeded in doing this. He had to mop up carefully placed Communist "pockets," and appears to have done so; he has been able to commence the real job of bringing a nation out of chaos. It is fair to note that he has had steady economic and military support from the United States.

As a result two new States had come into being: Vietminh, a firmly held Communist State, probably held solidly in the orbit of Communist China; Vietnam, a non-Communist western oriented State struggling to make its newly found independence viable. Laos and Cambodia meanwhile moved towards a greater degree of sovereignty. Another slice of the southeast Asian coast area moved out of the nineteenth century European imperial system into the stormy waters of twentieth century nationalist independence.

Much of the rest of this Indo-Chinese peninsula is occupied by the country of Thailand (which we used to know in school as Siam). This nation, a constitutional monarchy, had maintained its independence (though it lost some of its territory) throughout the imperial sweep of the European countries. It had ceased to be a despotism in 1932; it had sent many of its younger men to America or England to be educated; it had, for many years, an American legal adviser to its government. The independence of its 20 million people was fairly solid—until the Japanese invasion in 1942.

Thailanders are a practical people. They, or at least a good many of them, saw no particular reason to die heroically in a war they clearly could not win. They adopted a policy of non-resistance, changed their government, and put in a ministry satisfactory to and cooperating with the Japanese invaders. This it was believed would leave the life of the people comparatively intact; and so in general it did, though the Japanese not unnaturally took full advantage of the situation to obtain bases, rice supplies, and so forth. (In any case Japan had for years been buying rice from Thailand; Japanese armies could not be everywhere; non-resistance seemed like a good policy at the time.) There was also, perhaps, a feeling that the Japanese were at least Asian, though a Japanese is as different from a Thailander as a Scot is from a Spaniard. When the Japanese withdrew in defeat, some of the politicians who had followed the line of cooperation had entrenched their political position. They have substantial influence in the Thailand government today.

In the Thai case there was no substantial Communist underground though there were and still are occasional outbreaks of that coloration on the extreme north. Yet there is an exposed flank through Laos; and Communist propagandists have by no means overlooked the possibility of making adherents in Thailand. Thailand is aligned on the side of the Western Free World because it is a party to the Southeast Asia Treaty Organization (SEATO: United States, Australia, Philippines, Thailand, Pakistan, Great Britain, France) since 1955. A glance at the map, however, will indicate that a determined military push from Communist Vietminh could change the situation. Perhaps because Thailand never fell under a Western empire (though the European empires in the nineteenth century treated her badly), there has been no reaction against the West comparable to that in Indonesia.

Malaya—its official name is "The Federation of Malaya"—is again a collection of small States gathered by empire into a colony. Presumably it is presently headed for dominion status within the British Commonwealth. If Malaya is a single country, it owes that fact to the administrative unity given it by the British. Singapore (the Gibraltar of the Strait of Malacca) is technically not part of it, though a small island closer to the Malayan peninsula than Staten Island is to New York; but it is difficult to believe that Singapore will not eventually follow the fortunes of Malaya itself. An important fact is that while Malayans furnish the ethnic background, the dominant commercial group (which in time may well become the dominant political group) is Chinese. These have achieved their position, not by conquest, but by quiet immigration, patient industry and increase in population.

There is always the possibility that they may, one day, throw their lot in with Communist China taking Malaya along with them. Certainly that is the plan of the Chinese Communist organizers in Singapore and elsewhere in the Federation.

Nationalist propaganda followed the Japanese armies into Singapore in 1942, though the dozen or so States which compose Malaya present a difficult problem for propagandists. What was common to the area was the Communist organizer, engaged in constructing an "underground" composed theoretically of nationalists but whose backbone was probably composed of Chinese as well as local Communist guerrillas. After Japanese withdrawal these systematically upset the peace. Nominally their cause was "independence," and "anti-imperialism." Probably their leaders acted really in the interest of expanding the Soviet-Chinese complex, though capable British action prevented the movement from reaching the stage of full-scale belligerent conflict as in Indo-China. Persistent terrorism (the tactics were the same as those pursued in the early stages of the Vietminh seizure) made life extremely difficult. At the moment (1957) it seems to have been brought under control. Meanwhile in Singapore itself, nationalist and Communist propaganda, within the British tradition of free speech, keeps up merrily.

In sum, though the Japanese invasions did not establish the Japanese Empire over the Asian coast hoped for by the Tokyo imperialists, they did upset the rule of most of the Western empires. Young, inexperienced nationalist governments have taken over in countries whose problems even the most experienced administrators would find difficult to handle.

There is no question about the underlying emotion; in these countries it is, in general, Asia for Asians. There is no question about their immediate political objective; in practically all instances it is assertion and establishment of independent nationalism. There is no question about the difficulty: in practically every case the governments succeeding the old colonial governments (in the case of the Philippines, succeeding the United States insular government) have had to seek economic assistance and have secured it chiefly from the United States, though Great Britain has powerfully helped in her own area. There is no question about the Russian and Chinese plan: they intend to export revolutions aimed at making the young countries affiliated Communist states, if not outright colonies. The problem was and is whether the assistance these new nations seek and get will produce peaceful evolution.

3

And now it is time to face squarely the question of "colonialism." While the Asian coast presents the problem in a string of colorful crises, the problem pervades the picture of the Middle East and of the entire continent of Africa.

With the problem of colonialism must be bracketed that of "imperialism." In political semantics these two are "bad" words applying to the same subject. "Imperialism" means specifically the policy of creating and holding an empire in which one cultural or race group has power over the governments and affairs of different race or cultural groups. The dominant rulers are said to be "imperialists." The dominated areas are said to be "colonies." "Imperialism" describes the process from the side of the master. "Colonialism" describes the result from the point of view of the subject groups.

It is appropriate to state the case for imperialism-colonialism, not because the writer is its advocate but because in America, particularly, its contributions and results rarely get a fair hearing.

Let us begin with the results.

We have noted on the Asian coast the "nationalist" movements. These brought formerly subject peoples out from under the sway of western empires and set up independent nations in almost precisely the boundaries and with almost precisely the unity given them in colonial form by their former imperial rulers. The most striking case of an area not discussed in this study: India and Pakistan. It will do to illustrate.

There never was an "India" as it existed under the British Empire or as it exists today, until British rule gave it form. There was instead a collection of "native" States, principalities big and small, including great and powerful kingdoms and a complex aggregation of smaller sects and tribes under semi-feudal or wholly feudal rulers, and so forth. During the late eighteenth and principally during the nineteenth centuries, Britain extended, hammered and organized this subcontinent into an administrative unity to which British Prime Minister Disraeli gave a name, "The Indian Empire," and he placed its imperial diadem on the head of Queen Victoria. Even passionate Indian patriots concede that this unity of India was a British achievement. Its less spectacular but more important substructure was a more or less uniform British law, implemented by a more or less uniform British Civil Service, a more or less uniform Transport Service, and a common language for purposes of government which even today is English. With this came substantial peace throughout India. Native princes were not permitted to war on each other; order in the main prevailed in an area where earlier rulers or races ceaselessly struggled against other rulers or other races.

When the anti-colonial nationalist movement in India began, its protagonists sought, not to re-create the past, but to bring this British-outlined India out from under British rule as an independent nation with the administrative unity and common denominator provided by the British imperialists.

They almost succeeded. But the division between Hindu and Mohammedan gave rise to a secondary "anti-colonial" movement, that of Mohammed Ali Jinnah. He pleaded and agitated the cause of the Mohammedans, asserting that they would be no more free under Hindu than under British rule. The outcome was division of British "India" into the two independent countries we know today as India and Pakistan, the latter being two separate territories on the northern and northeastern tier of India. The boundaries were worked out as nearly as could be along ethnic-religious lines so that Pakistan should include most of the former Moslem population of India. As a result, about 86% of Pakistan's 77 million population are Moslems, the balance chiefly Hindu. The two new States—they are really "new" in the sense that no such States ever existed before —comprise the old British Indian Empire. They could not exist nor could they have entered the twentieth century were it not for the imperialist process. There may have been better ways to group and give common framework to disparate peoples, and the imperial-colonial process in many respects was anything but nice. But the world of the eighteenth and nineteenth centuries followed no other way.

To this must be added the undoubted fact that in some respects at least the imperialist governments did a better job for the average man on the street or peasant on the farm than had been done by the governments they supplanted. This is a controversial statement: it will be denied in some quarters. The writer can come to no other conclusion. If it had not been so, Western imperialism could not have maintained itself as long as it did. The actual amount of Western force and troops involved were always infinitesimal compared to the populations kept under imperialist rule. This could only have happened because, in the main, these populations had no urgent desire either to re-create their former governments or to shift to anything else in sight. Factually, the British Empire, and its Colonial and Indian departments in the nineteenth century developed a great number of civil servants and empire agents who sincerely, honestly and intelligently devoted their lives to bettering, so far as they could, the lot of peoples whose former local rulers had oppressed them almost beyond belief.

It was the imperial civil servant who stood (when anyone did) between the humble farmer or small businessman and the ruthless rapacity of his feudal chief, the incredible cruelty of the chief's retainers, the unlimited greed of the local money-lender, and so forth. It was an imperialist agent who did something—all too little—to make education available to part of the population, and who systematically endeavored to give first-rate education to many men. This is why Nehru and many of his principal lieutenants were educated at Oxford, Cambridge and other British universities. Western imperialism at least paid lip-service, and in the British case, real service to the idea that justice should be universal and that men and women were entitled to consideration as individuals.

The British practice represents perhaps the best development of imperialism; other empires did not do so well. Yet in most instances they represented a substantial advance over the conditions prevailing before they established their rule. The best proof of that lies in the fact that they did give the framework and design apparent in the emerging nationalisms of today.

All these services—and they were in the aggregate real—of course assumed as a major premise that the home imperial country would continue to have essential control over the fate of the subject countries. That is, that the imperial country would have primary position in trade, business and economics. It would have control of the geography, the manpower, the resources, in case of war. It could

draw on its colonies for soldiers to help when attacked. Also, in
most cases, the citizens of the imperial country, commonly of the
white race, assumed that they were "superior" and they commonly
handled their lives, their clubs, and their social relations accordingly. Even at best they were thus regarded as merely "good masters"; their chief merit was that they replaced "bad masters." The
sudden surge of post-World War II revolt struck many British as
a form of ingratitude, best summarized in a rhyme published in
Punch under a cartoon showing small emergent nations thumbing
their noses at Britannia,

> "She washed them and taught them,
> And then let them go,
> And did they say 'Thank you'?
> Not all of them. No."

Indeed it was clear that the first results of nationalist independence, of emergence from imperial rule, were not likely to benefit the
common man in the imperial sense. It was quite likely that his new
government in early phases would be less able to keep order. (Nearly
5 million were killed in border disputes as India and Pakistan separated. In the emergent State of Indonesia order even now is not
uniform throughout the former Netherlands Empire area.) It seemed
probable that the new governments would have a lower standard of
political morality and a higher incidence of corruption. It was almost
certain, over-all, that the organization of economics and business
would be at least for a time less efficient, less productive. In a material sense the question boils down to this—is it better for a people to govern itself badly, than to live well governed by someone
else? This would be the most favorable statement for the imperial
position. The articulate elements of the populations of the Asian
coast, and increasingly in Africa, have answered the question with
substantial unanimity: they prefer to take their chances with their
own.

To them, the rule of the "good master" was not good. Probably
their advocates magnify the slips, mistakes, bureaucratic stupidities
and occasional cruelties of the old empires (of which it is true there

were many). Certainly it was not their affair to urge the contributions which the empires made.

And there were always two powerful considerations in the background, if not in the foreground. The first we have noted: the white races commonly lived as superiors, liked to evidence their superiority, liked to live apart. The other was the economic arrangement prevailing between the imperial country and the subject countries. To this last we may turn for a moment, though the subject fills many books.

Trade and commerce of the imperial country followed, when it did not precede, political penetration and domination by the ruling empire. This was sometimes a search for supply of profitable merchandise which could be bought cheap in the colonies and sold dear at home. Later, as the industrial system grew in the nineteenth century, it became also a search for markets—areas in which manufactured goods could be sold to populations which had not developed their own machinery of production. Having a long lead in technical development, western countries could do both rather easily. Since there were competitive empires, each not unnaturally sought to restrict the profitable commerce so that the ruling country should get maximum benefit from it.

Meanwhile, however, the population of the subject countries developed men who themselves had capacity to construct factories and supply their own countries. It was widely believed and in many cases was the fact that the empire countries systematically endeavored to prevent their colonial subjects from organizing, building and financing these factories, or to assure that ownership of the great instruments of industrialization remained in the hands of the empire country and its citizens. The charge has probably been exaggerated; but unquestionably there was enough truth in it to hurt. Certainly during the latter part of the nineteenth century and the early part of the twentieth, the ruling countries steadily drew income and wealth from their imperial provinces.

The result was at worst comparative impoverishment of the subject peoples, and at best a substantial brake on their economic development. How far this went as a matter of economics is open to some question. To answer it, one would have to compare the actual economic fate of the country under imperial rule with the probable economic fate of the country had there been no such rule— a comparison of historical fact with a historical "might-have-been." Unquestionably up to World War I the imperial countries did draw out more than they put in, just as the United States has drawn out in profits at least as much as she has put in to the Latin American area. But a degree of territorial development, experience, education and even higher income went along with this process: economic progress can not be measured entirely by in-put and out-take. It seems fair to suggest that the position of the subject countries at the close of the imperial age was substantially worse than it would have been had these countries under capable organization and no trade restrictions been independent from the very beginning. But as we have observed, they were frequently badly organized and governed, or not organized or unified at all. Absent the imperial administrations they might well have been miserably organized and administered.

More important is the fact that at present most of these areas have obtained a frame, have obtained a measure of organization, have developed in varying degree national leadership and are prepared to begin now. They therefore not unnaturally desire to play the game of economic nationalism which their imperial masters played successfully during the past century. In the larger of the emerging succession States such as India and Indonesia there is area and population enough to develop wide domestic industrialization with substantial domestic markets. There is reasonable chance of obtaining without too much difficulty those raw materials not present in the country itself. The old doctrine that some races can not handle modern processes of industrialization and manufacture seems to be pretty thoroughly exploded as race after race attempts the enterprise, develops capacity, and crashes through with quite adequate plants manufacturing everything from steel to textiles. It appears to take about a generation of experience, coupled with appreciable effort in public education, to reach this result.

The wisest of the empires, Great Britain, has come to understand this. She steadily moves toward development of the remaining parts of her empire expecting the day when they can be turned loose, preferably in affiliation with the British Commonwealth of Nations. In greater or less degree, France, Belgium, The Netherlands, and Portugal have followed suit. In all cases, there has been powerful opposition within the imperial country: vested economic interests do not give up easily. In general, nationalism—anti-imperialist and anti-colonial—goes hand in hand with a powerful demand for local industrialization and technique fostered by the emerging country. The process has not been easy.

Even as they succeed the emergent nations run squarely into the fact that economics, as we have had occasion to observe, is no longer a nationalist affair. In mid-twentieth century it is almost impossible to be self-sufficient at all and it is entirely impossible for a self-sufficient economy to produce the standard of living attained by the great nations of the West. There is as yet no established international or world framework which can supply the finance, the transport, the adjustment by which production meets market, by which raw material flows to fabricator, across national lines. In brief, the dilemma of anti-colonialism is that the former colony attains an independent nationalism at a time when nationalism means less than it has meant for a number of centuries. Rarely in history have fifty years produced as many emerged and emerging sovereign national countries as has the first half of the twentieth century. Rarely in history has international (if not supra-national) framework equivalent to that once provided by the moribund empires been as necessary as it is at present. But empires can no longer meet the challenge. It is thus presented as a continuing problem to the next generation who must resolve it in their own fashion.

Review of the imperial system could not be complete without reference to certain new pressures which will certainly intensify the crises as they arise. Notable among them is that of straight population pressure—the outward thrust of races or groups whose population has simply outgrown their living space. Sometimes people of one race literally fear submergence by another more than they fear death. (When the Japanese Fleet and Task Forces roamed unchecked in the South Pacific, British New Zealanders seriously and anxiously considered whether, in case of invasion by overwhelming forces they should not kill their wives and children and die taking a Japanese with them.) Less dramatically, the large and relatively empty continent of Australia (population 9,000,000) watches the Chinese population (475,000,000 in Mainland China alone) steadily spill into the East Indian archipelagoes, and maintains absolute determination that it shall not enter and convert Australia into an Asian continent. Less vocal but certainly extant is a similar fear on the part of some non-white populations lest they be submerged and absorbed by other Asian populations, who, though Asian, they consider alien.

There are, of course, solutions like that prevailing in the American island group of Hawaii. There a number of races live together in relative happiness, each preserving its own folkways without substantial friction. But many people even in the United States (White Citizens' Councils, for example) oppose this kindly and successful solution. Whether in the case of a population take-over it could be achieved under other governments is not certain. In practical effect, the old imperial framework has resulted in erecting groups of relatively weak nations, frequently confronting enormously powerful blocs of other races. In the next half-century statecraft may well be put to its highest test in working out solutions for these problems.

4

Though the continent of Africa can not be dealt with here save in most general terms, it already outlines an enormous problem coming up some years hence.

For practical purposes, there are two Africas. One is an Arab-Egyptian-Berber-Mohammedan Africa north of the Sahara Desert which runs with few interruptions from the Atlantic shoulder of Africa straight to the Red Sea. Only the northern part of this is heavily populated. These countries have been touched on as we looked at the Middle East. They are less a problem of "Africa" than of the Mediterranean-Middle East complex and we do not follow it further here.

South of the Sahara is the vast area of Negro Africa. In current vernacular, "this is it." Completely divided among the Western Empires save for tiny Liberia and age-old Ethiopia, Africa presents squarely the problem of a vast subject race overlaid by the tiniest contingent of white ruling groups. The total population of Africa, even including the northern tier, is only 220 million. But of this, some 80 million are north of the Sahara and out of our present problem. This leaves 140 million, more or less, south of the Sahara, of which not more than 5 million are white by the most generous estimate—and 3 million of those are concentrated in the Union of South Africa at the southern tip of the continent. (Even in the Union of South Africa the 3 million of white European population is superimposed on well over 10 million Negroes.) In most of this Africa, Negroes are counted by millions but are governed by whites counted in tens of thousands. This sets up a terrible and dangerous unbalance. The real problem is how long 135 million Negroes will accept government by Western Empires (France, Great Britain, Portugal, Belgium), and by the local imperialism of the Union of South Africa operated by a white race which Negroes outnumber at least three to one.

One reason why the system continues is the fact that this is the imperial process in a quite early phase. There was no "Africa" of any kind save on a map (there may not be now) before the empires came, though there were transient primitive kingdoms of area and importance such as that of the Zulus under the mighty chieftain Chaka. But these were not ancient: Chaka, a primitive though mighty leader of spearsmen, had conquered his kingdom in his lifetime. He was murdered in 1824 by his half-brother Dingaan who continued the empire to 1840 when it broke up. In the twentieth century, Africa, aside from imperial framework, was quite simply a vast area divided among undeveloped tribes save in a few places like the Union of South Africa where small white settlements had dug in.

Now contact of twentieth century civilization with primitive culture presents a dilemma which no one has yet solved. Briefly, the question is posed whether (a) some sort of barrier should be erected preventing contact—as the Danes prevented contact in Greenland between whites and Greenlanders familiarly called "Eskimo." Or (b) whether full contact should be attempted, letting nature, economics and force take its course.

In either case the primitive gets the worst of it. If a barrier is built, land assigned and the primitive culture left alone, you have little more than a living museum on a vast scale; in Africa inside that museum may prevail customs and practices and conditions of indescribable cruelty attended by indescribable suffering. But if contact is open (the "barrier" or live-museum theory has always been the work of kindly, well-intentioned statesmen), primitive life is usually unable to cope with the ensuing situation. A minor disease may decimate the population. A stronger and better organized force tears to pieces the impis of tribal spearsmen. Organization of more or less modern farming and industry absorbs land which the hunter has used or the migrant wishes to traverse. There is always a tendency to compel labor to work for the white settler; the western property system finds no counterpart in the primitive mind. The end is almost always the same: a subject population whose culture has been disrupted ruled over by a handful of aliens. This is true even where the best of thinking and the highest of motives have guided the policy. It is worth repeating: the problem of twentieth century contact with primitive cultures has found no satisfactory solution.

Probably the best that can be done is to work pragmatically with the cultures as they appear, seeking their evolution towards an organization capable of entering and coping with modern civilization. The worst is to convert subject populations to a status not very much better than serfs—a status endured by Negroes in the South African Union today. One remembers that the slave populations of French Haiti once rose against and wiped out the handful of Frenchmen who ruled them. It was Toussaint L'Ouverture who illustrated graphically the possibilities by taking a handful of pepper, putting a few grains of rice on top of it and shaking his hand. The white rice grains simply disappeared.

Africa is in all stages of development. In some areas, notably

Nigeria and the Gold Coast (both British), an enormous amount of patient work has given a fairly high degree of unification and organization within, of course, the framework carved out by the Empire. Both colonies are verging towards the time (probably quite soon) when they will emerge as self-governing Commonwealth dominions. The United Nations is discussing the case of the Gold Coast, or Ghana, at date of writing. Should they then choose independence as against affiliation with Britain, the Asian pattern will have been repeated: the empire gives frame, outline and organization, and the succession State takes over. But there are great areas in Africa in which there has not been this patient work, or in which it has not yet jelled sufficiently to create a national framework. There, disappearance of empire would probably mean reverting to the primitive cultures described by the famous missionary David Livingstone and his rescuer, the explorer Sir Henry Morton Stanley. The colonial-imperial system would have ended; but no one can forecast what would take its place.

Probably (forecast is here at its most difficult) attempt would be made to organize the situation by the other imperial aspirants—the Soviet Union or China. Whether either would succeed better than the Western empires is an open question. It is far easier to destroy a framework in these circumstances than to build one. At the moment the Soviet Union is probably more interested in weakening Western empires and obtaining access to African geography than she is in doing the work of empire or substituting an equivalent under some other name. There are only 200 million Russians in the world, and they would have almost at once the same problems that are faced by the Western empires though they might tackle them with a different doctrine and a different point of view.

Already it is clear that the first and worst exacerbation of the colonial problem in Africa has come squarely to the fore: the problem of race supremacy. The government of the Union of South Africa has seen to that. Its policy has at least the merit of frankness (though in the writer's view this is where the merit stops). It faces squarely the fact that less than 3 million whites are almost completely dominant over more than 10 million Negroes and that the Negro population increases more rapidly. It insists that the problem is whether the white race shall continue to exist in the Union of South Africa, or whether it is fighting a rear-guard action in demography, its ultimate fate being either expulsion or absorption. It proposes to carve out some sort of position in which the white race shall have undoubted mastery over some part of Africa's surface, using whatever means may be necessary to achieve that end. Obviously this is almost saying to the Negro population of Africa that the result of white rule is to be permanent subjection or servitude; that the races can not live together on the basis of equality; that, in fact, the Negroes must either get rid of the whites or accept servitude in varying degree. One could hardly think of a better way of lighting a fuse towards explosion on a continental scale. When that kind of contest starts, little distinction is made between the white who has patiently and altruistically labored for the cause of the subject race, and the exploiting white oppressor. In blazing catastrophe, they all go down together.

This is the great difference between imperialism-colonialism in Africa under present circumstances, and imperialism-colonialism on the Asian coast. The Asian countries though disparate were in general not primitive (this was not true in all cases, but generally so). Their civilization in most cases is ancient and high. There was far more to build on. And, of course, colonialism in Asia is a century or more older than African colonialism.

Can an African transition stage be worked out, and will the current of forces in the twentieth century accept the fact that time as well as good intention and good policies will be needed? British experiments in Nigeria and the Gold Coast suggest that the job can be done, and in certain areas like these it is well towards accomplishment. But much of Africa has not come this far, and the times are impatient. Whether the modern wisdom of the British Empire, or non-national administration through United Nations trusteeships, or any other framework plainly designed to bring fruition to nationalist aspirations in a context which gives them a chance of success will be allowed opportunity of performance is a major question.

Probably crises in this direction will not occur all at once. At

least, this is to be hoped. Probably the Western empires by evolution of thought and sheer compulsion of circumstance will be
increasingly desirous of fair and moderate solutions and increasingly less anxious to fight desperate rear-guard actions to maintain
remnants of declining power. But will that enlightenment come too
late? Can the end of imperialism be put to constructive use? Can
some entirely new framework emerge? Or must the problem be
solved by the age-old method of naked force?

5

Where, in all this picture, is the United States?

She resigned ambitions to empire, giving independence to the
Philippine Republic. American diplomacy encouraged The Netherlands to work out freedom for the Republic of Indonesia. Even
during World War II Cordell Hull had been cautiously indicating
to Great Britain that the United States considered the independence
of India inevitable. In general, he counseled the Western empires to
set definite target dates upon which the colonies would become free
and independent. American diplomacy had steadily opposed the expansion of Japan's imperialists and their aggression against China;
indeed it was just this that led to Pearl Harbor. Both by word and
deed the United States government had been on the side of emerging
subject countries, while the steady current of public opinion in the
United States has opposed colonialism.

Nevertheless, with that record, most of the emergent nations as
they succeed, with the solid exception of the Philippine Republic,
have recently shown little sympathy for the United States. Some of
them have been forthrightly hostile. In Africa, of course, south of
the Sahara, the case has not yet arisen.

The situation is more puzzling to American statesmen because a
State emerging from empire almost automatically seeks assistance
from the United States to stabilize its economy. Morocco, for example, recently won substantial independence from the French Empire.
As new States frequently do, it found its finances and economics
in parlous state, and promptly applied to Washington for help.
South Korea had such assistance even before the Korean War, and

of course has had a great deal more since. The new Republic of Vietnam has had American aid in one form or another estimated to amount to $300 million a year. Indonesia has asked for and received assistance. What is it, then, that stirs up the anti-American current of hostility?

Time will answer some of these questions, for no certain reply can be given now. Obviously the United States is lumped with the white countries, and the bitter issue of race has never been too far from the surface in colonialism. The political organizations which took over as the Japanese withdrew obviously had been anti-American else they would not have cooperated with the armies of Tokyo. Communist propaganda, always present and frequently handled with skill, naturally fans the flame. If the United States is allied to the Western empires in Europe—as she is through NATO—she must of course (says this propaganda), make common cause with the old colonial Powers. In any case, the United States is pledged to "White Supremacy" in the Communist book: witness the segregation issue in the South. The United States has no large corps of men knowing the local languages, leaders and psychology to throw in, and has had little skill in organizing local parties as stout in America's defense as the Communist parties are stout in forwarding the Russian or Chinese Communist point of view. So the debate is one-sided.

Power-politics enter into it as well. The United States, though it has no imperial ambitions of its own, does have a powerful interest in assuring that the nations of the Asian coast, and the African nations as and when they march, shall not fall under the imperial sway of Moscow or of Peiping. In general, "independence" movements under Communist sponsorship have plainly been designed to transfer the colonial area out of the possession of a Western empire only to place it under substantial domination by one of the two Eastern empires. Like any prudent country, the United States tends to oppose arrangements by which her professed enemies would acquire use of the geography, resources and manpower of these border regions.

It was essential for Communist tactics to present this normal American interest as a stratagem of Washington or "Wall Street" to obtain the leadership and influence vacated by the retreating empires. For this reason Russian and Chinese propagandist hammered heavily the astonishing falsehood that United States armies in South Korea had attacked North Korea. Of course the simple and undisputed fact was that American armies had left South Korea, and attack came from the North Korean side. Perhaps the very anxiety of Americans to help aided the false propaganda; perhaps we should have been more successful had we stood a little apart, dealing with requests sympathetically but not volunteering. Again it is a "might-have-been" against a fact. The fact, unhappily, has been that the Communist ideas ride rather higher than American in most local circles of the Asian coast. "Capitalism" in those areas does, it is true, conform much more closely to the Marxian descriptions than American capitalism; and the history of economic exploitation by the imperial masters is too recent to have been forgotten.

It does not follow that this condition will last indefinitely.

One may reasonably suppose that the prehensile, imperialist quality of Chinese and Russian Communist policy will become plain before too long. The same nationalism which now expresses itself against the West and the United States would then find more solid reason to attack the real menace closer to home. But by that time if Communist organization is able to do a really good job of infiltration and to export a sufficiency of package-revolutions complete with trained native leaders, Moscow-printed propaganda, Czechoslovak arms, and so forth, it may be too late. In newly freed colonies the bulk of a population is usually supine, trying to take care of its individual affairs, while the politics of the country are handled by an active few. Providing this active few is a Communist specialty: there are institutions and schools for just this kind of organization both in the Soviet Union and in China.

None the less it must be noted that Communist governments have nowhere been established on the Asian coast as yet save directly by force of arms. Both North Korea and Vietminh were so established. Intrigues go on everywhere; but they have not yet succeeded in taking control of any government. Perhaps there is no reason to assume that they will be more successful in the future.

The writer believes, despite surface trends apparent in the last

few years, that the United States will eventually emerge as the natural leader and friend of the countries emerging from colonialism.
Given the present state of affairs, this is a bold prediction. But it
has more solid foundation than wishful thinking.

Historically and factually the American record in the twentieth
century has, on the whole, been remarkably good. Ambassador
Joseph C. Grew has a habit of saying "history will out," meaning
that as years go by the facts and their implications stand out while
the mists of propaganda and politics fade away. The massive fact is
that the United States did cause the break-up of the Spanish Empire
in 1898, and the result was to give birth, with American assistance
and blessing, to the independent nations of Cuba and the Philippine
Republic. In 1917, President Woodrow Wilson proclaimed the doctrine of self-determination of peoples. Out of that came, immediately, at the close of World War I, independence of the nations
formerly comprehended within the Austro-Hungarian Empire and
the old Russian Empire, namely, Hungary, Czechoslovakia, Poland,
Lithuania, Latvia, Estonia and Finland; and also a little later, independence to countries emerging from the break-up of the Turkish
Empire: Iraq, Syria, Lebanon, Jordan, and, one may add, Saudi
Arabia. The forces engendered did not stop there. Egypt won substantial independence from the British Empire after World War I,
partly as a result of the Wilsonian impulse and certainly with American supporting sentiment.

The precise and immediate cause of Japan's Pearl Harbor attack
on the United States in 1941, which brought America into World
War II, was American opposition to the policy of the Japanese militarists, and especially the Japanese attempt to conquer China by
force and make it part of the Japanese imperial system. When that
war was ended the United States (at the time the dominant power
in the Far East) did encourage the more or less peaceful separation
of Indonesia from The Netherlands Empire. Acting within the United
Nations, she opposed a Russian-Chinese attempt in 1950 to seize
South Korea as part of a communist imperial system and bore the
brunt of the ensuing war. More recently she has mightily supported
the now independent State of Vietnam (Indochina) threatened by

Russian- and Chinese-supplied troops from the North. This has accomplished more and gone farther in the direction of realistic anti-imperialism than any great nation has done in all history.

This fact must be set side by side with the actuality that the United States, an enormously strong military Power, co-exists in the Western hemisphere with twenty-one other countries (including Canada), any or all of which she could conquer militarily or dominate economically were she imperially inclined. Yet the Western hemisphere is almost the only area on earth in which none of its countries fears seizure or invasion by an overwhelmingly powerful neighbor.

Sooner or later this historical record will establish itself.

Again, the argument that American industry and capital is automatically "imperialist" and inevitably will fight to conquer markets —standard Marxian dogma—is economically fallacious. American capitalism has galloped a long way since the days of eighteenth and nineteenth century trading capitalism. Remnants only remain of the theory that mass-producing and mass-marketing modern enterprise, American-style, is interested only in developing raw materials in underdeveloped countries, and selling high price manufactures to the miserable inhabitants of these countries. American industry certainly needs raw materials and will produce or buy them abroad when it can. But to a modern American corporation, a "market" can be established only in a country having a prosperous population. If there is to be "market expansion" beyond the borders of the United States, such expansion can take place only in those populations which have improved or are improving their standard of living. That is, in countries which are rather rapidly developing.

This is the exact opposite of "economic colonialism" as practiced in earlier days when a poor population was thought desirable because it furnished cheap labor. There are still plenty of cross-currents, tough problems and old-style forces to be met. The main trends, however, are already apparent. They are exactly contrary to Marxian dogma.

The principal protagonist of the notion that the United States is a great imperialist is, naturally, the Communist propaganda machine. This is operated chiefly from Russia; to a less extent, from

China. But it happens that Russia and China are themselves the two most prehensile colonial masters and imperialists extant in the world today. It seems impossible that they should indefinitely prevent the rest of the world from realizing this fact. Perhaps the crucial unmasking has already taken place. As these lines are being written, the nominally Hungarian Communist government at Budapest called in, not Hungarian but Russian tanks and airplanes to butcher Hungarians by thousands and to destroy parts of the fairest Hungarian city. This was a naked force-move of the most brutal type of empire. Contrast between the American and the Russian systems is so striking that the densest or most prejudiced Asian, African or Near Easterner can hardly fail to draw conclusions.

There is plenty of cogency, to be sure, in George Kennan's observation that a certain healthy detachment from other peoples may be useful. American desire to be "liked" has to be bracketed with the fact that Americans abroad do not always observe the courtesy and consideration required of guests. There is wisdom in the insistence by experts that American aid should not be rammed down the throats of countries made to admit their inadequacy or necessity, as was the case in administering the "Point Four" and technical aid programs, 1949–1954. There is solid reason for refusing to accept as a good cause for American assistance threats that the applicant country will promptly call in Communist help from Moscow or Peiping. Understanding, sympathy and (except in case of real emergency) not being in too much of a hurry is a prime necessity in these matters.

For those countries suffering a bad attack of "nationalism" (we have noted that nationalism means less today than perhaps ever in history), experience may prove the best teacher.

The American economic system has plenty of faults, many problems, and some grave perils. Nevertheless it is much closer to realities than the dogmatic systems described by dogmatic communism. Theoretically, communism provides a method of organization, a means of conscripting capital, a process of industrialization and economic development, capable of mauling an undeveloped primitive country into a modern country within the space of a few years. Practically, experience has proven the results it obtains are anything but certain. Poland, underdeveloped but still able to maintain a high economic system, is (October, 1956) hungry and in want as a result of Russian-Communist control. Hungary, formerly one of the granaries of the world, today has not enough to eat. The Soviet Union herself despite formidable strides in manufacture and heavy industry is wondering how she can feed her population—though she is perhaps the richest country in the world in agricultural resource. Obviously something is wrong with this picture; the communist plan departs somewhere from realities which ultimately assert themselves in human life.

Even the savage facts of military defense should, in time, be brought into line with the essential task of peace-keeping in great regions—eventually perhaps on a world scale. The NATO or SEATO bases are today held up as an instrument of probable colonialism. They can equally be regarded as parts of an international defense system—the only kind of defense system that makes military sense in modern war.

It is not the business of the United States to destroy the remainders of the nineteenth century empires, however little faith we may have in imperial systems. Still less is it America's business to shore up or maintain the surviving imperial systems, however anxious we may, and indeed must, be to preserve the lives and cultures of our principal European friends and allies. They, like ourselves, must find their way into the world which the twentieth century is hammering out. It probably is our business to make clear the facts of economic and military life to the emergent countries. To point out that full military and economic nationalism is a luxury few, if any, nations can afford for themselves. Certainly it is not a luxury for whose enjoyment any country can expect much in the way of aid from abroad. The most convinced anti-colonialist must reckon with the fact that the end of colonialism can not mean erection of unlimited narrow nationalisms: the only end of that trail is economic bankruptcy and probably eventual military subjugation by some more powerful nationalist neighbor.

Properly examined, colonialism can be effectively ended only as

new international institutions are forged out. There must be set
up an economic regional, if not world, framework in which an
emergent colony takes place as a full-fledged member of a community of nations, enjoying the benefits but assuming the obligations of community life. Probably there must also be a framework,
for the time being, of regional defense, merging eventually, let us
hope, into a framework of world law, in which nations, old and
new, enjoy maximum security, and assume corresponding responsibilities for world order and, if need be, common defense.

I see no other solution. The individualist nation claiming and
endeavoring to act with absolute sovereignty, like the petty princes
of the Middle Ages, simply can not survive. Nor can the peace of
the world accept the risks involved when any great number of nations claim that position. The emergent countries make a moral
case against their former imperial masters; it is on that they base
their claims for independence. But the former imperial nations
also have rights; they also are custodians of the safety and the
welfare of the many millions of their own people. New institutions
must be able to provide for that degree of organization of economics, of safety, and of public order which the empires provided
in their time. They must also provide what the old empires all too
frequently did not: equality of opportunity and a measure of
assistance for the new members of the community.

The United States is in an excellent position to assist in making
these institutions. To take leadership perhaps, for it has statesmen
and students wise enough and tolerant enough and able enough
politically. Leadership should be an ambition of Americans in this
task. But leadership depends at long last on the qualities and characters of men. It ultimately comes to rest where it belongs.

BATTLE OF THE PAST AGAINST
THE FUTURE

1

LITTLE APOLOGY need be made for devoting a few pages to direct philosophical analysis of the twentieth century crisis. Essentially, the struggle has been between ideas of the past and a slowly growing conception of the future. It is also true that the present forces in being today were constructed around ideas and conceptions of yesterday and the day before. The unparalleled speed of twentieth century evolution, however, has made yesterday a great deal longer ago than the yesterdays looked back upon by our fathers and grandfathers. Modern technical invention, the spread of ideas, increases in population and immediacy of communication has seen to that.

This suggests that we are in one of those occasions in history permitting a new approach to the problems of peoples. Such occasions are a kind of dispensation granted by Providence, offering to men new and splendid opportunities. I believe such a time is approaching. It may even offer opportunity to attempt the greatest adventure open to men: the adventure of achieving freedom with order, of erasing lines of hatred, of healing wounds of centuries.

In 1945, an armistice ended the second world war of this century. President Roosevelt had sounded its battle cry: "Freedom from Fear; Freedom of Religion; Freedom of Information; Freedom from Want." These were to be freedoms for "all the peoples in all the lands."

More than victory or armistice was needed to realize these ideals or to bring peace. A decade was required to liquidate the hatreds of international war. Within human limitations this has been largely accomplished. The enemies of yesterday in Europe and in Asia are today allies and friends bound by pacts of mutual defense. France and Germany have joined to defend, to build and to enrich the civilization of Western Europe. America, Japan are forging instruments of a common life. Greeks, Turks, Yugoslavs have opened their gates to each other. Perhaps never in history have opposed peoples so swiftly sought each other's friendship.

At the same time, the danger of world war is in some respects less than it has been for several centuries. Science speaks equally to all who will listen. The conquest of the air has been made available to many countries and increasingly available to all. The Prometheus-like seizure of the atom has placed unlimited destruction in the power of at least four great nations. Combined with air power, it has made war almost useless as a means of accomplishing any human end save mass suicide. Fifteen years ago General Staffs could advise and politicians could accept war as an instrument of policy and could advance a dubious claim to predict the probable results of war. Today, neither statesman nor general dares predict any result save universal catastrophe.

Fifteen years ago most of the world accepted, fatalistically, the premise that most of the world's peoples must live in hunger and in want and much of the world added that these millions were condemned to a class war. The twentieth century now knows it has tools at its hand and resources at its command which in a generation can satisfy the needs of any people willing to open its arms to modern production. "Freedom from want" in the mouth of the dying President Roosevelt was a hope and dream, but in the minds of present statesmen, is a practical attainable possibility. With a little scientific help from the Rockefeller Foundation a country like

Mexico, hungry for corn, made herself self-sufficient for that food in a period of seven years; the same thing could be done in twenty-five years for India, or China.

The services of information throughout the world are better organized, and more accurate, more immediate, than any of which we have historical record. The miracle of radio communication permits that information to be broadcast almost instantly over the whole planet. For the first time every people has its capacity to communicate with every other people and all manner of men who live in the presence of each other. Even diversity of language, of habits, and of thought is ceasing to be a bar. The scientist in Rome, or London, or New York, or Paris, talks the same language as the scientist in Tokyo, or Peiping, or Moscow, or Stockholm, or Strasbourg. The engineer or doctor, the mathematician, the chemist, and the botanist have no difficulty in understanding each other.

So it comes about that the twentieth century has given its children the instruments with which to achieve the greatest revolution in history, liquidating all other revolutions, offering possibility of a world of freedom under law in which no individual is lost and none is forgotten, and whose product is peace.

2

Why is it with these tools at hand that the revolution of our time is only just beginning? In Europe, in America and in Asia, we find struggles, frequently bloody, as in Korea and Indo-China. These are wars, and like all wars, horrible; but the supreme horror of these wars is that they were the warfare of ghosts. The ghost of Karl Marx and the Paris communards fight the ghost of Jean Jacques Rousseau and the English liberals. The ghosts of Ivan the Terrible, of Peter the Great, and of the dead Lenin struggle with the ghosts of British, French and German statesmen-philosophers and ideas which were needed in their time—and which time has now overpassed and left behind—and are conjured up like revenants from unblessed cemeteries. In their name men are asked to hate, to kill, to seize power—and give it to egoists who have no

intention of giving it back. Huge walls are built by ghosts who fear
the clean, sweet air of reality. Barriers are built against information by other ghosts who fear that the sunlight of fact will be the
dawn driving them back to their graves.

These are our enemies, all of them. The work we have to do is
to unchain the living from the walking horrors of the dead. It is
said that this is a century of revolution. It is. So certainly it
should be. But the revolution must be for the young and living
and strong, the revolution of our own time, the revolution which
uses the limitless power given to peoples by nature and our own
time.

All the ghosts have organized armies of conscripts—living
conscripts of out-worn ideas with little reality today. The time has
come to reject them all.

What are they?

They are many, but of them six are the most active. They are
Capitalism, Communism, Nationalism, Imperialism, Race Superiority, Spiritual Supremacy. In the light of the twentieth century
world, these ideas have no right to enslave the living. Each has had
its day. Each has made its contribution. Each has had in it elements
which served the humanity of its time. Each has taught lessons,
many of them useful. Each has merged into the horizon of the
vaster twentieth century world. Each is entitled to its place, indeed
its honorable place, in the history of ideas and of human organization; but that place is in history and not in the present. Let us
examine them briefly.

Capitalism is a part of the honorable revolution of the eighteenth century—the struggle of men to escape from the feudal system of the Western world. To achieve order, property and land and
control over men had been assigned by the West to hereditary
princes, nobles and barons. The French physiocrats rightly considered that no man could be free whose economic life was dependent on any feudal lord, or on any king state which had
monopolized the powers of the feudal lords. Private property was
conceived as a means of freedom, liberating men economically as
well as politically. The British economists, and notably Adam

Smith, saw this and more also; it was a way of getting things done; especially a way of harnessing the strange new forces of steam and creating machinery of an infant industrial system. Industrialism outran the powers of any individual or the ability of any individual to hold and dominate the ensuing machinery. The individual foreseen by the French physiocrats and Adam Smith became merged in great corporations and organizations in which the British and now the American commercial organizations took leadership. These went beyond the boundaries of their respective nations: economics of the twentieth century knows no national boundaries.

But now, capitalism had ceased to be a matter of individual ownership; the heads of the great companies which carried on transport, mining and industry could not make of themselves lords of economy as the feudal nobles had been lords of land and men. Capitalist organization became, and now is, merely a way of getting things done—a type of organization of enterprise, outside the state, and ultimately responsible to public opinion. Even the property interest has become available to anyone who wishes to buy it. In America, the common funds built up for labor pensions and the like are buying, and in twenty-five years will own, the chief power over the American industrial system. Without intervention of the political state that industry is thus rapidly socializing itself.

But this is a method useful to some, extremely useful and successful in the United States, and possibly not applicable to other countries. It succeeds where, and only where, it serves individual life and leaves individuals free. We do not know, no one can know, whether this means of carrying on economics could be used by our friends, the peoples of Burma or India, of the Soviet Union or of Poland, of Spain or of Mexico. Capitalism is not a philosophy for which to fight and die. It is a tool, and a great tool, to be used or laid aside as the genius of any people directs.

Communism is the fruit of a later revolution—the attempt of a century ago to liberate peoples, especially of Europe, from economic distress. Then, the fear was that capitalism, born of the French Revolution, would merely replace the feudal nobility by a

"nobility" of ownership; the fear that princes of the land had
merely been exchanged for princes of industrial property. This was
really a counterrevolution; Karl Marx indulged many regrets that
the feudal ownership of land had ended. Today in Communist
countries, the attempt is made to force agriculture back to the
feudal mold in which great numbers of forced laborers work on
land owned and operated by a feudal agency, reporting to an overlord whose title is now not prince but "commissar." Not unnaturally, the experiment failed.

None the less the danger which the old Socialists and their Communist successors fought was real enough, and the descriptions
which Marx gave of the capitalism of a century ago were by no
means unjust. The British novelist, Charles Dickens, was describ-
ing the same conditions in his novels. But to combat them, the
Communist idea organized its armies under the name and slogan
of the "class-war"—the idea that there must be a perpetual and
bloody struggle, that the Communist ideal could be organized only
on the basis of a supreme and superlative hate, hate of half the
world against the other half. To a country like America which has
had substantially no classes, and in which property ownership is
a fleeting affair, this made no sense. The American proverb that
families went from the shirt-sleeve of the laborer through riches
and back to the shirt-sleeve of the laborer in three generations,
has proved a measurably accurate description. The balance of
power of the labor unions, owned by no one, offsets the power
of the corporations—owned by many millions.

A Communist state today struggles to accumulate capital and
to invest it in industrialism, as does capitalism itself. It also is a
way of doing things, not a philosophy. Its only philosophy—that of
the class war of hatred—is a dead idea. It is one of the enslaving
ghosts which we here must consign to eternal burial. Do anyone
of us care enough to die for it, whether a people chooses to organize its industry and economics through the State rather than
through non-statist organization? Each of us knows the genius of
our own people, and each of us will defend that. Yet all of us
will resist to the end the attempt to make hatred the conscripting

officer, calling up men to lie and spy and fight and to kill and imprison and maim. In the name of that ideal in 1947 Yugoslav guerrillas burned Greek villages and imprisoned Greek children. In that name, millions of men were, still are, held in slave camps in Hungary, in Rumania, in the Soviet Union, in China. In that name, great parts of Asia have been devastated and millions have been killed. It is time to end the ghost of Communism.

As a defense, a century ago, it may have had its place. It is not for us to judge history. Today as a means of dividing and enslaving thought and will, it should go back to its historical cemetery. Let others write the inscriptions on its gravestone.

Nationalism—another ghost of the past. It too had an honorable beginning; it too is entitled to its monument in our historical cemetery. The feudal lords who had brought a measure of order out of the chaos when the Roman Empire, the Mogul Empire and the Chinese Empire fell had their place in things. Yet they, human beings seeking place and power, were not content merely to give order; they sought to expand in great feudal empires. Big and little Genghis Khans struggled with each other. Life could not be lived that way. National states arose; they contributed order over greater areas. The king's peace in England gradually gave tranquillity to a country torn by feudal struggles and the Wars of the Roses. Louis XI, and, later, Richelieu and Louis XIV gave nation-statehood to France. In doing so they produced and fostered language, culture, poetry, drama, architecture, universities: an honorable contribution; let this be a spray of palm and olive on its monument.

Yet each served its time, and its time passes. For each indulged in its time a passion to make all other countries into its own image. Louis XIV sought to create a Europe in the design of his Versailles as Rome before him had sought to create a world in the image of the Capitoline Hills. A Britain thought of creating a world of English civilization. An America, half a century ago, flirted briefly with the idea of extending American life beyond the seas in the Pacific; and to the credit of its people, rejected the idea and pledged to set free, and did set free, the lands she had won by conquest of the dying Spanish Empire. So today the Philippines and Cuba are independent republics, masters of their own life and their own institutions. So also the British wisely reorganized much of the Empire they had acquired, conceding nationhood to its major parts and erecting the British Commonwealth of Nations. India and Pakistan are there to prove the point.

For, in fact, the twentieth century has ended old-fashioned nationalism as a principle of world organization and is gradually laying its ghost. Two American brothers in 1903 using a curious machine succeeded in flying through the air. Less than half a century later, machines fly above the sight of man with little reference to national boundaries traced on flat maps below. The economics of almost every nation came to depend, not on the resources of that nation, but upon its ability to combine resources drawn from all parts of the world. Save for two nations—the United States and the Soviet Union—no nation can feed and house and clothe its people as they desire, and no nation at all can make war except as a combination of many other nations. It is already evident that within twenty years neither the Soviet Union nor the United States will be able to maintain an isolated national existence—if indeed either can do so now. The twentieth century subtracted from nationalism its ability to maintain national life.

There remains of nationalism, then, the splendid contribution it did make and has made—its ability to develop the peculiar genius of peoples. The greatness of France is the greatness of the French language, and of French literature, and of French poetry, and of the French way of life. The greatness of China is its philosophical point of view, its golden gift of poetry and laughter, its ability to mobilize the genius of Chinese in their own language for China. But even this requires world contacts. We have in America mountain valleys populated by English settlers of 200 years ago, who became isolated in their mountain stronghold. They talk the language of eighteenth century England, they sing eighteenth century English songs, and follow eighteenth century English customs. But it is an England which no longer exists; these valleys have become merely living museums of the past. Even the greatest aspect of nationalism—its preservation and resolute defense of its peoples' culture—depended on hospitality to ideas and cultures visiting it, learning from it and enriching it. Paris is splendid among cities because through centuries it has been a supreme free port for ideas and men. Its quality as a world capital depended less on the far-flung arms of Richelieu or of Louis Quatorze than on the fact that it was a center where ideas were communicated.

So, it seems, the military and imperial phase of nationalism is gone. The foundation has been shot out from under it by airplanes and telecommunication, by economics and electricity, by factories and by markets, and most of all by the common sense of peoples who wish to be themselves in their national culture but wish to use for that culture the resources of the entire world.

Another ghost is imperialism.

This also has its history, and in great aspects its history also made its contribution. Let it also have an honored place in the cemetery of history, but—let it rest there. Few will deny that the empire which was Rome gave order, law, language and frame to rough tribes emerging from the barbaric period of history. Into its frame came Goths and Franks, Burgundians and Vandals, Scythians and Pannonians. In modern times the great frame of Rome still dominated mass migration. In my own childhood, outside the American hemisphere, the world was run by thirteen empires: the British, the French, the Austro-Hungarian, the German, the Italian, the Spanish, the Russian, the Turkish, the Japanese and the Chinese, with smaller empires like Belgium, The Netherlands and Portugal. For all practical purposes, this was the organization of the world. It gave frame and design to the nineteenth century. As centuries go, we think of the era as a plateau of international peace. Because of the British ascendancy, it has been called the Victorian Age.

Our twentieth century has dissolved these empires. No longer were their chief component parts semi-barbaric tribes. The invading Goths or Franks did not seek to be different from Rome— they sought to be Rome itself. Their efforts to conquer were not efforts to be different; they were in effect efforts to imitate. The

Huns who under Attila stormed towards Constantinople were not seeking to develop a "Hunland"; they were seeking to be the empire of Byzantium. Conquering militarily, they were conquered morally. The last great defender of the Western Roman Empire, Stilicho, was himself a Pannonian Vandal, not a Roman. But in the twentieth century, the peoples which are and have liberated themselves from empire have no desire to dominate or to be the empire itself. The Burmese sought not to be England, but to be Burma. The Philippine Republic sought, not to be America, but to be Philippine. India and Pakistan did not seek to take over London and rule the British Empire; they sought to be Mohammedan Pakistani and Hindu Indians.

Unlike the attacks of older times in which invaders sought to take over the culture of their former masters, the twentieth century has seen a formidable demand, people by people, for each to enjoy the privilege of its own peculiar culture, its own language, its own genius for getting things done—perhaps even its own right to make its own mistakes.

The twentieth century has learned that no people can long be held against its will in any empire. The ghost of imperialism has proved unable to mobilize armies strong enough or forces great enough to hold in the culture of a master country peoples who wished the culture of their own. The ghost of imperialist Communism can fare no better, as any Pole, Czech or Hungarian, any Roumanian, Bulgarian or Lithuanian can testify.

Imperialism made its contribution. It gave for a period order to the world. It set up communication over vast areas. It permitted a measure of free flow of ideas. It developed a measure of international commerce. But because no people will long be morally tributary to any other people, it has ended its work, save as in its closing days it gives orderly and healthy birth to peoples who seek to be and to express themselves. So it is that no current statesman can now talk seriously of forming an empire. Even those—there are some in Moscow and Peiping—who attempt the fact, are afraid to use the name. Even as we have been stating the problem, the lust which Stalin had to annex the countries of Middle Europe—the days when by his choice his head appeared on the coins and postage stamps of captive countries and his statues adorned their public squares—has vanished.

We must recognize that the end of imperialism left an unfilled place in the life of nations. The fact is that no nation can live to itself or defend itself alone. Each must thus move inside a complex of nations. The empires did supply such a complex for their constituent peoples. As they pass, some new twentieth century instrument must take their place. The form must leave to each people the full independence of its culture and its life: but must also organize for each people the necessary services required for economics, for defense and for a common denominator of law permitting peoples to hope for freedom from fear, freedom of information and freedom from distress.

Another ghost, a diseased werewolf, may be disposed of with brief contempt. The ghost of race superiority has occasionally stalked the world. Its cries still whistle down the wind. It was thought until Hitler committed suicide in 1945, that the Nordic might be a "master race." Well, Nietzsche is dead, and so is Hitler. It was thought that only some races could organize, could manage, could be technically profound, could operate twentieth century industry. We know better now. Every race that has had opportunity has demonstrated its skill; Parsees and Hindus operate steel plants comparable to the best in Europe or America. Italian, French, Spanish technology, each has its triumphs. Slavs can organize great factories and liberate atomic bombs. It may be a Greek, a Turk, a Burmese or a Japanese who will penetrate the secrets of the cosmic ray. South American Indians in the Andes were able to live and maintain a civilization in areas which the white Europeans have not yet been able to master. Mexican Indians proudly construct beautiful and well-planned cities. Each race awaits, and each demands its turn. Anthropology joins with history in showing that when the tools of civilization are open to all peoples, there is no master race.

3

Yet as we take leave of these ghosts it is fair to remember that
they, like men, contributed both good and evil in their time. As
in the case of men, the good they have done survives. Capitalism,
a century ago, did introduce industrial organization into the world
and created some superb mechanisms for satisfying human wants
and needs. The Communism of a century back did play its part in
preventing a divine right of property from establishing itself in
place of the former divine right of feudal nobles and princes.
Nationalism did permit the organization of peoples and development of culture. Imperialism with all its faults did give a measure
of world organization, replacing the anarchy of nations which prevailed before 1815. Attempts to claim spiritual monopoly did none
the less spread knowledge and great conceptions over vast areas.
Even ambition to be a master race may have expanded some
understanding of technology and organization.

It is not the intellectual and spiritual achievements of the old,
living organisms we deny or bury. It is their companion were-
wolves of outworn organization we inter: the greed developed
under the old capitalism; the hatreds and cruelty fostered by Communism; the aggression born of nationalism; the denial of personality that went with empire; the bigotry born of religious fanaticism; the arrogant conceit of race superiority.

These, the revenants borne down the twilight breeze, we must
exorcise. With them go the men vain enough, weak enough, cruel
enough, or mistaken enough to use them as instruments of policy,
or politics, or organization. The time has come to clear the way
for the great twentieth century contribution to history.

4

What are the conceptions we can use as powerful lights on the new
way?

Clearly the first is that the world is destined to become one. No
longer do we learn of distant Cathay only when a Marco Polo

comes back to Venice recounting his experience after years of absence. No longer does a Russian learn of the west only because an occasional foreign adventurer makes his way to a Moscovite capital. No longer can any nation say of any other nation: "Its affairs do not concern me." No longer can any group say of any other group: "We can not get along with them." No longer, indeed, can even our great religions say of any other religion: "This must be blotted out." We can not go back to the days when the disciples of Mohammed sought to compel every Frank to become Moslem or die. No longer can we accept the idea that a state is supreme in its sovereignty and therefore beyond the law. Fundamentally we must think and speak and work for a principle of world organization which is universal; which is legitimate precisely because it is universal; which becomes illegitimate precisely to the extent that it violates universality. The fault of the ghosts we have just consigned to their graveyard was that each, despite its merit, sought not to unify but to divide, and in dividing, to set up one group as masters and others as subjects. One group as enemy to others.

There can be division even within universality. Indeed there are occasions when division is essential. Defense is essentially division; yet defense is necessary. But defense need divide no nation or people from any other nation or people unless it is attacked. At base, the only justification for division of peoples is the right, indeed, the duty, to defend a principle. True division is set up by a policy of attack. Rightly, Article 52 of the Charter of the United Nations permits reciprocal agreements for defense within a framework of universal order. Rightly, because when the universal order is attacked, a crucial division has already taken place; the defender seeks to re-establish universality, the aggressor to destroy it.

Clearly also, and directly connected with universality, is the principle of the individual.

More than a century ago, the German philosopher, Hegel, told his students that the law of life exacted freedom for all individuals and that freedom consisted in the capacity to make a choice. But the individual granted that capacity was under a companion duty: the duty to seek the universal. His choice must be therefore towards the universal—but it must be *his* choice. Because no man can ever have a full knowledge of the universal principle, and because, even if he did the understanding of principle changes as time goes on and knowledge grows, new apprehensions will be made by individuals. Maintenance of the dignity of the individual is the only instrument granted to humanity to apprehend the growing measure, the lasting values of universal principles. Suppression of any individual diminishes by so much humanity's ability to put itself in harmony with universal order. It follows that every individual, everywhere, is of interest, be it a Chinese coolie, in a village, an Egyptian fellah, an Andean Indian, a laborer on a Calabrian farm, a Negro in the American South, or a Mau-Mau in Kenya. In little or in great, each of these contributes. A mighty man like Albert Schweitzer may apprehend and contribute to millions; humbler men and women only to one or two; but human conception is the sum of all of their apprehensions in a single world.

For this reason, our twentieth century revolution must be resolute in asserting and defending the dignity of individuals, wherever and however they may be found or placed. Each man must be approached with respect for what he is.

For the same reason, the dignity of each culture must be approached with reverence and respect. It is, in fact, the common expression of individuals of like language and experience; culture is the expression of a group which is able to communicate within itself.

Protection of individuals, like protection of groups, extends even to the protection of conflicts. Ideas, conceptions, lines of thought, inevitably struggle with each other. Like component fragments of an atom, they are constantly in motion, constantly in conflict, constantly opposed. Yet from their struggles, they create pattern. It is right that they should conflict, and interact. Out of this interaction comes greater understanding and greater cultures. This universality of which we speak is not static. It develops; the universality of tomorrow will certainly be quite different than that of today. So indeed it should. But apparently the instrument of its progress is the constant conflict of ideas, propounded by individuals, contributing to an ever-flowing stream of human thought. The harmony arising out of this pattern of idea-conflict is what we call civilization.

These two principles, universal order and creative individuality, always modifying each other, are essential to the free world. Without free individuality, any human attempt to establish order becomes static and sterile. Without constant search towards universal order, any individual effort becomes mere anarchy.

The motion towards a humanely workable system is necessarily the effort of the human mind. This works by constructing pictures of ideal society. This, the "ideal pattern" used by many philosophers, notably Max Weber, is the working hypothesis upon which there is constructed a community, a state, a free world, in time— as we hope—a community of nations under law.

There will never be an ideal pattern to end all ideal patterns. Each pattern will constantly be upset by some individual who has apprehended some greater attribute of universal order. We shall never find the golden moment which the Devil offered to Faust, to which we say "Linger awhile, thou art so fair." The human mind of a free world can never declare itself satisfied. In Goethe's epic, damnation followed the occurrence of that moment. An individual, a community, a nation, perhaps even a race, conceivably might reach the point in which his mind or all minds in it stop growing, stop perceiving, consider that they have apprehended the universal—and then have no further function, save survival till eventual death.

Our free world can never do this. The greatest strength of the free world, indeed, is precisely in the fact that it recognizes, assists and demands the right and capacity for every individual in it to continue striving. It can accept the idea that human life is polarized in part by individual striving and part by the search for a pattern of order. But it requires that the pattern shall be given political reality by the free act and will of the individual. It requires that the individual shall be protected in his freedom precisely because he seeks some pattern within which his neighbor as well as himself can use and enjoy that freedom.

5

We have set out a philosophical pattern at some length because it alone gives reality to practical applications of statecraft.

World War I was perhaps the last of the eighteenth and nineteenth century European wars. Nationalist states struggled to preserve their position. If Czarist Russia or Austria or Germany could secure hegemony over stated territory—particularly mid-Europe and the Middle East—that nationalist state would have increased its power. This was considered an end in itself. Then from beyond the Atlantic came a disturbing idea: the principle of "self-determination of nations." Mr. Winston Churchill later observed that the world was entitled to something better than that as a result of the struggle which ended in 1918. Perhaps he was correct, for the principle of self-determination of nations spelled the end of the empires which until then had given the world the only order it had known since Rome. The principle, history seems to have decided, was right; the lack was of some companion principle capable of bringing self-determining nations into a common pattern of world order and world law.

World War II was a specific struggle over philosophical principles which squarely raised the entire problem. The German Nazis flung out against the world a principle which recked little of self-determination of nations, but did promise a kind of tormented and cruel order—the principle of world empire under a master race. Not unnaturally the world, most of which is not Nordic, rejected the principle. In retrospect it is surprising that a Hitler could lead as many Europeans as he did behind that strange and evil banner.

Following Hitler came a second affirmation of order—the Stalinist version of Leninist Communism. As Hitler had set out his theory in *Mein Kampf*, so Stalin had set out his in *Essays on Leninism*. This, too, had its attraction. As in the case of *Mein Kampf*, the individual in Stalinism had no rights and no existence save as a part of the State. In Communst theory, there must be a master dictatorship claiming to represent a master class, perpetually struggling against another class. All individual life was the life of a soldier enlisted in the class war under absolute domination by a small group, the central bureaucracy of the Communist Party. There could be no peace until this war had been won all over the earth. Therefore, according to Communist theory, all of life, all of human activity, was part of the ceaseless warfare. After it was won—if ever—perhaps a Nirvana of classless society might be obtained. It was no accident that, as Hitler's armies went down, the Russian armies took their place.

The logical victor over Hitler was, of course, Stalin, just as the logical victor over the ghost of Stalin will be the free world. Stalin's principle of order was a dictatorship claiming to speak for the oppressed classes throughout the world—the Marxian "proletariat." This was a wider conception than any brought out by Hitler or Rosenberg or Streicher. Yet it still spoke in bitterness and for only part of the world. Great parts of the earth, in Western Europe and notably in the United States, had liberated themselves from the necessity of having a "lower class."

For fifty years, the United States had been working on a quite different theory. American thought had not the slightest idea of enthroning the proletariat. Still less did it think of enthroning any small group of men who claimed personal power in the right of the proletariat. The American idea was to arrange a form of life in which there was no proletariat; in which every individual had at his own command life in any class in which he chose to be. The differences between class and class were differences of personal taste, which men might change if they so desired. The laborer might cease to be a laborer if he wished to save his money and go into business and be a bourgeois. The child of the tenant-farmer could, if he wished, go to a university and enter professional life. The son of a blacksmith could become President, as Herbert Hoover in fact did. One reason for the mighty tension between the Soviet Union and the United States is precisely because the world which the Soviet Union claims to oppose does not exist in America, save in residual remnants. To manufacture a class of war in America, the Communists had to invent an upper class against which to fight, and their attempt has become ridiculous.

Freedom, however, is an attribute produced only by a general pattern. For it means not merely freedom from fear of a neighbor, which a respectable system of laws supplies in any community or any state. It means also freedom from fear that an invading army will seize a man and his family and his home, or that invading airplanes will wipe him out with an atomic bomb. In older days, when nationalism was strong on earth, a powerful national government could assure in some measure immunity from fear. General Staffs considered that their primary business was to secure immunity from invasion to the people of its country. In the present days of intercontinental aircraft, and in the coming days of guided missiles, no nationalist government, no nationalist army, no nationalist system of defense can assure this immunity. The great regional combinations today put together by the free world—the Organization of American States and the North Atlantic Treaty Organization—attempt with a degree of success to obtain immunity from invasion or attack for great areas. Yet eventually, as we know, this can only be done through world organization. Because of this, the free world, despite many discordant voices, rising from its individualist system, will always seek the creation and strengthening of the United Nations. Should the United Nations unhappily fail, the free world would have to reinvent a similar institution.

Americans, for the moment, stand at the very top of an economic pyramid. Never in history has an entire population of 170 millions as nearly achieved freedom from want. Yet most American students know now that America will be able to maintain this only if comparable results, so far as desired, can be achieved by their neighbors. But economic adjustments, the spread of technical information, the free flow of transport and raw materials are essential to all countries desiring to produce enough to satisfy the wants of their peoples. We all live against a background of world transport, world markets, world arrangements. There can be no victor in the race against freedom from want. The race can only be won by most if not all of mankind, else the apparent victory vanishes. The world in which a Babylon, a Byzantium, a Rome or a Berlin can be rich at the expense of an impoverished world ended somewhere in the early part of the twentieth century. The economist tells us that freedom from want can only result from widespread distribution. The Marxian who talks of capitalist warfare to secure markets is talking a language the modern economist has long since discarded; he knows that a market can not be "conquered" but has to be constructed. Conquering slave areas accomplishes nothing; modern enterprise need not enslave cheap labor. What it needs is to set up rich populations for whom it can produce and which it can serve.

Free minds of free men and women acting through free nations, working in a framework of universal order permitting them to attain and use the resources of the twentieth century; this is the basis of the free world revolution of the twentieth century.

CHAPTER Two

PEACE AND ITS INSTRUMENTS

IN A WORLD so complex and passionate, it is easy to assume that foreign affairs can never be controlled, must always be matter of chance, can only be lived through from day to day without governing concepts or justified hope of improvement. The emotion is natural; to yield to it is fatal and absurd. Factually the world is no more stormy than it always has been—probably less so, for an increasing body of unifying elements are appearing. What has happened is that all parts of the world now live in immediate contact with all other parts. All problems are thus known—more or less—and all conflicts are apparent; this does mean that any problem may become a world problem and a world danger. Tools of solution are nevertheless steadily being forged. Even more important, underlying conceptions of general acceptance are steadily gaining strength. They are not adequate now, and may not become so for many years. Yet progress is apparent. Despite setbacks, the progress is never wholly canceled.

"World problems," it is true, will never be "solved." We shall never, probably, achieve a Nirvana of perfect peace. Perhaps the world would be a rather uninteresting place if we did. What we probably can do is to pose the recurrent problems more clearly, and gradually make possible their control or solution with less human agony than in prior generations.

238

We here study some of the concepts and tools offering possibility of resolving problems. These are examined from the point of view of "American interest" because national interest is still the familiar, almost the only, understood language of foreign affairs. The writer is clear that in our case "national interest," accurately apprehended, must be coincident with the development and general benefit and welfare of a community of nations. The only other American position would be to use our present (but relatively diminishing) preponderance of military power to conquer an American empire—and be quick about it. That, for a century or so, might hold the situation—though the success of the gamble would be doubtful at best and the end might well be national disaster. Actually, the imperialist alternative is not open to American politicians. America has distinctly rejected this solution. Her people have neither aptitude nor inclination for empire. The only other possible line is to work through regional and other arrangements towards an eventual world commonwealth.

1. *Peace*

Peace is the undefined, unrealized ideal of ages. It has engaged the yearning of human hearts through all recorded history. Yet, surprisingly, we know less about peace than about any other human ideal.

We think of "peace" as tranquillity; absence of war or threat of war; a state of affairs in which men and women live, love, rear children, work, play, develop themselves, without threat of foreign invasion. This is what almost everyone wants—or at least says he wants. There have always been small groups who believed they could gain by war; there have always been very large groups indeed who were prepared to make war in defense of certain ideas they held dear: for example, their religion, their country, their social institutions.

The overwhelming consensus of desire for peace nevertheless never really dies. The words of Isaiah (they are engraved in the marble of the United Nations building in New York) were written six hundred years before the birth of Christ, and no one has improved on the statement,

". . . and they shall beat their swords into plowshares, and their spears into pruning hooks: nation shall not lift up sword against nation, neither shall they learn war any more."

Yet to students, peace is something infinitely more complex than mere absence of strife or threat of strife.

Peace is a result, not a condition. It arises from a balance of forces, not from mere absence of disturbance, just as white light is a perfect, balanced blend of an infinite number of other colors. Peace is a positive, not a negative. We know this without really knowing how it is achieved, though we are slowly beginning to disentangle some of the main elements. Some day a historian-philosopher will write for us an analysis and history of peace; here only the most elementary components can be discussed. Indeed, not too many of them are known or understood.

Historically, as noted elsewhere, peace has never existed in the abstract. It has always been the "peace of" someone or something. Even today if you are arrested for a "breach of the peace," you would find that the complaint in the Magistrate's Court accuses you of having broken the "Peace of the State of New York," or, if in England, the "Queen's Peace." Behind this is a fascinating, ancient, continuing bit of history. Never, so far as this writer can discover, has there been any peace which did not "belong" to an individual or to a governmental institution.

In the days of the Roman Empire, Roman armies and government carried with them "Pax Romana," the Roman peace. This meant that no one could take up arms against his neighbor and no group against another group: use of force was strictly reserved to the Roman authority, and no one else could resort to it. Romans insisted on this partly no doubt for military protection (armies almost automatically try to disarm and break up any force movements other than their own in the vicinity). But to have satisfactory civilian life it was even more requisite to maintain this outlawry of unauthorized force—this is called "public order." After all, no one can do anything much if he has continuously to worry about roving brigands, or if when he plants a crop he has no reasonable likelihood that he can harvest it, or if when he leaves his house in the morning he can not be sure it will not have been rifled or burned when he returns. "Public order" is thus the first strand in the cord of peace.

But "public order"—tranquillity of a sort—is itself a composite. You do not have "public order" very long if a wrong committed by one man or one group against another man or another group goes wholly uncontrolled or unpunished. If the dominant institution—say a Roman imperial governor—wants to have order in his province, he can not expect to have it if men can murder or wrong their neighbor leaving the neighbor or his family no redress. Absent some sort of compensation, that neighbor and his friends will form revenge squads; they will repay evil with evil, in ever expanding circles of growing disorder.

In consequence, "public order" is dependent on the existence of a second institution: law, administered by some tribunal to which any party aggrieved can have reasonably prompt access. The Peace of Rome existed because conquering Roman armies and governors took with them Roman law and Roman judges— unless, of course, they found a highly developed system of law already there which they could use. "Public order" which meant a measure of tranquillity thus involved first an overriding executive institution which was the sole custodian of force; and second, a generally acceptable system of law administered by a court or its equivalent. The Peace of Rome was called that precisely because Rome assumed the custodianship of force (and monopolized it) and also provided a system of law and its administration.

To work, law must not only be there and readily available; it must also be generally accepted; that is, it must more or less satisfy the prevailing idea of ethics, fair play and decency. This is the quality of "justice": there has to be not only law and its administration, but both have to be "just." Since conditions change, sometimes rapidly, and ideas of justice change, laws have to change too. The over-all institution (in the illustration we are giving,

Rome) had to be able to make changes and modifications so that the law and its administration more or less satisfied the population.

Now we begin to see why there can not be merely "peace." There has to be peace as the result of some system. And so peace emerges throughout all history.

For example. In the violent days of the Middle Ages when little feudal lords struggled with their neighboring barons, the Catholic Church undertook to establish the "Peace of God." In this case God was represented by a very immediate, well organized and powerful institution, the Church. For practical purposes, the "Peace of God" merely meant that fighting had to stop at certain places, notably churches. Within those areas no one could draw a sword or continue a battle. As in the case of Rome, the Church had its own system of law and its own courts to administer that law. The "Peace of God" would have meant nothing had it not been for the fact that the Catholic Church, then divided into powerful arch-bishoprics and bishoprics, represented not only spiritual but temporal force, and had its own courts of justice. The Bishop's house and his cathedral were frequently redoubtable as castles; he had his own armed force of police, and his courts had the Canon Law. At one time, even, the Church propounded and in considerable measure throughout Europe maintained the "Peace of God" in the form of what was called the "Truce of God"—a ruling that all fighting everywhere must stop on Thursday night and be adjourned until the following Monday morning. Amazingly, this happened. It was convenient: the soldier-peasant could go home and attend to his crop if he were near enough; from the point of view of the Church, he could attend Mass on Sunday.

Somewhat similar history brought about peace in England, and later in the Anglo-Saxon world. There the "King's Peace" originally meant that in the presence of the King or within stated limits around his castles no one was allowed to use arms. The King's soldiers were generally on hand to enforce this. The King himself sat as a judge to provide justice in case of complaint. To extend this peace, the King himself went from place to place in England holding court. Eventually the "King's Peace" was expanded to prevail wherever his representatives or judges held courts. Still later it was applied to the highways which he ordained for peaceful travel of himself and his subjects. (Such highways still exist in England—which is why "King's Highway" is a familiar phrase.) Off the road a robber dealt only with local people who might or might not enforce order. But if he robbed on the "King's Highway" he became a "highwayman" and the King's soldiers went after him, which was a serious affair. Gradually the "King's Peace" became the peace of all England. In America the various States of the United States inherited that peace, which is why if you get into a brawl you are accused of a "breach of the peace of the Sovereign State of California" or Michigan or Massachusetts, as the case may be.

The institution in this case was first the Royal Government of England; later, in America, the government of the American State. Even today (so far as the writer knows) there is no "peace," national or local, which does not thus "belong" to some governing institution claiming monopoly of force, and equipped to administer justice under law. Equipped also to change laws when grievances appear. Probably prepared also, as we have seen, to assure conditions within which people have the economic means of life; populations do not support or suffer misery in sweet reasonableness for very long.

So, we see, peace needs more than good will. It needs an institution which can control the use of force by others than itself, and that in turn means that (when the chips are really down) the institution has or can command force sufficient to quell disorder. In international affairs there have been steady and disappointed efforts to create just such an institution for many years; and the world is strewn with mementos of these attempts.

In the early twentieth century it was considered that if international law could be established, and if there were a court capable of interpreting it, this would be enough. As a result, a permanent court of arbitration was established by a convention signed at The Hague (Netherlands) in 1907. The late Andrew Carnegie gave it a magnificent palace. But no nation had to take its disputes there, the court had no way of enforcing its decisions, the judges could not prevent any nation from resorting to arms, and the institution was incomplete.

Later, as a result of World War I, and at the insistence of President Woodrow Wilson, the League of Nations was established. This was an attempt to supply the overriding "institution." But it also had no force, no compulsory power, no ability to make law, and no way of enforcing order. It was thought in 1918 that the good sense of all nations would lead them to join, when necessary, in repressing aggression, lending force to the League of Nations for the occasion. When, however, the nations of the world did not lend force to the League of Nations to prevent Mussolini from attacking Ethiopia in 1936 after refusing to arbitrate his disputes, the League of Nations was, as an institution, bankrupt, and presently fell to pieces. Mr. Sumner Welles bitterly observed at the time that when the experiment creating an institution was tried again it must have some force under its control; and of course he was right.

A third, more difficult component of this balance we call "peace" is that of adjustment. Many conflicts of interest do not yield to "law," either because there is no applicable law, or because both parties are right as they see it. These conflicting interests must either be fought out or they must be compromised—there is no other way. Compromising involves not merely striking a bargain, arranging to divide, or settling a dispute; it involves also convincing both parties or groups that they are better off for having settled it along the lines worked out. In foreign affairs these are usually what we call "political solutions," meaning that they are arrived at by negotiation rather than by arbitration or judicial process. Arranging them peacefully is the work of diplomacy. Obviously in any peace system, recourse to force by any nation must either be impossible or else be so dangerous and difficult that neither side will choose to fight instead of to deal. There must therefore be in any institution of peacekeeping a means of providing political settlements as well as of repressing disorder and enforcing a rule of law.

These are the barest requirements for a peace system, as far as we presently understand them—if indeed the word "understanding" applies. An institution capable of assuring peace must have mechanisms and resources enabling it to meet them, else it becomes an empty debating organization. This is why the work of devising, supporting, maintaining and directing institutions of peace preoccupies the minds of many men in all countries. These men may be dreamers. They may be starry-eyed; some may be impractical; and some are living more in the future than in the present. But without them the world would have little hope of achieving peace.

2. *World Government*

Anyone who thinks that world government is a present possibility is no realist: it is presently impossible. Equally, anyone who fails to work towards it simply does not know the world in which he lives. Within the span of two or three generations—possibly less— we are likely to face a situation in which either a measure of world government is an accomplished fact, or we may all be dying (rather horribly) in the effluvia of a world struggle which may not even afford the drama of war.

Let us try to face the facts. Any government in any area is a more or less artificial construct which gives form to the desire of the overwhelming majority of the governed for some method of keeping order, settling controversies, carrying out measures in the general interest, and so forth. Accurately analyzed, government thus recognizes and gives effect to a general desire to be governed. Building the desire, crystallizing institutions, creation of confidence in those institutions, has been the work of many years, based on folkways and habits evolved through centuries. Absent these elements, any charter or constitution setting up a government is a paper document without force. The government can not induce or compel action; the governed feel no obligation towards it; and the fabric either falls apart or never gains enough solidity to exist at all.

"World government" nevertheless does exist in certain extremely limited aspects now. When it exists it is—let us use the bad word—"supra-national." It is imposed on the United States, as on all other countries, by sheer force of circumstances which bring into being the desire to be governed in those aspects—and confidence in the method evolved.

There is, for example, international distribution of radio wave lengths, and a sort of "supra-national" regulation of radio communication. This has existed since 1928. In that year a conference on radio communication was held in Cairo, Egypt, and the rough outlines of the ensuing Cairo Convention have regulated the air waves ever since. This regulation survived both Stalin and Hitler, and its chief structure continued even through World War II. It is in effect today. The force—"sanction" in the old vocabulary—is not that of international force. It rests in the fact that either you regulate distribution of frequencies in radio, or nobody can use radio for communication at all. Every country is therefore faced with a choice: will it observe (in general, at least) the rules of distribution, or will it abandon international—indeed, in large measure, national—radio communication. Such abandonment can be coupled with engineering devices making it difficult for anyone else to use radio communication either. If everyone tries to use all the air waves at once, obviously no one's radio transmitter can convey a message. Actually, every country in the world finds on balance that it prefers to communicate by radio more than it wishes to prevent others from communicating. Therefore it observes, more or less, the terms of the Cairo Convention and its successor conventions.

This is not to say that this form of world government is not flouted from time to time and that the world law—that is, the agreed distribution of air waves—is not broken. The Soviet government breaks it every day with its "jamming" operations. For that matter, practically all law of any kind is broken quite often in certain detailed aspects. The important fact is that the general plan and distribution maintains itself. As a result, you can listen in on Radio Moscow or Radio Peiping or Radio Argentina if you have a good enough radio receiver, and, in general, a Russian or a Chinese or an Argentine can listen to the Voice of America if the Voice of America really wants to be heard.

A second form of world government has to do with health and quarantine rules. This is very recent. During World War II the United States Public Health Service established liaison with the American Department of State at the instance of Surgeon-General Thomas C. Parran. This gave public health its first chance to speak a piece officially in international affairs. At the close of World War II, a conference was held which set up, under the auspices of the United Nations, the "World Health Organization" (commonly referred to as WHO). This organization has worked out certain international practices and quarantine rules; and has begun an all-out attack on certain kinds of disease.

Again, "sanction" is imposed by physical and pathological fact rather than by power. Countries can either protect themselves against certain kinds of disease, or they can let it go and suffer. Few, if any, countries, once apprised of the facts, care to risk uncontrolled disease, and consequently with some degree of conviction, join in the common policy. Certain kinds of disease anywhere may strike anywhere else; no one is safe unless everyone is safe. Though the field is still in its infancy, greater areas of recognizable universal interest are steadily appearing.

A third virtual world government exists in the field of civil aviation. If planes are to fly internationally, certain uniformity of practice has to exist everywhere. Regulations in international airports have to be approximately the same throughout the world if planes are not to crash in confusion. Air towers have to talk a language which can be understood by all pilots, and must speak in terms which plane crews of any nationality can comprehend. The International Civil Aviation Organization (ICAO), created at the Chicago Air Conference of 1944, sits in Montreal and rides herd on rules and regulations. Breach of practice can be brought before that body. ICAO has no force to compel acquiescence. But civil aviation planes (which are very expensive) and passengers (who value their lives) simply do not go to areas where regulations are not observed. Again, each country has to choose whether it wishes air transport linking it to the rest of the world or whether it chooses to live within itself.

Until relatively recently much of the Communist world did elect to live within itself. It did not join the Chicago Air Conference. It displayed no interest in having much air communication with the world outside Iron Curtain countries. The attitude has somewhat changed since Stalin's death. It appears likely now that Communist nations also are finding air communication with the outside world desirable for them. But to have it, sheer force of necessity requires that they acquiesce in, and generally observe, the chief regulations of ICAO. Otherwise, the system breaks down.

A fourth area is unquestionably coming up. This is control of atomic radiation, an issue dramatically posed in the recent campaign between Governor Adlai Stevenson and President Dwight Eisenhower. Briefly, the underlying situation is this.

Atomic bomb explosions and possibly also some other uses of atomic energy increase the radio-active content of the ether and upper air. The effect of this can be tremendously toxic, since a "fall-out" results. This reaches the surface of the earth and enters the human body through food or other absorption. The extent of damage to human health which may be produced by the present fall-out is as yet unknown. Its growth could have terrible consequences. It might merely produce lingering and horrible disease like leukemia or bone cancer. But, in greater intensity, the "fall-out" may change human genetics so that children would be born monsters.

The extent of danger is as yet not thought to be great. There is a degree of present taint in the entire air, but, unless increased, it is not sufficient to produce serious effects—probably. But not certainly. When this taint "falls-out" and enters food of animals or of human beings, some evidence suggests that it becomes gradually concentrated in bone structure or otherwise; thus even an almost imperceptible taint in the ether or in the air can be concentrated to toxic proportions. One estimate holds that the air already has in it

25% of the amount human beings could safely take; if three times its present content be added, human life would be in danger. Continued increase in this taint in a generation (this means, in the lifetime of our children) could produce the most sweeping and hideous changes in conditions on the entire planet. The prevailing scientific opinion is that if continued for a few years, we will approach a horrible borderline which, if crossed, could cause the mutation if not the end of much of the human race.

This is not the kind of situation in which any sane person cares to take chances. We literally enter an area in which failures of the fathers will be visited on the sons even to the third and fourth generation, and after.

The only presently possible method of resolving this situation is a world-wide agreement, enforced by the circumstances. For the moment, ability to explode fusion and fission atomic bombs is limited to a few great powers. But it is a trick that has been learnt, and it is steadily getting easier to do. Possibility that every nation-State may explode big or little atom bombs or may engage in other use of atomic energy which will further taint the atmosphere and further increase the "fall-out" raises possibilities too grave for any nation, great or small, to contemplate. A United Nations Committee has been assembling the facts. To this writer, it seems a practical certainty that sooner or later (and, for everyone's sake, we must hope, sooner) tacit or explicit world agreement will be reached. That agreement will command assent; it will be, factually if not theoretically, supra-national. Atmospheric poison, like disease and radio frequencies, knows no national sovereignty or boundaries. It is itself worldwide and supra-national. So the answer must be supra-national—another area of world government is emerging.

How far these disparate points in a common denominator of world action will build into a single structure can not now be foreseen. Almost certainly there will be an increasing number of situations whose circumstances demand this sort of solution.

They may be economic. For example, demand for world rule of great international waterways like the Strait of Malacca, and the canals of Suez or Panama. The Suez Canal crisis of 1956 indeed suggests that some action along that line may not be far off. In that crisis, the Egyptian government under Colonel Gamal Nasser expropriated (that is, took by "eminent domain") the shares of the Universal Suez Canal Company which is an Egyptian corporation. This, under international law, the Egyptian government had a right to do. But there was strong suspicion, backed by a few actual instances, that the Egyptian government intended to control in its own political interest the transit and traffic of the Canal, giving Egypt a powerful leverage over the wholly non-Egyptian economic life of Western Europe, the Mediterranean and other parts of the world. Discussion has thus far failed to reach (though it may later) the point of declaring the real interest: transit of the Suez Canal is a matter affecting the economy of the entire world, and the lives of hundreds of millions of men and women outside Egypt's borders. The entire world may find it necessary to "expropriate" the Egyptian nationalist interest, just as the Egyptian government has expropriated the nominally private interests of the owners of shares of the Suez Canal Company.

For that matter, the time may come when control by any one country of a single essential natural resource is subjected to overriding control by the world in general. At the moment this seems distant. Should, however, one country or small group of countries establish domination over the only supply of, let us say, oil or some similar resource essential to the life of the rest of the world the consideration of overriding world interest again might come in to play. President Woodrow Wilson forecast some such development when he discussed inclusion in his fourteen-point peace program after World War I equal access to the natural resources of the world; and the principle appears in the Atlantic Charter put forth by Prime Minister Winston Churchill and President Franklin D. Roosevelt. This development lies at the moment in the far future: it is given here as illustration to suggest the pressures toward world government solutions of certain kinds of problems.

Possibility of supra-national control over resources and activities presently within the nationalist control of each government or country commonly provokes antipathy and violent political reaction in some circles within every country. Some elements in the United States inveigh against "one worlders," "starry-eyed dreamers" who would sacrifice the sovereignty of the nation to vague schemes of world betterment, and so forth. These reactions are neither as wise—nor as unreasonable—as they sometimes seem to their adherents and opponents. In their favor it must be said that a government ceding some measure of control over any subject matter formerly considered "internal" has exchanged a situation over which it has control for one over which it will not have control; and there is always danger that "world government" may be bad government. In opposition it must be noted that the world is growing increasingly smaller, that the activity of any country increasingly affects other countries as well; that the United States, for example, might find itself in trouble because Belgium chose to withhold uranium, or Canada cut off the supply of nickel. As population grows, economics becomes more tight. Scientific development demands materials beyond national borders. The imperatives of a growing number of situations increasingly demand wider regulation than any one government can give. Situation by situation these imperatives may well demand action as circumstances demanded action in the cases of radio communication, civil aviation and world health; and as they are urgently demanding action in the case of atomic radiation. We have to be prepared for them, and to deal with them as they appear with wisdom and with charity, powerfully inspired by common sense.

3. *International Law*

International law is another long-sought goal, as an instrument of peace.

Growth of international law has proceeded thus far without benefit of the pressures which are bringing every indication of world government. Few external circumstances as a rule impose it. Until the United Nations or some similar institution is recognized as custodian of peace and public order, and until it possesses a degree of force, military, economic or moral, capable of administering and applying international law and requiring adherence to it, that law rests on the slender base of universal consent. The only "sanction" for its enforcement is the moral pressure which the rest of the world may apply to the law-breaker.

International law, like any other law, is a body of rules intended to govern conduct. Eventually, there must be that agency of enforcement and administration which as we have seen is essentially a part of "peace" or "public order." Through some centuries, these rules have grown slowly into a substantial system. It is not a thoroughly satisfactory system. Few systems of law ever are. Its greatest weakness lies in the fact that in the abstract international law may determine the legality or illegality of any act and it may decree the right of aggrieved parties to compensation or redress; but there is no way of assuring the rules will be effective. Most violations of international law never come before any court; though the International Court of Justice is established as the principal judicial organ of the United Nations, it sits in idle splendor at The Hague, hoping that occasional cases will be brought to it. More often, breach of international law results in diplomatic protest or possible diplomatic claims which accumulate dust in Foreign Office pigeonholes for decades. This is what happens when moral force is the only force behind law.

"Moral pressure," so dearly loved by pacifists and by politicians who do not wish to assume the burdens of action, is nevertheless at once the weakest, and the most powerful, force in the world. It will not stop a single bullet. It will not prevent the dispatch of a single guided missile, or prevent a single massacre. The chorus of disapprobation in other countries amounts, in the eyes of the hard-boiled "realist," to using nothing more than words. The "realist" uses weapons or other real force to effect his will in violation of accepted rules of international law. To men like Hitler and Stalin moral pressure meant little or nothing. Women could cry. Priests could condemn. Intellectuals could babble. International organizations could pass resolutions. Who cared?

Yet international law backed by this weak sanction does have power. More careful statesmen understand that. Moral disapprobation, which today expresses itself in words and pious sentiment, tends also to carry with it fear of the law-breaker. A secondary effect is to induce all hands to strengthen their armament so that they can defend their interests in realist as well as in moral terms. A third effect is to inspire some countries to band together to undertake restraint of the law-breaker, even at hazard of war, in fear lest the next victims of his uncontrolled will may be countries not yet on his schedule of attack. Continued course of law-breaking commonly leads to the formation of a coalition of countries to seek their common defense, and, if need arises, to meet the attack before attack is loosed on them. It is not an accident that the two men who most flouted international law, Mussolini in Italy, and Hitler in Germany, slowly brought into existence the coalition which finally crushed both of them. The story ended with the lynching of Mussolini by an Italian mob, and the suicide of Hitler in the ruins of his own capital.

The fact that breach of international law produces effects like these commands respect even of men and countries which have little interest in the law as such. It is the reason why capable statesmen and diplomats in planning their moves take the greatest pains to be (or at least to appear to be) on sound international legal ground. It is the reason why when Communists move to attack another country they are careful not to move Soviet or Chinese troops but to put their troops into the uniforms of the country they attack or to call them "volunteers," to insist that their campaign of conquest is a "local" revolution instead of armed aggression. (International law condemns an aggressor who nakedly moves his armies into foreign territory. But international law condemns interference in domestic problems and domestic movements, however violent. Therefore, every device is used to make an operation appear a "domestic" affair with which the rest of the world should not interfere.) This is the reason why Colonel Nasser, about to seize the Suez Canal with Communist connivance and arms as part of a Russo-Egyptian scheme to dominate the Middle-East—a vast violation of international law—was careful to proceed by expropriating the shares of the Universal Suez Canal Company, an Egyptian corporation. It is the reason why Britain and France, who rightly wanted to stop him, made a grave mistake when they simply moved their armies instead of acting as a provisional peace-keeping force until the United Nations could assure peace. It is the reason why President Truman was careful in the Korean crisis to obtain a vote of the United Nations Security Council authorizing defense of Korea instead of merely ordering the American army to move in.

Some realists say that all this is mere sentiment. If you mean to do a thing, do it. Why waste time setting the stage? This, of course, is simply mistaken—and it is also wrong. Mistaken, because the results of flouting international law in the long run can be disastrous. Wrong, because the only way the world can really come to order and law is through steady observance of international law; even lip-service is better than no service. Until the erection of the United Nations there was literally no way of establishing legality of many international actions. Now there is such a way—provided, of course, the United Nations really functions. There was substantial justification for naked force-moves in the nineteenth century and earlier because there was no way of expressing international conscience. As of today, there is; or at least, there can be.

The remarkable fact about international law is that it does continue to exist and grow, that its principles do have acceptance and that from time to time they do result in the recognition of rights and the imposition of duties. Its remarkable quality lies in the fact that although sovereign nations can not be compelled to conform to law they do so, if only because it is convenient and to their apparent "interest." There is a sufficient accumulation of matters and cases which have been thus settled or determined to indicate a slowly growing conviction by most governments that compliance with international law is to their advantage.

In result, and as a consequence of the work of many patient, often frustrated men (to whom the world owes a great debt), an impressive body of international law has been built up, commands at least lip-service, and is available for present use. If the growing pressure of the modern world convinces all governments that compliance is to their interest, or if increasing method of enforcement is found, one of the raw materials of world peace is at hand.

Whether the present body of international law is adequate may be questioned. Originally it was said that the only subjects of international law were sovereign "States." Private citizens, wronged groups, or non-governmental interests had no standing as plaintiffs or defendants. The Union of South Africa, being a sovereign State, might claim that international law was violated; but her huge Negro population (not being a sovereign State) however wronged, being merely individuals could not. This limited the usefulness of international law. More modern thinking breaks through this legalistic wall and asserts that men as men can complain that the recognized human rights have been violated and that these human rights had a measure of recognition and protection in international law itself. A noted international jurist, Professor Philip Jessup, indeed insists that there is already a "transnational" (or, if you like, "supra-national") law because human problems in some categories are universal; and as a result international law affects not merely States and governments, but individuals as well. This line of thinking is still in its infancy. But it clearly forecasts at least probability of development, as and when international law finds its institutional framework or a system of world public order which is essential to true peace.

You will not create international law by writing out a Code, or organizing a court, any more than you will organize a world government by drawing up a constitution and inviting the politicians of the world to sign it. Systems of law, like institutions, are built from the bottom up, not from the top down. When they do come into existence, when Codes of Laws are drafted, or constitutions are adopted, they have force because they describe, recognize and define an already existing body of opinion and practice.

Thus, men who dream of world order, men who work (frequently in quiet desperation) to enlarge understanding of international law, the growing body of people (like yourself as you read) who seek peace and institutions making it real, all add to the body of sentiment. In time, there will be so many of you that you can not be denied, and that politicians and statesmen can and must construct the institutions of peace.

4. *Disarmament*

A theory which dies hard is that automatic peace may be achieved through disarmament. There is not, in fact, much evidence to support this theory, and, if anything, less ground for believing that disarmament will be possible except as a result of a well-organized world peace. Save in certain limited aspects, disarmament is more likely to be a result of world peace than a cause of it.

At one time it was supposed that wars were systematically stirred up by commercial companies which manufactured armament; a United States Senate Committee headed by Senator Gerald P. Nye spent an endless amount of time endeavoring to prove this case. Fifty years ago intrigues of that kind stimulated by armament makers perhaps actually occurred though they were more actively pursued on the stage in George Bernard Shaw's "Major Barbara" than in real life. There is no ground to suggest that this sort of activity goes on today. In the free world, modern business is more afraid of war than of any other single occurrence. War means that the government steps in and takes control. It means that prices are fixed. It means enormous increase in taxation. All too frequently it means currency inflation. In point of fact, big business interests at present are probably more convincedly pacifist than any other single element in the population. In the Communist world, the politicians, not the armament plant managers, control the situation.

More serious is the theory that large armaments, and large armies, navies and air forces themselves engender explosive preconditions of war. Nations engaged in an armament race almost invariably fear and suspect each other. There are frequently military experts who believe that "preventive" war should be commenced at the time when the position of their country, in terms of armies, munitions and weapons, seems most favorable. Particularly this is true, at present, when the element of surprise, or "first round," may be determinative. A first attack with atom bombs, for example, may be sufficient to crush the enemy; if you do not do it he may; therefore, to be the attacker is to have the advantage, while to fail to be the first may cause destruction of the nation.

It would be pleasant to dismiss these considerations as merely fantastic. Unhappily we have had one disastrous illustration of just this reasoning: the Japanese air attack on the American fleet at Pearl Harbor on December 7, 1941. It was also more or less controlling doctrine in the German General Staff during Hitler's time. It is fair to note, nevertheless, that the case of Pearl Harbor is the nearest to an authenticating event—and there are other explanations for that besides mere military advantage.

The probable fact is that modern war engages too many vast consequences and involves taking too many risks for any rational group of politicians or generals to commence it merely because they command temporary military superiority. On the technical side, while attack may prostrate the opposite country, it is almost impossible to prevent reprisals which might totally devastate the attacking country. On the political side, there is no way yet devised of bringing a useful political result out of that kind of war. There remains the possibility of a madman or fanatic in control of a great government —a possibility that can not be ruled out. Adolf Hitler was undeniably psychotic. There is some reason to believe that Josef Stalin was very nearly that when he died (or was murdered) in 1953. Near-Eastern fanaticism has been apparent in some of Nasser's moves; Communist fanaticism in some of the Soviet Union's. On the other hand, the incalculable dangers of the situation make it somewhat more likely that a madman or fanatic may be restrained or assassinated by his own people before madness goes too far. But there is, none the less, some possibility that war may result from mere possession of war tools of great destructive capacity.

Lip-service to the idea of disarmament has been prevalent in most countries, yet the disarmament job never has been done. A serious attempt was made by the United States in 1922, when under the leadership of Charles Evans Hughes a naval disarmament treaty was entered into designed to stop the naval armament race between the United States, Great Britain and Japan. The attempt was noble; the result ridiculous. Certain categories of larger ships and gun bores were banned; but the fire power and range of the remaining ships and guns were increased. It may fairly be said to have been an attempt doomed to failure. For one thing, technical evolution in weapons and other things move so fast that specific limitations made today look ridiculous in the light of tomorrow's inventions. Disarmament, to be effective, has to go very nearly all the way, and in any event, no one will start disarming until everyone else does. There is always one recalcitrant who will not start, so discussions become futile. A United Nations Committee on Disarmament established under the United Nations has been discussing disarmament for the past several years, thus far without the slightest success, though the desperate attempt continues.

But we may be reaching a point at which limitation and control of certain kinds of armament will be imposed by the sheer weight of facts. This will not be true disarmament: it will rather be control of certain classes of weapons. Two such cases are already discernible: control of atomic bombs (certainly of the large ones) and control of intercontinental (perhaps small as well as large) guided missiles. We may be approaching a situation in which every nation must give up these weapons and others like them or everyone's life becomes unendurably precarious.

The growing and imminent danger of contaminating the atmosphere and resulting contamination of food and of the human body has already been noted. Guided missiles are apt to fall into a somewhat similar category.

Guided missiles at relatively short range exist now; and they can be fitted with atomic warheads. Possession of these at date of writing is, probably, limited to a few powerful neighbors: the United States, Soviet Union, Great Britain, France and Canada. So long as the range is fairly short, worry over their use is limited, though even today, great damage could be done in crowded areas like Western Europe. The danger is not yet worldwide, though experts insist that within a short space of time (say, five or six years) rocket-type missiles will have a range several thousand miles, and that bombardment of one continent by another could take place. This would mean, for example, that Chicago, Cleveland and Detroit (all high-priority targets because of their manufactures) could be bombed by missiles discharged from Leningrad or Archangel or that rockets carrying hydrogen war heads might be loosed from Buenos Aires against Cairo. Probably within fifteen years it will be possible to bomb any place on the planet from any other place on the planet.

Should the United States decide to start that kind of war (which God forbid), she might from a rocket station in Kansas plant hydrogen bombs in every capital in the world. Moscow could do the same from Novaya Zemlya or Stalingrad. Neither is likely to try, for one very simple reason. The first bombing would undoubtedly reduce the life of the bombed country to hideous devastation. But no such attack could safely assure that from the ruins of the country so attacked there would not come an answering volley which would crush the attacking country with equal horror. It still is impossible at once to devastate the entire surface of any large country. Because of this, in the long run, neither country will gain too much by insisting on having these weapons in their hands when neither dares to use them. There is at least a theoretical basis for limitation.

Capacity to use weapons of this kind would rapidly cease to be the monopoly of a few great nations. With crews to use them they can be "lent" or given to other countries. In time, they will be capable of manufacture by almost anyone. Once that takes place, the tiniest country, say, Egypt, Denmark or Ecuador, Thailand, Afghanistan or Iceland, could threaten the world or any part of it as effectively as the Soviet Union, Great Britain or the United States. The greatest Power in the world would then exist by sufferance of the smallest. Also, the danger would be greater. Large Powers as a rule tend to become somewhat more responsible and more restrained than many smaller ones in these matters, if only because they have more to lose. Smaller countries, especially those whose reactions are semi-primitive, or whose mental habits permit them to consider their own death as glorious provided they destroy enough of their enemies, tend to be less responsible. Once these weapons are available to everyone, there is the possibility that guided intercontinental missiles carrying hydrogen warheads might be loosed by an inflamed Cairo mob; or that a band of defeated, desperate revolutionaries in some Asian or African city might in their death-struggle use this type of destruction as a last measure of defiance.

These risks are not great now. They will become increasingly real in the coming years. Guided missiles and atomic bombs were Buck Rogers fantasies until World War II. The atomic bomb became a reality in 1945. Limited guided missiles became manageable at least as early as 1953. In ten or fifteen years, more ability to manufacture and use these weapons is likely to be common throughout the world.

Circumstances at this point impose control; and when they do, there will be agreement, and that agreement will be kept.

It will then become at least permissible to hope that the area of agreement imposed by circumstances may be increased by good sense. For by that time we may be dealing, not merely with simple destruction by bombing but with more sweeping though creeping destruction—by contamination, let us say, of the Gulf Stream, or of an entire sea. The human race will then have to decide whether it wishes to allow any tiny fraction of it to wield power to destroy great parts of the rest of it. We may then begin, at long last, to deal rationally with the subject of disarmament.

Possibly even earlier, though we can not tell. It is a goal which appears unattainable. Equally, it is one which must never be abandoned.

As we explore this long vista of unabandoned, disappointed dreams it is easy to be discouraged. Discouragement is natural—and unwarranted. Serious students of history know that theoretical conceptions of yesterday tend to become the desires of today and to crystallize into sudden action tomorrow. An American author, James Branch Cabell, once observed that man is the only animal who plays ape to his own dreams. Probably dreamers of yesterday have already traced the plans or at least indicated the major outlines of today's and tomorrow's institutions. This is why no realist worth his salt fails to respect and pay attention to the great dreams, however impractical, of the idealist. The day is likely to come when their thinking has reached so far into public opinion that realism demands its satisfaction. The twentieth century has proved that if it has proved nothing else. Actually, the intelligent realist is little more than a jobber-contractor and construction manager who builds into today's structures the conceptions of yesterday's thinkers and intellectuals—(the "Lords Spiritual," as we observed in the beginning) —as time and circumstances require, and as building materials become available.

5. *The United Nations*

Attempts to create an institution which should guarantee peace go back a long time. For the purposes of this study, we need not go over the historical record. Enough to say that at the close of World War I, under the inspiration of Woodrow Wilson, the old "League of Nations" was created. Its Covenant entered into force on January 10, 1920. But the United States had already changed its mind; President Wilson had made it the primary issue in the Presidential campaign of that year. In November, 1920, the election of President Warren G. Harding decisively registered American unwillingness to enter the new international institution.

The League of Nations Covenant had many defects, not least of them being that it was primarily a league of the victors in World War I. A greater defect was that it failed to have direct contact with peoples and, of course, had no force to compel compliance with its decisions. Undoubtedly it did engage the best of the efforts of many men in many nations. But it could not mobilize action sufficient to prevent Mussolini's Italy from breaking treaties, intervening in the Spanish Revolution, and generally terrorizing the Mediterranean. It could not take effective measures restraining Hitler from gradually converting the German Republic into an imperialist Nazi empire. It is the nature of any government that it ceases to exist the moment its inability to govern is demonstrated. For practical purposes the League was dead in 1938.

World War II created a different situation. As always, the agony of war looses the hopes of peoples for permanent peace. These were crystallized in some sense when Franklin D. Roosevelt and Prime Minister Churchill met on the deck of an American warship off the Canadian coast and drew up the declaration of "common principles" known to the world as "The Atlantic Charter." This document forecast not only principles of peace but the creation of some permanent system for assuring it.

That was in August, 1941. Less than six months later the United States was at war with the Axis coalition. President Roosevelt then proposed an agreement designed to bind together the many countries defending themselves against the Axis Powers. The writer, with Dr. Herbert Feis, drafted a declaration binding all these countries, the Soviet Union included, not to make a separate peace or armistice with the enemy and also declaring that they all subscribed "to the common program of purposes and principles embodied in the joint declaration * * * known as the Atlantic Charter." It remained to give this document a name. President Roosevelt pondered it overnight, and (as he recounted the story to the writer) went to visit Winston Churchill, then a guest at the White House, early in the morning. The British Prime Minister was in the bathtub. President Roosevelt called to him, "I suggest we call this 'Declaration by United Nations.' " Churchill put his head under water and came up with a spout. "I think it will do," he said. So the declaration, and from it the present world organization, got its name. It was signed on January 1, 1942, by twenty-six governments.

Preparatory conversations looking towards a world peace-keeping organization were conducted during the war. In October, 1943, Secretary Cordell Hull visited the Soviet Union. He obtained the "Moscow Declaration" of which one clause provided that "the united action pledged for prosecution of the war will be continued for the organization and maintenance of peace and security." In August and September of 1944 conferences were held at the famous estate of Dumbarton Oaks in Washington between representatives of Great Britain, the United States, the Soviet Union and, a little later, of China (then, not Communist). A draft charter was prepared. As the war moved to its end, a conference was held in San Francisco, resulting in the signature there, on June 26, 1945, of the "Charter of the United Nations." By it the organization of the United Nations was constituted as it exists today.

The United Nations did more than merely organize a new League. It picked up and attempted to create so far as possible the existing institutions which might give a m∪asure of peace to the world. Its central function was, of course, adjustment and settlement of international disputes by means other than war. To give effect to that, the United Nations Security Council was to sit in permanent session; the United Nations alone has, in theory, the right to authorize and to make legitimate use of force by any nation. Its design contemplated that it was to have control over an international force of some kind, though this has never been effectively organized save for the specific purpose of repelling Communist attack in Korea, for minor operations, and, more recently, for occupation of the Suez Canal area.

In addition, there was established the International Court of Justice, which continued in slightly different terms the Permanent Court of International Justice at The Hague which had been formed in 1907.

Specialized agencies were also contemplated, and they have been added to the United Nations group of institutions. The International Civil Aviation Organization (ICAO), devised to function as an agency in the United Nations, had been organized in December, 1944, at a conference over which the writer presided. It has its headquarters in Montreal. The International Labor Office (ILO) which had been formed in 1920 for the purpose of exchanging views and collecting information was carried forward in amended form. It has headquarters in Geneva. An Economic and Social Council was set up into whose operations the international labor organization was integrated. The International Telecommunication Union, foreshadowed in the old Cairo Convention but given form in 1947, was later coopted under the same general authority.

Provision was made for regional pacts in the interest of common defense and regional welfare, of which the Inter-American Pact, agreed to at Chapultepec, Mexico, in 1945, later given form by the Treaty of Rio de Janeiro in 1947, was the earliest. The North Atlantic Treaty Organization (NATO) created in 1949 was the most powerful. Other less far-reaching agreements have been concluded.

Most important of the conceptions was the theory that use of force in international matters was illegitimate, except in immediate defence, or as authorized by the United Nations—or pending action by the United Nations, by a regional peace-keeping authority. This meant, in substance, that the use of armed force by any nation to settle a controversy with any other nation was an outlaw proceeding, and that it was the duty of the entire world through the institution of the United Nations promptly to end such outlaw use and to settle the controversy itself. This was a conscious attempt to create an institution in which "the peace of the world" belonged. It took account of the principal components which, we noted, make up the vast and delicate balance we call "peace." There was to be a system of order; the Security Council, or, if need be, the General Assembly of the United Nations, had jurisdiction over that. There was to be a system of law in settling disputes: the Court of International Justice was to discharge that function. There were to be specialized agencies to deal with the essential needs of international life: economic problems, telecommunication, aviation, labor standards. A little later came the specialized agency for world health.

There was also outlined a system of "trusteeship" which had general jurisdiction over colonial areas. It is designed to assure that the governments of such areas shall work for the welfare of the peoples within them, and that colonies shall gradually be brought to a point where they could become independent nations as the old imperial system comes to an end.

This was, and is, the most nearly complete system for giving a measure of world order and world peace ever devised. It falls far short of completeness. It still depends primarily on governments, and there is always danger either that a majority of governments will not wish to act in the situation, or that one government or group of governments so strong that it or they can not be coerced will decline to accept a world system or conform to United Nations action. Also, there is danger that a majority of governments in the United Nations Assembly will create an intolerable situation for some part of the world. Critics of the United Nations have sometimes asserted that this made the entire plan meaningless. When law or concrete action is necessary you can not be sure that the Assembly will take the necessary action. True, but no one has yet advocated dissolving the government of the United States because the Congress of the United States does not always legislate promptly or effectively when problems press. It is said that the Security Council is useless because the "veto" power has been reserved to five countries: United States, Great Britain, Soviet Union, China and France. This objection has force, but there is no way to overcome it now. None of the great Powers (least of all the United States) are quite prepared to be bound, without their consent, by actions of the Security Council. In any case it is their active assent and cooperation that is needed—not the legalistic fact of a majority vote, supposed to bind the dissenters. The institution is not yet strong enough for that, simply because there has not as yet been time and experience sufficient to build universal acceptance of and solid faith in the institution. As the United Nations increasingly builds its prestige, that day, one must hope, will come. Yet, for that matter, no one proposes throwing overboard the Supreme Court of the United States because it occasionally makes a decision which it can not enforce.

In less crucial detail there are many criticisms which have force. Admission of new members of United Nations rests in large measure at the will of the dominant members so that some important nations are compelled to remain outside. Obviously the concept of the United Nations also requires that all nations shall be in it and not out of it. But equally, to be inside and to be a member in good standing does presuppose good-faith acceptance by the entering nation of the primary obligations of the United Nations: to settle affairs peacefully without use of force. It was, for example, perfectly sound to refuse to entertain an application by Communist China for admission to the United Nations while her troops were fighting for the purpose of seizing South Korea. It would have been mere mockery for her to join in a pledge that she accepted an obligation "not to resort to war" or

> "to refrain in her international relations from the threat or use of force against the territorial integrity or political independence of any State or in any other matter inconsistent with the purpose of United Nations."

Yet, in the main, the United Nations contemplates a universal system of which every State shall be a member, in which every State renounces the use of unauthorized force and to which every State will bring any situation which threatens a breach of peace. The companion agencies are designed to consider and act on problems which require solution if human beings are to live in moderate comfort and safety.

The United Nations is already an institution: this has been accomplished during its first ten struggling years. It is not yet a wholly strong institution. Were two or three powerful nations to secede, or were many weak nations to act irresponsibly, it might become powerless to discharge its function of compelling order, and simultaneously providing law and administration of law in which grievances could be stated and wrongs redressed. Yet in the period of its existence the world has seen mighty tensions—for example the Cold War between the Free World and the Communist world. Also the tense animosities in the Middle East, the Soviet drive to bring all that region into her Empire; and the great problems occurring as colony after colony sought independence from the old imperial system. Despite these mighty collisions, no great Power has proposed to secede, nor proposes to do so at the present time. Apparently, on balance, the danger of being out is infinitely greater than the danger of being in. The chance of being compelled to refrain from action or of being coerced by unjust action within the United Nations is less than the danger of attempt to be alone.

The writer believes that there is growing confidence in the United Nations and that as in the case of the United States of America and its Supreme Court a century and half ago, the institution is establishing itself bit by bit, and case by case, gaining strength and standing and acceptance as it meets the crises of the time. Its history is too short to forecast its permanence and solid establishment: it is still weak enough so that it could be wrecked. But problem by problem and day by day it looks better as a peace-keeper, and more able to meet problems before they lead to war. Meanwhile, war itself as an alternative looks more horrible, less productive, more likely to result in hideous carnage in which there can be no victor. We have moved a long way since 1938 when the old League of Nations expired. Indeed, we have moved a long way since 1945 when the United Nations was little more than words on paper and a dream and hope in the hearts of many men.

For the strength of the league rests precisely on the fact that it does recognize and does give defined form to a body of sentiment which is practically universal. In this respect it has the basis of a true institution and goes beyond the status of a mere intellectual's dream. It picks up and carries forward the work of some centuries in international law. It gives effect to those areas of human action in which world regulation of some kind imposes itself by circumstance. It finds its moral support in the condemnation of war, and practical support in the fear of what war does and may do. It offers hope, perhaps tenuous, but still appreciable, in the areas of economic adjustment, relief from distress and relief from the burdens of armament.

All these motives have existed for a long time; this is why when the old League of Nations failed, its equivalent, or rather a better instrument with the same purposes, had to be reinvented. If the United Nations were to dissolve tomorrow, the world whether in peace or in catastrophe would have to get at the task of re-creating it, just as when the Confederated States of America formed in 1775 failed to meet problems, the federal union of the United States of America had to be formed in 1787. The United Nations is not merely a dream of "one worlders" though it certainly embraces their dream. It is an institutional expression of universal necessity.

Will crises arise which rip the United Nations apart? Perhaps; but crises do not last forever, and if that happened we should be grieving over the time lost, binding up the wounds—and desperately seeking to re-establish the United Nations. Perhaps the job could be better done. More likely, as it seems to me, the United Nations will emerge crisis by crisis in better and stronger position. It will have its ups and its downs. Some crises will be met with courage and strength. Others will perhaps be skimped or avoided. The record so far is good; the average of capacity has proved high as international affairs go. There is, in the writer's judgment, more likelihood that the United Nations will grow in prestige and strength than that it will crack up.

At all events, sane Americans must hope so. Absent the United Nations, our country would enter a period of international anarchy at the precise time when anarchy would be most costly to us—leaving aside consideration of the rest of the world. A late twentieth-century war fought with weapons of poison and blast already available would be enough to cripple our entire civilization—if it did not destroy our civilization altogether.

These are large phrases, not to be used lightly. That they are not used lightly will be clear to anyone who cares, for example, to read the National Academy of Science-National Research Council report on the biological effects of atomic radiation, or who has had the slightest acquaintance with the research of the Air War College of the United States Air Force. It is a case of finding viable organization of world affairs, or of awaiting the end of this phase of human life on our shrinking planet. The United Nations has made a fair start towards becoming the means by which that organization can be attained.

Peace-makers, the New Testament promises, will be called the children of God. When such men and women appear, there will be both idealists and realists among them. They will have earned their blessing.

CHAPTER Three

ECONOMIC TOOLS FOR
PROMOTING PEACE

1

THE REVOLUTIONS of the nineteenth and early twentieth centuries forcibly brought forward the idea that individuals were entitled to at least a minimal economic position. Marxists went further, asserting that the entire position of man was based on his economic status. Liberals, without thus discarding the spiritual and intellectual development of personality as the chief end, nevertheless believed that man though endowed with all political rights could not be really free while he was condemned to a life of grinding poverty, misery, or hunger.

Simultaneously, the idea emerged (in the teeth of a good deal of history) that peace was chiefly bound up with economic problems. Marxists maintained that capitalist countries inevitably needed markets outside their own country after they had reached a certain period of development. They then were constrained to invade and make imperialist colonies of underdeveloped areas, or weaker countries. Eventually, capitalist countries inevitably clashed: French or German capitalism would find itself struggling against and at last making war on English or American capitalists for markets in Africa, Asia or other "colonial" areas. Factually, in the nineteenth century, commercial interests did, when the competitive struggle became acute, cause their governments to take diplomatic action, and sometimes military action, to secure control of the areas involved. Even today accepted Marxist doctrine assumes that capitalist countries will eventually go to war with each other over markets. Peace, it was therefore thought, required a new handling of world economics.

The Marxian description was not wholly inaccurate as a description of world affairs in the seventeenth and eighteenth centuries. The British government had backed the operations of the British East India Company and that company actually was a forerunner of empire. Spain and Britain had fought for control of the seaways. The nineteenth and early twentieth centuries did somewhat better. The French pushed into North Africa, just as the British had pushed into Egypt. On one occasion the two systems clashed in 1903 on the Egyptian border at Fashoda, but subsequent negotiation avoided war. German policy under Kaiser Wilhelm II had been to demand a share of colonial empire for the German Reich; this was the thrust of its demand for "a place in the sun" and had obtained some measure of satisfaction.

Nonetheless, in the nineteenth and twentieth centuries, the imperialist (or capitalist) powers had, on the whole, avoided wars for strictly economic reasons—wars which they had been unable to avoid in the sixteenth and seventeenth centuries. Certainly they avoided major wars for economic advantage, though the Russo-Japanese War may be an exception.

Though nations had developed some ability to accommodate themselves in economic matters, one school of thought (Economic Determinism) nevertheless steadily maintained that economic maladjustment must be a powerful contributing cause of war. It is often said even now that a poor country cannot live alongside a rich country without substantial danger that peace will be broken, and that a population existing in poverty will either tempt the strength of a more prosperous neighbor, or will be tempted to try to secure by force the economic advantages of those nearby.

Realistic observation scarcely supports the thesis. The United States, an immensely prosperous country, has lived in substantial peace with Mexico, a relatively poor country, for a century. The strains between the two countries in the decade from 1914 to 1924 arose less from economic causes than from disorders in Mexico following the fall of Porfirio Diaz in 1910. Friendly Mexican-American relations survived the expropriation by the Government of Mexico of American and British-owned oil fields in 1941. A better illustration of danger to peace arising from economic disparity is in the Far East. The Japanese empire unquestionably coveted the markets and commercial privileges capable of being developed in China and in Southeast Asia. The Japanese doctrine of an Asian "co-prosperity sphere" (a euphemism for an enlarged Japanese empire) did arise concurrently with the growing power of the Japanese military party. Economic considerations undoubtedly did play a great part in the decision of the Japanese government to attempt the seizure of a part of China (the Shantung area) after World War I, and again to launch an invasion of China by manufacturing the "incident" of the Marco Polo Bridge in 1937. It is true that island Japan, like island Britain, depends for her national existence on her ability to draw raw material from outside her own country, and to export her manufactures to foreign markets. Even so, there is no clear evidence that the militarist party in Japan was animated primarily by economic motives, just as there is no compelling evidence that the German industrialists who backed Hitler in his internal schemes in 1933 were the moving force leading to his policy of foreign aggression. The writer cannot, therefore, agree that economic considerations are anything more than a contributing factor entering into the vast complex of forces which determine war or peace.

Nevertheless, economic factors are of first importance in international relations. Without question, each country should and must concern itself with the economic conditions of its neighbors as well as of itself. The reasons are twofold.

The first, and most important, is idealist in character. Much of the human race is—fortunately—so constituted that it cannot unconcernedly watch a neighboring people struggling with misery. Alternatively, a people in misery and dissatisfied cannot indefinitely

observe an adjacent population in great prosperity without wondering whether the cause of disparity does not lie, at least partly,
in international relations. Nondiplomatic problems invariably arise.
A prosperous country may seek cheap labor from its depressed
neighbors, importing—with such labor—problems for future generations of untold complexity. (The most pressing American problems today—race relations in the South and on the Pacific slope
—proceed directly from importation of cheap labor in times past.)
A poor country seeks to better its position by exporting goods and
underselling in foreign markets; this leads to tariffs, reprisals and
other disturbances of trade relations. No country, certainly not the
United States, can show a clean bill of health in dealing with these
problems. They emerge as problems of immigration or of tariffs
and trade restrictions, or as internal campaigns, "Buy American,"
"Buy British," and the like.

On the cold diplomatic side, tensions thus created eventually
may shift world balances of power. A people seeking economic
improvement tends to throw in its fortunes with that nation or
group of nations most hospitable to its economic interests. If, for
example, the Western world were to refuse to purchase the products of the now renascent Germany and Japan, those countries
would almost necessarily be compelled to seek closer working relations respectively with the Soviet Union and Communist China. In
each case, a price could be exacted. The Soviet Union could insist
(and is insisting now) that to obtain hospitable economic treat-
ment, present-day Germany must abandon the NATO alliance.
Communist China would undoubtedly seek to detach Japan from
her present partnership with the United States and the West. If
neither result has yet come to pass, it is partly because the United
States has wisely given economic support in both countries, and
partly because neither the Soviet Union nor China has the kind of
economy at present which can offer to Germany and Japan, respectively, enough economic advantage to counterbalance their relations with the West.

But it would be a bold prophet who asserted that this condition
would last indefinitely. In the case of Soviet Russia, it is clear that

in a relatively few years she will achieve an economy comparable to that of the United States. The conclusion must be that though economic relations may not be a prime cause leading to peace or war, they are a powerful contributing consideration determining the alignment of nations. Such alignment may prove decisive in case political, philosophical, or emotional factors lead to war. Put differently, economic factors have not, of recent years, caused wars. They may have, and in future probably can determine what alliances and groupings will take place, and which group wins a war in the event of its occurrence.

2

The not unusual concurrence of idealist and realist factors have therefore pushed forward the problem of economic arrangements tending to make for greater international stability. These may be called economic "tools" for peace—at all events, they are powerful contributing forces to a state of affairs in which war may be less likely to break out, or may appear less attractive to one or another group.

Economic measures for peace-keeping differ widely from political operations. For political operations turn largely on the attitudes of peoples, and are thus more or less within the control of peoples themselves. Economics, however (besides being a dismal science), is severely limited in impact at any given moment of time. The twentieth century has demonstrated that in aggregate economic resources and economic capabilities are potentially almost unlimited (at all events no limit has yet been verifiable); but at any given moment and place there are only definable supplies of goods, natural resources and services. There is only a definable present "effective demand" or willingness to consume products. We are thus not operating in the unlimited plane of idealism, but are limited by actual supply, actual effective demand, actual transport facilities, actual willingness to exchange.

We can calculate forward. We can say that in the predictable future at a stated price level, there will be a calculable increase in the supply, let us say, of copper or sugar. We can say that in the event that a given national economy, for example that of Spain, increases in productivity and prosperity, it will then consume a predictable additional amount of copper or sugar. In any case, international economic arrangements have to be based on existing circumstances modified by estimates of the more or less predictable future. They can rarely go beyond this. The fallacies of attempting economic arrangements beyond present or predictable future limits are obvious; attempts to build on strictly idealistic grounds are doomed to disappointment. For this reason, perhaps, attempts made in the United Nations, and also in the Organization of American States, to set up declarations of the "economic rights of man" are little more than pious expressions of hope to the extent that they overpass present economic capacity or reasonably predictable increase in that capacity over a relatively short span of time. Properly speaking, political tools for peacemaking are essentially philosophical and idealist. Properly speaking, economic tools are essentially matters of finance, engineering and transport.

With, however, one stunning qualification. Economic capacity is the result of the minds of men, of their background and motivation, their will, psychology, religion or philosophy translated into social organization. Economists know little about this: they merely recognize the fact. A group of Mormons could push into a singularly unpromising area in the Rocky Mountains and in a relatively short time, substantially without aid from the outside, build the strong, prosperous and capable community which is today the State of Utah. A group of men and women, the same in number, but with a different religious, philosophical or educational orientation, attempting a like settlement, might either have starved to death or produced a flabby community of no particular significance. There is an interaction between political and philosophical orientation and tangible economic engineering. In evaluating any measure of international economics—whether it be a credit offered by the United States Treasury or the Federal Reserve Bank to the government of Brazil or Great Britain or Vietnam in Indo-China, or a capital loan made by the Export-Import Bank to finance the construction of a hydroelectric power development in Chile or India, whether it be a price stabilization agreement to assure an orderly price structure for sugar or wheat, or encouragement given to an American company like Sears, Roebuck & Company to establish stores in South America—this idealist factor is always present. In some situations, the result will be to stimulate within the country economic forces which will make for the growth of that country and the prosperity of its people. In others, the measure may temporarily prolong a period within which the economy of a country does not face its own problems but lives on borrowed time—and money.

In consequence, economic measures designed to assist international relations and to create a basis within which peace is more easily kept must be judged by two standards. The first is whether, in terms of straight production of goods and services and their distribution, the specific objectives are good in themselves. "Good" in this sense means, do they provide more goods and services, and assist in assuring that goods and services shall actually meet and satisfy human needs. The second criterion is whether the measures tend to stimulate creation. Do they in result start a chain reaction so that the production and distribution stimulated in turn brings about greater will and capacity for more production.

This is why many of the phrases frequently used are really meaningless. It is loosely said, for example, that countries having capital should "export" capital to those which do not. But export of capital may mean any one of several things. Capital may be invested, for example, in a copper mine or an oil well in a foreign country. Let us assume the enterprise is wholly owned, organized and staffed by the capital exporting country—say Britain or the United States. The product is taken out of the ground and shipped elsewhere for sale. The profits will build up in the home office of the enterprise—New York or London. When the operation is over, the capital has been returned, let us hope with a profit, to the country of export. Little necessarily remains in the country where it was spent save a worked-out mine or a depleted oil field. The only receipt the country thus "developed" obtains is the fact that during a certain period of time laborers are paid for their work; there is no net increment, or only a small increment to the life of the country.

Contrast that with a different form of capital export. Sears, Roebuck & Company, for instance, has invested a considerable amount of capital in Sears, Roebuck stores in Brazil. In addition to that, they have by appropriate buying contracts stimulated the manufacture of goods in Brazil; their representatives say rather proudly that more than nine-tenths of all the goods they handle are Brazilian. The net result not only distributes goods and services in Brazil; it stimulates Brazilian enterprise to supply such goods and services, and thus acts as a catalyzer. A naked loan to a foreign government—say by buying the bonds of Peru or of Haiti—gives to the governments of those countries funds which they may spend. These may be spent to buy arms, or build government buildings, or to build roads or electric power plants, as the case may be. The first leaves nothing behind but a debt which the taxpayers of the country have to pay. The second leaves a tangible monument, which may or may not be productive. The third may open up a new region and stimulate activity. Thus the problem is not merely one of export capital; it is also that of supplying an element in the economic situation which leads to greater lasting productivity within the country receiving it, leaving behind an increment of permanent productiveness.

End product of capital export thus really depends *on the forces within the country which the capital can liberate;* this, in turn, depends upon the human resources of energy, intelligence, honesty, and industry available within the country which receives it. The United States, for example, did receive a very limited amount of capital from Europe a century ago, but the bulk of its capital it manufactured for itself because of the habits and education of its people. Other countries of comparable size and resources have not done so well. Even today, formation of capital is not thoroughly understood by economists; yet the problem of capital export on analysis becomes quite as much that of inducing capital formation than of direct capital export.

The moral to be drawn is that in any economic operation in international affairs, the human or idealistic dimension is perhaps quite as important as the cold arithmetical calculations of cost, probable production, market for the product, etc. Especially when economic plans are being drawn to assist the maintenance of peace, political and psychological factors are at least as important as the arithmetic—although prima facie the arithmetic limit must prevail.

3

With these considerations in mind, we may examine some of the principal economic expedients which have been used.

Economic instruments in aid of reconstruction of peace in the post-war period have been many. They fall into four main classes:

1. First, there are the measures and organizations designed to liberalize trade and reduce trade barriers—the theory being that trade and commerce between nations betters their economic position and creates a better atmosphere for the organization of peace.

2. The second group, intimately connected with the first, consists of financial instrumentalities whose object is to relieve international economy from the strains caused by unbalance in foreign exchange. Obviously unless all trade is to be by by barter, settlements have to be made in money. But, in a world in which seventy odd countries insist on having their own currency, unless each country's trade is roughly in balance (that is unless its exports are roughly equal to its imports) its currency and exchange rate will go high or low. Further, since nations will sell and export to some countries and buy and import from others, the credits they gain when they sell have to be balanced somehow with the debts they incur when they buy. Part of the price each country pays for nationalism in finance is the danger of having its national money so cheap that it will buy nothing abroad, or so dear that nobody can afford to buy from it.

3. Third is the process of direct relief—straight out loans without real expectation of repayment or outright gifts by a coun-

try or group of countries to another country or countries for the purpose of assisting them through an assumedly temporary crisis.

4. Fourth, there are arrangements, some private and some public, looking towards direct international or supra-national economic organisms doing their own trading, their own distribution, their own production, their own banking, and the like.

All of these methods are technical, and any one of them has behind it a literature capable of filling a library section. One of the best single volumes on the subject, *Trade and Payments in Western Europe—A Study in Economic Cooperation, 1947–1951*, by William Diebold, Jr., was published by the Council on Foreign Relations in 1952. The European experience, comprising as it still does the great bulk of the world's international trade, lies at the heart of the problem. To be complete, such a study would have to add studies on the Asian economic measures under the so-called "Colombo Plan" and on some of the principal measures taken between the United States and various of the Latin American countries in the Western Hemisphere.

The first and most traditional type of measure is aimed at reducing trade barriers and thereby making expanded commerce between nations more nearly possible. The problem is politically complex in the extreme. Liberalizing trade is a splendid principle; Secretary Cordell Hull spent his life endeavoring to give effect to this policy. But, in a tightly organized world, when any country sells to any other country it must sell something that that country does not produce, else it takes a customer away from the local producer. When, for example, European steel or Japanese textiles sell in the United States, there is an immediate outcry from the American steel or textile mills that foreign interests are taking the bread out of the mouths of American producers and workmen, and demanding tariff or other trade restriction protecting the American. Foreign countries operate in exactly the same manner. Especially after World War II, trade restriction took a somewhat new form. Governments estimated how much of certain kinds of products they were prepared to purchase from other countries, and fixed "quotas" of allowable imports. Frequently they required agreement by the countries from which they were prepared to buy, that these should in return purchase stated products from them. Other devices even more restrictive were adopted.

The dilemma posed was real. In classical economics, each country should produce what it can manufacture for export most efficiently. It could, presumably, sell these goods in a free market more cheaply than others. It would be more advantageous to produce such goods and sell them and in turn buy more cheaply other goods from the most efficient foreign producer than to try to develop a self-sufficient economy.

Unhappily, in this, as in applying other aspects of *laissez-faire* economics, the human waste can be considerable. It is no consolation whatever to an American textile mill driven to bankruptcy by foreign competition to be told that the rest of the United States has gained by the process, since it bought foreign textiles at a lower price. Further, the effect of such an arrangement is always to give advantage to the highly industrialized and technically efficient countries. The writer was on the Board of Directors of the Export-Import Bank when a loan was granted to Brazil for the purpose of constructing its first steel plant—the famous Volta Redonda plant of today. American steel producers argued against it, contending, rightly, that they could sell steel to Brazil at a price less than Brazil's cost of production. The fact was true. But it did not answer the economic argument of Brazil: she could not, indefinitely, export agricultural produce in amounts sufficient to purchase her rapidly growing need for steel. In effect, *laissez-faire* economics would mean that Brazilian purchases would always be greater than Brazilian exports; Brazilian exchange would drop rapidly; in time Brazilians, with their own money, could not buy at any reasonable price (in their own currency) the products they needed from abroad. The logic of that would suggest that Brazil should annex herself to some steel producing country—a *reductio ad absurdum* which obviously appeals to nobody.

As long as the world is cut up into a considerable number of countries of varying degrees of size, there appears to be only one practicable approach. Each country must produce a considerable portion of its needs of all kinds, or, at least, must produce sufficiently for itself so that the amount and variety of products it must buy from abroad do not reach unmanageable amounts. Large and well-developed countries, such as the United States and probably such as the Soviet Union, can do this by themselves at present. Smaller or less developed countries have to find their way into regional arrangements by which each region is, though by no means self-sufficient, nearly enough so to be able to handle the situation. At all events, up to date, no better method has been found.

The two first groups of economic instruments mentioned above are really groping in this direction. In a rather desperate attempt to open trade after the war, each country negotiated trade agreements with its neighbors; some 200 of these were in existence at the end of 1947. At that time these were approaching shipwreck on the hard financial rock of unbalanced exchange. The country that needed more kept on buying more, or trying to. The supplying country naturally wanted payment but the buying country had insufficient money of the supplier, and the supplier frequently was unwilling to accept payment in the buyer's currency, or in the goods the buyer had to offer in exchange. An attempt was therefore made to meet the situation financially.

By now the Marshall Plan had come into existence, and with it, the Organization for European Economic Cooperation, which exists today. Its long-range objective was stated to be "integration" of European economy. Ideally this would mean eventually a single economic system for the seventeen countries constituting it, as complete, perhaps as the economic system in which the 48 American states operate within the United States. Practically, of course, the group could only stimulate gradually increasing connections or devices so that national frontiers would be less of a barrier than they have been heretofore.

An early fruit of this grouping of countries was a European "Payments Agreement" granting to each country the right to draw exchange—notably dollars or gold—from the group in order to pay its balances. This went through various stages and forms; out of it came the European Payments Union of today, which has functioned since 1950. In part, the European Payments Union must be ascribed to the initiative of Mr. Paul Hoffman, at that time Administrator of the Marshall Plan organization (known as "E.C.A.," the initials standing for "Economic Cooperation Administration"). He had been hoping that the European economy would move towards integration. On the financial side, therefore, he sought an arrangement relieving the endless difficulties arising because the European countries in their post-war situation could not balance their exports and their imports. When they could export, unhappily they often could not export to countries which could pay "hard" currency (money having a high value) and, therefore, could not pay for purchases from countries requiring payment in such currency. After complex negotiation, the European Payments Union was evolved.

Under it, the Bank for International Settlements (an institution born out of difficulties after World War I), calculates the debtor and creditor position of each country in the Union every month, and settles balances. Between times, the central banks of each member country grant to other countries whatever credit is necessary to keep trade and payments moving. Each government settles its accounts with the Union. Part of the debt must be settled either in gold or dollars; the rest can be covered by credit or debit entries as the case may be. To start the Union off, 350 million dollars were given to the Union as working capital by the Economic Cooperation Administration. The members of the Union manage the organization through a council of seven. There are provisions which make it to the advantage of each country to endeavor to keep its trade in balance. The European Payments Union has not needed further assistance from the United States and can, at least in part, tend towards broader commerce between European countries.

This is a strictly regional organization. Conceivably, if the world ceased to be divided into two concrete and opposed systems—the Communist and the free world system—the Union and regional organizations like it might become obstacles to a single world system. For that reason, both in the United States and Great Britain, whose ultimate objective is a free-world commercial system, there have been doubts and criticisms. These are justified in the general sense that any regional system is a makeshift, or "second-best." But economic diplomacy, like political diplomacy, is the art of the possible. Since World War II, we have not had a world working on a single economic system as we did during the Victorian Age. The regional system accomplishes a partial transition from the inadequate nationalist economics of separate small countries to an economic system for a region more or less capable of handling its own needs. When a full world system can be developed (as one day it must emerge, though who knows when), it should be possible to make the transition from the regional to a world-wide system— possibly with less difficulty than has been encountered in building the regional system.

Financial instrumentalities, however, really relate to symptoms and not to causes. They are apt to emerge first because economic troubles present themselves commonly as financial problems: this country, or this merchant, must buy but cannot pay except in currency of his own country which no one else wants. Behind that local crisis is the deeper problem: should not international trade and economics be so handled that the problem need not arise? In the Victorian world, commerce between countries was sufficiently widespread and sufficiently in balance so that these problems as a rule did not become unbearably acute. Primarily, all countries being less populous and developed were more or less self-sufficient. International trade was a relatively narrow margin over internal national economics which in the main took care of themselves. The twentieth century world allows no such easy assumption. When populations were satisfied to live at or near a subsistence level, to shelter themselves in houses built of local materials, to clothe themselves in fabric that could be spun and woven from local flocks, to feed themselves with the products of their own soil, their need for foreign commerce was not great. At the time of the American Revolution (which was brought on in part by a British attempt to restrict American commerce), the dispute arose over relatively small items of which the thirteen American colonies had need. Tea, for example, spices, sugar, luxuries, were items which had to be sought abroad.

A modern population, however, will need great quantities of products which may not be found within its borders. For example, the world moves largely on wheels driven by petroleum, and all countries do not have oil wells. Metals of all kinds, standard as well as rare, are essential; but all countries do not have iron ore plus coal to smelt it, or copper, zinc, lead, tin and so forth. Some of the staple products indeed whose use is growing rapidly are concentrated in a very few countries—for instance, tin, which is supplied chiefly by Malaya and Bolivia, or rubber supplied chiefly from southeast Asia. The small margins of international commerce which would supply the needs of an eighteenth or even a nineteenth century country would be insufficient to keep its economic life going for more than a short time today. As populations increase, and even more as they demand a standard of living consonant with modern technical production, necessity for international commerce increases.

Recognizing this, some countries, notably Belgium, Netherlands, Luxembourg, have attempted within their own regions to open the gates completely, setting up the equivalent of a free trade area between themselves. Part of the stimulation for this has been the example of the United States. The far-seeing wisdom of the American Constitution provided that commerce between states should be solely in the jurisdiction of the federal government and as a corollary it followed that no state could impose restrictions on such commerce. Due to this perhaps more than to any one cause, the United States was able to achieve a commercial and economic progress unexampled in history. The three small countries mentioned above, whose organization is known as "Benelux," quite consciously hoped to improve their respective positions and quite consciously hoped that other European nations would join them. The problem proved more difficult than perhaps had been anticipated; "Benelux" has indeed achieved a notable improvement in the commerce and development of the three countries, but it has had to struggle with the natural desires of groups within each country to maintain a protected position and not to have to suffer competition which a nationalist economy might exclude.

Can the job be done over larger areas? Western Europe is considering such an area organization at date of writing. The question remains unanswered. The writer believes that it can, without minimizing the difficulties. But it will require the best of political ability, and probably also a considerable use of government aid to cushion shocks to individual groups of producers whose special position necessarily suffers when, entering a larger area, they must encounter competition from others whose costs may be less, whose efficiency may be greater, who (because temporarily they pay less to their labor) can undersell.

In this group of tools for international peace must be set proposals for integrating agriculture. Agricultural markets in production are among the stiffest obstacles to liberalizing trade. A farmer, not unnaturally, wishes to be sure of a market and sure of a price. If the system does not provide these, he asks his government to see that he gets both. In most countries, including the United States, there is a program of one sort or another for supporting agricultural prices, commonly in the name of "stabilization." Sometimes this takes the form of direct government price-support as is done in the United States. Other countries limit imports of foreign agricultural products, thereby maintaining domestic markets for their own farmers.

More enlightened students of the subject, among whom must be mentioned former Foreign Minister Dirk Stikker of The Netherlands and later Minister of Agriculture Mansholt of The Netherlands, propose a "single market" in agricultural products. Frenchmen and East European agricultural men have reached a somewhat similar idea under the name of "the Green Pool." In its more dynamic form, "the Green Pool" plan is a suggestion that all countries in the group shall coordinate their measures for supporting agricultural prices and markets. As yet these ideas remain in a state of discussion; the difficulties have never been worked out. The necessity for some such plan grows with the years; but so also do the difficulties. Farming is today no longer a handicraft, but a process of manufacture.

The illustrations given above are all diplomatic expedients in the West European area. They are illustrative of other and wider attempts though obviously the need for liberalizing trade and removing financial barriers to payment is greater in that area than perhaps anywhere else in the world.

The United States, as the product of Mr. Cordell Hull's initiative, has a statute permitting the American government to enter into reciprocal trade agreements with other countries. In effect, the American government can bargain, proposing to reduce its tariff barriers towards any particular country in exchange for like reduction by the other country. This is a direct diplomatic tool in the hands of the United States—limited, of course, by the fact that reduction of an American tariff commonly occasions political outcry by any American area or interest affected.

The bilateral agreements thus envisaged have been theoretically put on a multilateral basis since the formation of a group of countries prepared to engage in such negotiations under the "General Agreement on Tariffs and Trade," familiarly known as "GATT." This agreement was signed in Geneva in 1947, and called for more or less regular negotiations among its members, comprising all of the principal trading countries of Western Europe (except Switzerland), plus the United States. The organization has done some good work, but far too little for real solution. The European idea would be to create a European regional area with a preferential system—low tariff barriers within the region, higher tariff barriers against nations without. The American position has always been against preferential trade areas, since the United States in theory looks forward eventually to "one world" in which trade can flow relatively free from barriers among all countries. It cannot be said that any of the countries involved, including the United States, is really prepared to take a violent plunge towards free trade.

None the less, it is clear that the bottle-neck of international economic diplomacy lies in precisely this area. Unless commerce

can proceed on a scale capable of taking care of nationalist necessities, the smaller countries are doomed to poverty or perhaps
worse. It has been noted that pressures are steadily growing more
intense. Politically we shall reach a point at which some countries
are in such bad shape that they must chronically be bailed out by
gifts (possibly concealed as loans), to make up for the unbalances
created by restricted foreign commerce. Or else, they will fold up.
It would seem probable to this writer that within a relatively few
years some sweeping new approach will be needed. Meantime, regions will work out their most pressing problems by bi-lateral
accords among themselves. The Communist world, of course, will
be proceeding on the basis of regional international planning (and
compulsory adherence to it) much as Nazi Germany did when it
controlled most of the European continent.

Here indeed lies a substantial danger to world peace and to the
world situation. Nazi Germany, having created a region within
which planned economy was the rule, used the leverage of the
entire region to force other countries into her economic system.
Soviet Russia, certainly if she gets on with Communist China,
could do the same thing. If she is comparatively liberal in dividing the commerce-pool and its products with her associated or
captive countries—as Nazi Germany was not—a system might be
created to last for a considerable period of time which would be
a powerful antagonist to the free world system since it could attack
any single nation in that system. It could threaten loss of needed
supplies. It could offer as bait a substantial volume of needed purchases and possibly threaten competition in a number of ways. To
a weak country in the Middle East, Southeast Asia or Latin
America the pressure might become irresistible.

Diplomacy has simply not caught up with the problem of free
commerce. It probably can do so if sufficiently pressed, as pressed
it is likely to be.

The third group of expedients—next after liberalizing trade and
removing financial restrictions—can be fairly classified as direct
relief grants. There are a number of such operations in existence
today.

The first was a straight relief operation carried on as the war closed by the United Nations Relief & Rehabilitation Administration (UNRRA). The bulk of the contribution to this was made by the United States; it was aimed at straight-out feeding and supply of countries devastated by war, accompanied by a certain amount of more fundamental aid to such countries (for example, Greece) as had suffered most from occupation or invasion. This occasioned a certain ironic amusement among some of the countries asked to contribute to the fund, notably the Latin American countries. These pointed out that their own standard of living was lower than the standard of living of the countries they were asked to relieve, and wondered whether they had not as much standing to receive as to give. But UNRRA was designed to relieve from the results of war, and the point was not pressed.

As UNRRA came to its end, it became clear that great parts of the world were still in difficulties. In considerable measure this sprang from the fact that the war had destroyed the capital assets of the countries involved, or, that during five years of an exhausting war, they had exhausted the machinery, tools, capital, necessary to rebuild their cities, put new machinery into their factories, re-equip their railroads, and so forth. Great Britain, very hard hit both by war destruction and by war depreciation, was in difficulties and made no bones about saying so. Her great daughter, Canada, voted gifts—undisguised gifts—amounting to more than a billion dollars. But the real load was picked up by the so-called "Marshall Plan," suggested by Secretary of State George C. Marshall, and later vigorously urged by Mr. Acheson first in private life, and afterward as Secretary of State. A large American "loan" was first granted to Britain under circumstances which made it tolerably plain that it would not be repaid—Lord Keynes, the British representative who negotiated it, was particularly blunt in pointing out this fact as he explained the need for the "loan." But the combination of loans from the United States and gifts from Canada were insufficient, and a larger-scale plan had to be evolved. The Marshall Plan was the result.

Relations between a giver and a beneficiary are always difficult.

Gratitude is always a dangerous emotion; international gratitude is peculiarly unstable. The giver has a right to suggest policy; and the United States as donor endeavored to steer the Marshall aid money as much as possible towards rehabilitation of foreign capital assets. This was sound as a policy. It also raised every possible kind of problem. To do the job at all was so much a political miracle that criticism is ungracious. In the light of hindsight, one regrets that the Marshall Plan aid was divided between the various recipient countries, and that as a result, while it strengthened the national economies involved, it set them up once more as competing elements. In retrospect, if the Marshall aid had been steered through great groups, for example, the Council of Europe, we might have been farther towards cooperative nationalism and further away from the competitive nationalism which is now emerging. Cooperation in some measure was achieved by organizing recipients into the Office of European Economic Cooperation. Factually at the expense of some fifteen billions of dollars paid by the American taxpayer (and, it must be added, without causing him undue hardship) the capital assets of most of the European countries were rebuilt. The results showed up in 1955 as the gross national product of all of the aided countries increased to a point well surpassing their pre-war productivity. From being necessitous buyers who could not pay, most of these countries became honest traders with products to sell against products they needed to buy.

A scheme like the Marshall Plan, translated through O.E.E.C., necessarily must be pragmatic. It has to deal with things as they are; it can not insist on orderly reorganization of a country before it grants relief. Critics of Marshall Plan aid say, for instance, that the results in Germany were to reequip German industry—and to make 400 new German multimillionaires. Or that, in Italy, present distress was relieved and Italian productivity restored, thereby stabilizing a system in which an entrenched class of rich, parasitic nobility could maintain itself, while the poor merely subsisted.

There is truth in both charges. But to have stood over a country and demanded (in effect) a social revolution as a condition precedent to granting aid would have meant assuming an intolerable responsibility. Americans do not have any sense of inspired certainty as to how other countries should run their affairs; they have too much trouble running their own. The time element in any case would be incalculable. In large measure the Marshall Plan resulted in strengthening economy in the recipient countries—and in maintaining the social status quo. As the probable choice was between that and letting the Communist powers change the status quo, the decision to be pragmatic was perhaps a wise one.

As a diplomatic instrument the Marshall Plan probably did prevent subversion of the West European social system by Communist agitators; unquestionably it did promote welfare and stability. It probably prolonged the social and economic status quo within each country involved; it probably prevented some major social changes which are bound to take place in those countries where wealth-distribution is bad. Probably the Marshall Plan made possible an evolutionary rather than a revolutionary development of affairs. Possibly also the Marshall Plan promoted a reasonable development of the military alliance we call "The North Atlantic Treaty Organization" (NATO). Technically the two are not dependent each on the other. But it is probable that the willingness of the European countries to enter the NATO organization was influenced to considerable extent by the fact that they were already sharing some of the fruits of the American economic system through Marshall Plan aid.

For practical purposes, Marshall Plan aid drew to its end in the year 1955, though unexpended edges of it still exist. Its termination seems not to have brought disaster to NATO which now stands on its own feet as a frank defensive military alliance.

A like experiment on somewhat different lines is the so-called "Colombo Plan." In this case, Great Britain is the chief donor, though the United States, Canada, Australia and New Zealand participate; the recipient countries are, respectively, India, Pakistan, Burma, Indonesia, Ceylon, Nepal, Laos, Cambodia, and Vietnam. In 1954, Japan came in as a donor, Thailand as a donor and recipient. Again the principal objective is to supply capital to the recipient countries to enable them to build up their own economies.

Almost automatically the Colombo plan countries became a
"group," and the group had political as well as economic significance. In large measure the area was emerging from colonial
status—a transition less easy than sometimes supposed. As the
British Empire withdrew from the East, some grouping was indicated and the Colombo plan supplied it. The territories involved
are clear that they have received benefits from it; the extent and
degree of such benefits can hardly be calculated at this time. As of
1955 somewhat more than eight billion dollars had been funneled
into the area, chiefly to build up capital assets and increase the
productivity of the countries affected.

The Colombo Plan, in part, was aimed to bring the countries
in question into a group with the hope (perhaps doomed to disappointment), that the group might resist Communist imperialism,
Chinese or Russian. In part, also, it was an attempt to counter
the old Asian cry that Western colonialism sucked resources from
the East, giving nothing in return. It might be noted, on the side
of the West, that no Asian country has ever shown the slightest reluctance in exploiting dependent areas under its control, and that
the worst of Western economic colonialism has never exploited the
Asian masses with the ferocity frequently displayed by local politicians and property owners. But politics in economic affairs as elsewhere often do not arrive at justice.

The important fact about both the Marshall Plan and the Colombo Plan is that they aimed less at spot conditions than at building capital resources. They both represented a conscious attempt
to bring modern technical resources for production to areas which
had not achieved them. In Europe it is clear that the experiment—
almost unheard of in recorded history—had a great measure of
success. In Asia, the returns are not yet in. Both experiments suffer
from one cardinal lack of theoretical knowledge. "Capitalism," so
called, knows amazingly little about itself. Mr. Justice Louis D.
Brandeis once remarked that no one understood a billion dollars.
Students, since his time, have become increasingly aware of the fact
that no one understood where the billion dollars come from, or
to put it differently, how capital is formed. In part at least, capital

is a combination of saved up ability to command and mobilize certain kinds of resources for the purpose of creating productive plants, and facilities. But it is also a reflection of the desires of the local population in question and of their habits, their level of education, and their essential psychology.

Capital, in the sense of ability to mobilize resources, existed in the Middle Ages. Men understood then how to build roads, houses, ships. The genius of the time, however, wanted something else; and much of medieval capital is found in noble churches— for example, the amazingly beautiful Cathedral of Chartres. Twentieth century thought suggests the population of the time ought to have wanted better housing, better roads, better conditions for the masses. The fact was that eleventh- and twelfth-century peoples actually did want splendid spires and jewels for the Madonna. A civilization based on the handicraft principles of Mohandas Gandhi would want one application of capital. A population inspired by the modern American idea of life would want quite another. There is always the problem of determining whether a plan like that of Secretary Marshall or of Colombo is essentially designed to realize the actual desire of the population as then organized and governed, or whether it is essentially a missionary enterprise designed to offer them a new philosophy and a means of realizing its results.

4

Aside from regional economic instruments, three attempts have been made, none of them altogether successful, to use economics as a tool for world organization and world peace. These are, respectively, the International Monetary Fund and the International Bank, both set up at Bretton Woods as World War II closed; and the Food and Agricultural Organization, which is a specialized instrument of the United Nations. All three were designed to complement the United Nations which was in process of being born.

The International Monetary Fund was designed to work towards international convertibility of currency, relieving the immediate postwar situation. At the time, international convertibility of cur-

rency had virtually ceased, except to the extent that the war economics of the Allied Powers, backed by the production of the
United States, gave more or less arbitrary ability to the various
Allied countries to command resources from the Allied pool.
American productivity was the primary base. The Monetary Fund,
a complex and technical financial instrument, put a pool of foreign exchange, created for the purpose, at the service of the
member countries. It has had a material, if modest, influence in
allowing free exchange of goods during the immediate post-war
period.

The International Bank, commonly known as the World Bank,
was designed for something else. Its fundamental idea is not too
different from that of the Colombo Plan and the Marshall Plan,
that is, to make capital available to countries having need of it,
but through loans to be repaid rather than by gifts or grants in aid.
The International Bank has thus acted as a lending agency and
(incidentally) as a kind of friendly counsellor to countries which
sought loans from it. A distinct limitation has been the fact that it
insisted on doing business primarily with governments, thus
strengthening the grip of governments on their own economic
processes. For example, one of the standard public utility enterprises in Brazil is owned by the Brazilian Light & Power Company,
a private concern. More capital was needed by this company for
electrical development to meet the growing population on Brazil's
East coast. The project, as a project, had every merit. But the
International Bank could not make the loan to the company until
the government of Brazil guaranteed it, so that for the first time, this
private enterprise was virtually forced to become, to some extent,
governmental in nature. The International Bank has proved a
good and useful instrument within its limitation, namely, that it is
nothing more than a conservative, traditional money lender. It is
not clear whether money lending alone, on classical terms, really
fits the needs of twentieth century development. Increasingly it is
clear that capital in underdeveloped countries must be built as well
as lent. But this is not primarily the money lenders' business.

5

Behind and below the multilateral economic instruments are a whole series of private arrangements made by one government with another. The United States has made many such arrangements, some of them designed to assist peace, more of them designed to forward its own trade. It has repeatedly lent money to Argentina, though the results were chiefly to give dollar exchange to Argentina with which to pay out accumulated unpaid debts for American export. It has made similar loans to Brazil. It has entered into buying arrangements by which it agrees to purchase copper from Chile, tending to stabilize the economy of that country which depends heavily on copper to provide foreign exchange for Chilean necessities.

It has entered other arrangements designed to assist economic development. It entered into a wheat pool arrangement with wheat producing and wheat consuming countries whose ultimate motivation was to assure a minimum price of wheat with maximum distribution from wheat surplus countries. It has entered into a sugar agreement by which the United States agrees to admit stated quotas of raw sugar from other countries to America—the sugar, of course, being purchased by American companies to be refined and resold to the American consumer. Other similar arrangements, less formal in character, have been from time to time used to stabilize situations where wide price fluctuations would harm producers.

The worst that can be said about these arrangements is that they do not, as a rule, alter fundamental unbalances between production and ultimate consumption—the stability they gain is apt to be temporary. The best that can be said for them is that they do provide periods of time within which producing countries can cope with their own problems—though countries frequently do not avail themselves of the borrowed time. Cuba is still essentially a one-crop country, depending on the price of sugar for her economic life. Wheat prices are still primarily artificial. The case for stabilizing by means of price is still an unproved one.

Of more interest—and equally, more controversial—are purely

private economic arrangements made between private companies to balance the economy of their respective industries. Probably if the whole truth were known it would be found that more economic stabilization is carried on in this manner than by all of the governmental machinery we yet have evolved. This is done through organizations known as "international cartels."

A cartel is at bottom an agreement between companies in which each is assigned a particular market, or a share of the market, the others agreeing not to compete, and in which some mechanism is devised to make production roughly equal to consumption. All the elements of a true "planned economy" are present. In classic economics this is a crime: the cartel does not allow free competition, free play of economics, compel production to adjust to consumption, or allow price fluctuations alone to equalize production-consumption. In the United States, cartels are illegal under the antitrust laws. Outside the United States, they are in general the rule and not the exception.

Thus, from 1928 on, there was virtually a world cartel in oil. We have seen that it helped in the tangled areas of the Middle East. The major oil companies agreed in that year that each of them should preserve that percentage of the market it then had. Further they would pool facilities, tankers production and so forth. General distribution of interest was thus worked out, which evolved during the years. In substance, American oil companies did not invade the European markets; the European companies did not invade the American market (though Shell retained a bridgehead it had established in the United States). Later, when Iran nationalized the Anglo-Persian Oil Company's installations there, the cartel group picked up and supplied the markets previously taken care of by Anglo-Persian. Still later when the dispute was settled, the cartel group again undertook to market the product which now entered once more into the world trade.

On the continent of Europe, such arrangements are so common as to be the rule. It is indeed difficult to see how, in an area chopped up into a number of small countries (for this purpose, France and Germany are "small"), there is any alternative—un-

less, of course, Europe were able to integrate itself into a single
marketing area which it apparently is not. The coal and iron cartels
of the Ruhr and the Saar indeed have been elevated into a single
supra-national organization for the purpose of working out an
European market without restrictions for coal and steel. But while
nationalism rises as World War II recedes, the future of such experiments, however bold and well conceived, remains problematic.

6

While a large amount of work has been done in the economic field,
it must be admitted that, surveying the scene, the results, though
substantial, fall far short of meeting the real issue.

The twentieth century has unlocked forces apparently demanding new frames. An advanced, technically competent country like
the United States can almost set its level of production where it
wishes, given a reasonable period of time. Producing nearly half
of the manufactured products of the world now, it could establish
itself as producer and supplier for virtually the entire free world
and the Soviet Union as well. Not improbably a rapidly renascent
Europe will be able to do almost as much within two or three
decades. The problem is clearly not one of production: the capacity to do that is established. The problem is how to distribute that
production throughout the world so that each people makes a contribution to economic supply and draws from the economic supply
what it needs. It is once more, on a world scale, the problem of an
economy which is potentially abundant; at long last the problem
resolves itself into defining the position of the recipient. What
must be demanded of him, what can he contribute, what entitles
him to share in the economy of abundance? Mere gifts of surplus
do not answer the question; beggars or dole receivers are not
happy. Countries in that position seek to escape by every means
in their power. Yet the old process of exchange—purchasing from
the supplier, selling goods in return to him or in international trade
so that accounts balance—seems not to have fully reestablished
itself. Virtually, the world is asking that a prime producer, like the

United States, shall produce for itself and not for others. Others ask to be put in the same position as the United States, able to produce what they need. But world geography does not permit this save (possibly but not probably) in the case of the very largest countries; and smaller countries are unwilling to sink their nationalism and group themselves into large areas merely because economics suggest this would be a good thing to do.

Hence the dilemma. The world is unwilling apparently (and, in view of the human cost, perhaps rightly) to return to the free trade principle beloved of classical economists and more or less established by the British Empire in the days of the nineteenth century. There is, indeed, no certainty that the system would succeed if reestablished. The world is unable to work out any system of barter capable of establishing an area economy at a level its people are willing to accept, save as the fruit of a dictatorship like that of Hitler or the Soviet Union. It is clear that in the next fifty years, we shall struggle with the problem, probably striking out lines which would seem fantastic if stated today. But then, it must be recalled that many of the economic expedients familiar fifty years ago would seem fantastic now; and that the palliatives of our present expedients would have seemed equally fantastic to our grandfathers.

CHAPTER Four

RETHINKING AMERICAN FOREIGN POLICY

WE HAVE RANGED WIDELY in this primer of international crisis. It is time to return to our own country. For the predictable future, the United States and its people can only use the foreign policy of their own government as the primary instrument for avoiding or meeting crises.

Clearly, some plainly stated criteria of judgment are needed. At least two vast lines of motion are presently going forward:

First, the United States is perforce moving from a world made up for the past four centuries of nationalisms into a world where nationalist conceptions alone no longer are sufficient answers to or methods for solving the problems either of the United States or of any other country.

Second, there is a conflict, moral and philosophical, and it poses a struggle, not between economic systems (Communist-capitalist) but between a conception of man as a being of supreme significance and a conception which reduces him to the status of a tool or counter in a social-engineering problem.

These propositions, as will appear presently, are not abstractions. They require a change in orientation, lead to different strategy and call for different tactics in meeting current and future problems.

Foreign policy for the United States is built upon:

1. Its objectives, which in the main do not change.
2. Its long-term strategy—the general choice of forces and developments upon which the United States relies in moving toward its objectives.
3. Its "policies," that is to say, the considerations which direct its tactics in all given situations—whether it be the question of independence for Algeria or the problem of dictatorships in the Caribbean Sea; which determine the attitude taken toward disarmament at any given moment or toward the usefulness of a large "foreign aid" program.

Current discussion of American policy commonly revolves around tactical questions, because they are immediate and spectacular. Perhaps for that reason too little time has been spent on the deeper questions.

Objectives of the United States are determined primarily by the desire of its people for peace, prosperity and welfare. The United States does not have an acute desire for national glory, has little urge toward world supremacy, does not feel that it must impose its people as rulers or its ideas as primary organizing factors. Factually, its people want peace, immunity from possible attack, economic relations which permit continuous advance in genuine well-being, and access through communication to the cultural treasures of the rest of the world.

These have been the objectives of the United States since she attained her present continental limits in the nineteenth century. "Nationalism"—determination of foreign policy substantially by squaring it with "national interests"—was an adequate base which served quite well up to World War I. America could then defend herself alone. She then had, substantially, the needed materials for a rapidly growing economic life. She thought war unnecessary to realize her own needs—thought wars between other countries were undesirable chiefly because they threatened her own quiet development.

Developments, economic and technical, political and philosophical, during and following World War I changed that with typical twentieth century violence. Philosophically, Leninist and Stalinist Communism, ascendant in Russia, and the contemporaneous rise of Nazi-Fascist philosophy translated themselves into international political action. This forced into American consciousness the fact that the leaders of other nations did intend to impose themselves and their philosophical ideas on all other countries in the world, including the United States. They were prepared to and did mobilize armies, economics and ideas to achieve that objective. Change in the pace of American economic life was no less drastic—change which had been experienced by a few other nations but now was being brought home to all save the most primitive countries. The national base was no longer great enough for the expanding American national economy—a situation Britain had faced in the case of her own economy earlier.

Most violent of all are the present demands of defense. American politicians consider "internationalism" a naughty word, if not actually subversive. Perhaps, unless "internationalism" is carefully defined, they have a point. But Air Force, Navy and Army officers know better. In their business, some form of "internationalism" is not a question of opinion. It is a matter of existing fact. Their mandate has not changed: they are still there primarily to assure the immunity of the territory of the United States from the consequence of attack and invasion. But they can not do this solely from American territory. Their radar net (the now famous "Dew Line") is in a foreign country, Canada. Their air bases are in Greenland, Iceland, Great Britain, Saudi Arabia, Morocco and many other countries. Access to that geography, to the countries controlling it, and to conditions permitting them to operate their bases is a physical necessity if they are to do their job. An "international" system—of some sort —is, for them, no theory but day-to-day practical life. Its geography, complicated enough now, will probably become more exaggerated as airplane ranges enlarge and as guided missiles eventually make it possible to threaten any country, anywhere on earth, from any other country, anywhere on earth.

It follows that for the United States, as for most other countries, a strategy of unmodified nationalism does not realize her objectives because it simply does not fit twentieth century fact. A new base must be sought.

Evidence that American foreign policy needs rethinking need not be formulated here. Some symptoms may be mentioned in the fields of philosophical-political operations, economic operations, and defense.

The nearly unanimous testimony of competent news correspondents affirms (and the writer's own travels verify) that the propaganda of the United States is working against rather than for American prestige, and this not because of faulty technique but because basically the Government of the United States does not stand for any ascertainable philosophy. America's "inability to take sides," as Raymond Cartier put it (*Paris-Match*, March 24, 1956), has antagonized public opinion in Europe and in Asia. The reason is that the United States Government does not really comprehend that it has and must maintain a philosophical and moral position. It has confined itself to seeking allies against "Communism," meaning against the Soviet Union, ignoring the fact that "anti-Communism" does not equate with freedom.

Economically, the United States has pursued a policy of "foreign aid." By absolute standards, it is the most generous economic operation known to history. But our Government has steadily refused to face the necessity of a degree of economic integration with the actual international bloc of countries whose combined economies must be handled together and made to balance and advance if the economies of any of them or of the United States are to be sound. In Gunnar Myrdal's phrase, the alternative is between an integrated economic system and catastrophe. American policy has yet to adjust to that fact.

Militarily, a greater attempt to meet realities has been developed, perhaps because the factors are more obvious. We do have NATO, and an inter-American defense system of sorts. We may be able to build other such systems elsewhere. But, as any military expert

knows, such organizations are no stronger than the political and economic relations on which they are based. NATO is struggling with
this problem now. No one comes into a military international complex merely to defend someone else's country. Without an underlying
foundation, military arrangements could vanish over night, as Napoleon's system crashed in 1813.

It follows that the strategic bases of American foreign policy must
be rethought.

The force of a convinced philosophical position can and should
be the first and greatest determinant in American foreign relations.
Properly applied, it determines everything else.

For the United States, the central philosophical conception is the
limitless and unique value of human beings, either because (as religious men would say) they are all children of God, or because (as
rationalists would say) they each and every one of them have capacity to apprehend, however dimly, the universal order with its freedom, its order, its beauty and its deep joy. This means that the United
States is basically pledged to those spiritual and intellectual movements, political organizations and governments which offer to the
human beings they affect or govern the greatest opportunity of self-
development. Such opportunity implies order under law; no man
has freedom in anarchy. It implies economic systems which do not
rest on slavery or bondage or the equivalent and which distribute
their products with moderate justice. It calls for military systems
whose function is to protect this deep freedom from outside attack,
interference or oppression.

For practical purposes, this means the United States must stand,
throughout the world, for democracy—though obviously it cannot
impose democracy and in any case democratic mechanisms and organization will differ widely from country to country depending on
customs, stages of development, and social competence. America
must either stand for that or be, as she is sometimes pictured, a crude
opportunist, linking herself temporarily with any or every party or
government or force which at the moment may seem advantageous
to some immediate end.

This, it will be noted, is something quite different from the struggle of "capitalism" against "communism." It recognizes that there is no virtue in "private enterprise" or vice in "statism," as such. The question in either case is: What do these systems offer to, or exact from, the individuals living within them? The United States is pledged, for example, to seek a Poland in which Poles are in control of their own lives. The ideal is a great one. It is a matter of indifference whether a Poland which does offer peace and life-content, liberty of thought, and opportunity for free economic and spiritual development chooses to operate its railroads and factories by private corporations or by the State—always provided the underlying values are realized. Under either private or statist systems (there are dangers in both), men and women may be reduced to economic bondage. Under either system, conceivably, they may be vouchsafed the materials for a freer, larger life. The American philosophical thesis tests not the form but the content of any given social organization.

Wherever there is a square conflict between the philosophical conception of the value of free men, and a conception which denies that value, the United States must either "coexist" or fight. "Fighting" in this sense will almost certainly occur ideologically, no matter what Americans desire. There is no way to stop discussions; indeed, the discussion is what really counts. Fighting militarily is, of course, the last of all possible resorts; it is really justified only when an opposite ideology threatens by force to impose itself upon the United States or upon an area in which the United States can control events. In general, victory for individualist freedom within order anywhere in the world strengthens the United States. Loss of that freedom in any area anywhere weakens the American position.

Strategy in American foreign economic policy proceeds from a similar premise. Americans believe, with solid reason, that the American economic system has provided a higher standard of living for more people in a larger area than any known to history. They are dimly aware that this plateau of achievement cannot be indefinitely maintained for the United States if she lives in a complex (as she must) in which the other constituent countries are not moving toward like achievement. Here also, emphasis is on the human content of a system rather than on its form. If oil, steel, electricity, transport and credit are so used as to give opportunity and content to individual life, it is a secondary question whether they are produced and made available in private enterprise (as in the United States), by mixed companies (as in Great Britain), or by state-owned facilities, as perhaps they must be in smaller or less developed countries. For American requirements alone, a high degree of exchange with many areas far beyond United States borders is essential; yet it is clear that no such exchange can be continuous save on a more or less equal basis—or at least on a basis by which the less-favored areas are moving toward equality with the United States.

This implies not "foreign aid" but integration. We do not think New York, New England and Pennsylvania engage in "foreign aid" when capital and goods flow from them to Arizona, California or Oregon to create the American West.

"Foreign aid"—justifiable in the immediate postwar emergency— has ceased to be valid in great areas. It does not buy friends or convert doubters. It does not even assure that the peoples of the countries aided will share the benefits. Mishandled, it can mean that a shaky or corrupt government is bolstered up, or that an inadequate and oppressive economic group increases its take at the expense of the consuming and laboring public. At its diplomatic worst, it can lead to a degrading position in which the United States "bids" for the "privilege" of aiding a country against some other bidder, say, the Soviet Union. Here again strategy has to be rethought. We are really seeking a viable organization of international affairs, regional at first (perhaps world-wide in a later generation), by which American economic policy safeguards and forwards American advance along with comparable advance in the economic welfare of companion peoples. The ultimate test is human quite as much as it is statistical. Finance and commerce are means to the end, not the end in themselves.

United States military interest follows the same lines. Again, the geography not only is not American, but probably differs from economic geography in considerable degree. Primarily, American military interest is defensive. But because there is, now, no limit to the possible incidence of any war anywhere, or to the impact of any aggression particularly when sparked by a hostile philosophical force, we are committed so far as our resources permit toward peace-keeping and repelling aggression. Yet in evolving military defense measures, it is essential that the United States does not find itself arming governments pledged to a hostile philosophy. Nor does it follow that we should regard as "hostile" countries which, because they can not be defended by a military combination, consider that their hope lies in being able to maintain neutrality.

Defensive military strategy today for us, as indeed for everyone, does involve continuously larger units of territory comprising many nations. But we have not reached a point where every country outside our military net is necessarily an enemy. Also, military and territorial usefulness is by no means the only test. Only in war is one justified in making military expediency the primary criterion of action. In peacetime operations, the United States can often lose more safety by weakening the political structure of her multinational defense complex than she can gain through temporary access to an air base or naval station. It was a moral and philosophical force, not a military arrangement, that gave the United States access to the geography of most of the world during the recent Korean conflict.

The foundation piers of American strategy in foreign relations lie therefore:

1. In philosophical consistency in the ideas and forces the United States undertakes to represent and support throughout the world.
2. In changing its economic policy from one of "aid" to one of building an appropriate economic community.
3. In developing a military organization in conjunction with other nations, capable of defending the community which emerges from the first two forces—including, of course, the United States.

On this basis we can deal, tactically, with the very grave problems immediately presented to us. The more pressing are discussed as illustrations.

Conflict with the Soviet Union and its attendant economic and political complex—the so-called "Communist world"—is the largest and most spectacular of these. The Soviet Union obviously does have a reasonably clear base for its foreign policy. It has had political consistency—a philosophical conception which has thus far been bitterly hostile to our own. It does have an integrated international economic complex. It is building a supranational military system which, as the Korean War showed, can be offensive as well as defensive, and is dangerous to us precisely because Leninist-Stalinist Communism has made no secret of its intent to impose itself on the entire earth.

But American tactics pursued in that conflict clearly need revision. The United States assumed, and certainly in Stalin's time rightly, that any Communist maneuver anywhere in the world was a part of the "class war" and universal struggle carried on against "capitalism" with the United States as the ultimate target. We need not abandon that assumption. But we can recognize that there have been spectacular developments in the Soviet Union. Our immediate problem is how to evaluate and treat them.

We need not enter into personal judgments of the men composing the present Soviet Government. It is not the business of the United States to determine whether Bulganin and Khrushchev (who served Stalin in his bloodiest days) are now in a state of grace entitling them to admission to heaven. It is not too important even whether they are sincere in what they say. The real point is whether any shift in the position of the Soviet Government reflects evolution at work in the Soviet Union itself and whether it liberates forces there which will tend to give reality to the words the Soviet leaders have been uttering. Some kinds of political declaration have irreversible effect.

Among the declarations made by the Soviet rulers are that "personal government" is no longer tolerable in Communist policy; that the policy of terror is no longer good Communist doctrine; that individuals accused of crime are presumed innocent until proved guilty and that confession is not good evidence of guilt. Now whatever the mentality of the men who made these declarations, destruction of Stalin as tyrant-dictator makes it immensely more difficult to re-establish, for a time at least, another tyrant-dictator. A population freed from the shackles of a twenty-year terror will resist (and has the will to resist) reimposition of terror. Accusation by State police will not, for a time at least, convince a Russian community that the accused is guilty, and the Soviet Union is by that much less a police State. So, for the time being, forces have been engendered which tend to give greater measure or dignity and freedom to 200 million Soviet Russians and may one day assist 80 or 90 millions in the captive Iron Curtain countries.

This is an advance—ever so tentative but still an advance—toward the American philosophical ideal of free human beings. Far from being immediately rejected, the statements should be welcomed and encouraged. We need not, must not, lower our guard. We need not trust the men who make the declarations. We may well assume that fear or self-interest dictated what conscience would not compel. We need not hesitate to condemn relapses into brutality like that in Hungary in 1956. The important fact is that one step was taken in the Communist world tending somewhat toward what we consider a civilized base. We should encourage rather than repel it.

Communication with the Soviet Union by travel, and direct contact, has been made somewhat easier. Again, this should be welcomed. We may assume that a Russian coming here does so to accumulate information useful to his State and perhaps useful against us. We may take for granted that Americans offered access to the Soviet Union will be, if possible, recruited into the Communist camp or will be inspired to the fullest practical degree with respect for the Communist system. Making all allowance for that, the communication permits Americans to know the Communist world more nearly as it really is—even after assuming "guided tours," flattery, and concealment of many things. Even so, we will emerge knowing more about the Soviet Union than we did before. Conceivably, we might give the Soviet Union a rather better understanding of the United States.

For, in the long run, we have to make up our minds that either there will have to be evolution within the Communist world moving toward a tolerable basis of peaceful life with us, or there must be

World War III, which may end an era of human life on this planet. American life in the past forty years has been evolving with great rapidity. It must be assumed that Russian life was not wholly frozen when Lenin seized power in 1917. Sane Americans must hope for developments in the Soviet Union which will eventually bring about a condition of civilized peace. The single alternative is nuclear war.

We have better basis for this hope than abstract reasoning. As we have observed, the problems of managing an empire increase by the square of its radius. There are plenty of signs that the Soviet government is no exception to this rule. The Communist imperial regime has not been able to stamp out the fierce individualism of the Iron Curtain countries in the mid-European strip; and as Communist China emerges she assumes the shape of a colleague preparing to rival Moscow, rather than that of a dominated people and territory. Should Russian influence extend itself over the rest of the Asian coast, and over the Arab world, there is much to suggest that the huge combination will fly apart. American policy, therefore, not only can but must look toward evolution in the Communist complex. It should be prepared to assist the process.

The philosophical basis used as guide in the foregoing suggestion is no less useful in dealing with other tactical problems of the Communist-free world conflict. China, for example, has not, so far as we know, gone far towards recognizing humanity and human beings, within China or anywhere else. Her government hovers near that horror-laden fog where mass-men pushed by dictators kill without distinction, where a neighbor country like Korea is merely a field of forcible political exploitation, where life means little, where terror is the chief guide. There is little point in recognizing or otherwise moving toward the Chinese Communist position unless some measure of increase in freedom and individual dignity for the Chinese and surrounding peoples is accomplished thereby.

The same considerations lead to a different conclusion with respect to Eastern Germany and the captive Mid-European Iron Curtain countries. Clearly, conditions prevailing before the Soviet Union seized these countries during and after World War II cannot be restored. Probably, indeed, they should not: the peoples and life in these countries, as in the rest of the world, have evolved in the past twenty years. But it does not follow that the brute Russian imperialism which Stalin imposed there needs to be recognized as a "fact of life" (as Khrushchev insists) or that it is vain to commit our resources to solving the problem (as George Kennan suggests). We can recognize that the Soviet Union will not, and perhaps should not, permit Hungary, Poland and other adjacent countries to become a military area from which a new Western invasion could be hurled against the Soviet Union. (The United States certainly refuses to permit any similar use of Mexico or Latin America.) The economic resources of the region fall partly into a complex whose center will be Russian, partly into another whose center lies in Western Europe. But it is one thing to say that. It is quite another to "accept" the fact that this huge area and its peoples can be permanently deprived of control of their own culture, lives, social development and human and political self-determination.

The mid-European crime committed was human, and that crime at date of writing continues. Whether, as devaluation of Stalin continues, it will be realized that his policy in these countries has likewise been deprived of logical base and whether Russian policy will change accordingly is not known. What is sure is that the United States can not accept as permanent the present Soviet control over these countries without denying the main philosophical premise of American thought and action. How far it should go in seeking liberation at any given moment depends on circumstances. But there should be no question of the direction of American policy.

Colonialism and the attendant rise in Asian nationalism is, next to the conflict with the Soviet Union, probably the greatest single problem. Oversimplified thinking suggests that America should be "anti-colonial" and stops there. This is sound as far as it goes. The implied premise is that all colonial civilizations tend to denigrate human beings and their development within the colony. Yet the deep test is human. Little would be accomplished for human beings anywhere, for example, were Moslem countries from Morocco to Egypt cut loose from colonial ties simply to become infamous slave-trading or piratical tyrannies like the Barbary States of the nineteenth century.

The test of policy is not primarily ending a political form, but assuring that new development adds to, rather than detracts from, human dignity and freedom within the area. This question is not always as open-and-shut as most Americans believe, nor as it is commonly stated by foreign accusers of the United States. In every case, it seems to me, the United States, convincedly anti-colonial in principle, has both a right and duty to ask that the anti-colonial forces and politicians in the area shall offer solid prospects of human dignity and life to the peoples they aspire to govern, and of responsibility toward other peoples in their international conduct. There would be no virtue in an independent Algeria which promptly falls to killing or exiling a couple of million resident Frenchmen, or to a renascent Arab League that can think of nothing better to do than devastating Israel and killing a million-and-a-half Jews. Criteria of sound anti-colonial policy must include the reasonable conviction that the peoples are not exchanging colonial rule for a permanently worse local tyranny, or ending one colonial tie to fall immediate prey to a no less brutal Communist imperialism. The peoples of colonial or dependent areas can make, and do make, moral demands on us. We have equal right to make moral demands on them, their leaders, and the forces which move them.

A third constellation of problems—probably first in real importance to the United States—is found in the Western Hemisphere. Canada aside, this is a group of 21 nations of which the United States is most powerfully developed while the rest are, in the main, relatively poor and undeveloped. A twentieth century economic renaissance is sweeping the continent; a variety of economic and social revolutions no less profound than the political revolutions of Asia are in full progress. Oversimplified thinking again has led the United States to exaggerate the sound conception of non-intervention and scrupulous respect for the sovereignty of her twenty associates to the point of refusing any judgment of them at all—pure Quixotism. So, in form and fact, the United States has made the mistake of treating corrupt dictatorships with the same cordial respect as in dealing with honest and forward-looking democracies. Once more in Cartier's phrase, our "inability to take sides" has produced the impression (as the great Argentine, Gainza Paz, observed) that we do not care. A dictator with an army has received military assistance, though the chief effect is to rivet his chain more heavily on his people.

Following our revised strategy, in every case the criterion should be whether assistance given tends to make for a better developed and developing people or merely tends to buy the favor of a local tyranny. Had we followed this line of thinking throughout, in military and economic assistance, and in political orientation, our situation would be better than it is today. Actually, we treated a Peron with as much if not more generosity, seeking to buy off his insults, than we offered loyal governments struggling to give welfare and freedom to their people.

Latin America also squarely poses the problem of moving toward economic integration. Canada and Latin America between them already account for half our foreign commerce. We need this commerce not primarily to make money for our merchants and manufacturers, but to supply essential materials for our own economy. Little serious attempt has been made to work out a hemispheric system for finance, capital development, orderly marketing, gradual equation of standards of work, and the like. Yet, a hemispheric system moving toward integration and capable of adding other areas as economic necessity becomes evident must be the beating heart of any American effort. If the hemispheric complex ever breaks down, the United States ceases at once to be outstandingly significant in world affairs. All this suggests a re-examination of our economic and military acts in the American region.

The three illustrations here given could be multiplied. The criteria suggested can be applied to small problems and great. The result would be a steady, consistent effort in foreign affairs. We shall have opponents, and certainly disagreements, in great areas. But even enemies, opponents and doubters would respect a consistent policy of the United States, and such a policy would consistently move toward realization of the ideals on which American objectives are based.

The heir to those ideals must almost certainly be a world organization. This is why the United Nations was constructed; why it exists; why if it were to dissolve its rebuilding would be an absolute necessity. For, as nationalism lost its logical base in World War I, regionalism is quite likely to become obsolete in the lives of children already in school. Historians, a couple of centuries from now, will probably discover that the twentieth century conflict is pounding out the premises for world law in an era still to come.

If well conceived, American foreign policy in the next generation may establish the claim of the United States to greatness.

Crisis is evident as this manuscript goes to press. Currently it is most acute in the Suez and Arabian area of the Middle East. This crisis will pass. Others, perhaps graver ones, will follow in that same region. Similar crisis exists in the Mid-European strip and others are building there also. In slower tempo, crises are gathering off the Asian coast, and in Africa. In farther distance a huge crisis is forming where Slavic Russia meets the Orient. Few prophets are hardy enough to forecast a tranquil second-half for twentieth century statesmen.

Yet, for the first time in some years, the writer is optimistic.

Crises, like symptoms of disease, reflect conditions requiring solution which have not been squarely met. The present crises seem to be of a nature compelling governments, politicians and more reflective elements in public opinion to think through and meet real issues, instead of devising temporary palliatives and calling the process a "policy."

The Middle East crisis of 1957 is an excellent illustration. On the surface it began when Egypt asserted her "sovereignty," and expropriated the shares of the Suez Canal Company. The Powers discussed this action legalistically and got nowhere. "Sovereignty" does give Egypt the right to seize the shares of an Egyptian corporation. But sovereignty does not and can not give Egypt the privilege of controlling for her own political purposes a waterway used by half the world even though it lay wholly in her territory. Certain Arab nations followed the Egyptian example by refusing to permit export of oil from their territories to Western Europe. As sovereign countries, they had legalistic right to do this. But the world will hardly accept the right of any country in the name of its "sovereignty" to paralyze the lives of many millions of people beyond its borders because the accident of geography gives it control over a necessary resource. Sooner or later both the mid-European States and the rest of the world thus have to face the implacable fact that the economics of modern transport and oil supply are not national but international. This means that the needs of many peoples living under many nation-states have to be recognized, balanced and accommodation made. The result has to be embodied in some form of organization or institution which recognizes at once the internal freedom and economic rights of the Middle Eastern countries and also the needs and rights of those other peoples which depend on Middle Eastern oil and waterways.

At the opening of this volume we noted that the twentieth century had been dealing with its problems in nineteenth century terms: had been assuming that the Nation-State was the unit of solution, whereas (with few if any exceptions) Nation-States are no longer viable either as independent units of economics or defense. The current Middle Eastern crisis, and every successor Middle Eastern crisis demands solution on the basis of modern facts rather than older dogma, and admits of no other. Though the process of seeking adjustments under crises stress will be both painful and dangerous, at least we are beginning to grapple with real problems. In that there is hope.

The same observation holds for the mid-European crisis in Hungary and Poland. Essentially the problem there is that the Soviet Empire undertook to solve the mid-European problem by making ideological and military colonies out of peoples whose assent and loyalty she did not and apparently can not command. Her failure has jeopardized her control of them for purposes of defense and has substantially destroyed her use of most of the region as part of her economic fabric. Eventually, the Soviet Empire, and the West as well, must find ways by which these countries are restored to their internal sovereignty, but also are built into a fabric which adds to the safety both of Russia and the West, and whose production, so far as it has external significance, is available on equitable basis to either or both as need may indicate. Again the problem posed is a real one; and nothing but a real solution will serve. When it is squarely faced we shall be at the beginning of the long road out of our difficulties.

The Latin American problem, less spectacular, less appreciated, and therefore less understood, presents in less acute form the same difficulty and the same hope. A hemisphere, most of whose economic affairs are now matters interchanged within the hemisphere itself, can not indefinitely run smoothly on the basis of twenty-two non-related systems; eventually, the high factor of unity which interdependent economics creates has to be reflected in principles and institutions which meet rather than deny actual needs. And a hemisphere whose chief requirement for protection is common defense against attack from outside has steadily diminishing excuse for building twenty-two competing military systems while essential capital construction needs of a continent and a half are unmet. Here also as problems arise, they indicate and outline the real questions at issue.

Possibility always exists that any of these crises may lead to general war. All things considered, the chances appear to be against large-scale conflict. Never before (so far as I know) has every General Staff so thoroughly agreed with every other General Staff that the outcome of all-out war is unpredictable and its results incalculable and that "victory" is drained of most of its meaning. In most previous historical periods behind every war was a calculation; one side or other considered it could be won, and believed that from victory certain areas could be seized or certain results be obtained. These are not the present calculations of the General Staff of any country capable of unleashing a general war. By consequence, pressure to find solutions other than by war is perhaps greater than has ever previously existed. Even the miserable expedients by which in the last decade wars have been carried on without becoming general— use of "volunteers" in foreign uniforms, exported package revolutions and the like—are wearing so thin that they can be resorted to only with steadily increasing hazard.

Repetition of the world struggles which wracked the first half of our century is avoidable in the foreseeable future. Opportunity does exist for a century of peace (imperfect and broken in limited areas but still, generally, peace) more soundly based even than that of the Victorian age.

Capacity to achieve that peace will depend chiefly on capacity to recognize fundamental problems, on courage to confront them, on willingness to explain them to operative public opinion, on wisdom to resolve them, and on determination to build the new institutions which an expanding era demands.

It will be a splendid quest.

INDEX

A

Acheson, Dean, 287
Aden, 152, 162
Aden, Strait of, 120, 153-54
Adriatic Sea, 91, 93, 108, 114, 130, 133-34, 138, 149, 178
Advisory Defense Committee, Inter-American, 72
Aegean Sea, 130, 132, 134, 151, 160, 162
Afghanistan, 119, 123, 152, 154, 158-60, 185, 259
Africa, 43, 74-5, 94, 151-53, 156, 180, 199, 202, 206-207, 210-12, 216, 270, 311; see also North Africa
Africa Korps, 168
Aguinaldo, 189
Airlift, American, 113
Air War College, 8, 268
El Alamein, 157, 168
Albania, 131-34, 139-40, 143, 146, 174
Alexander the Great, 132, 155, 161
Alexander II, 95
Alexandria, 168
Algeria, 9, 297, 309
Algiers, 172
Allenby, General, 157, 164
Allied and Associated Powers of World War I, 29, 96

Allied Powers (World War II), see Grand Alliance
Alpine passes, 133
Alsace-Lorraine, 98, 184
Amazon, 75
America, see United States
American Declaration of the Rights and Duties of Man, 77
American Expedition (World War II), 105
American hemisphere, see Western Hemisphere
American Revolution, 282
American Telephone and Telegraph Company, 26
Andes, 229
Andorre, 13, 98
Anglican Church, 28
Anglo-Persian Oil Company, 294
Anglo-Saxons, 80, 88, 242
Anjou, House of, 20, 98
Annam, 194
D'Annunzio, Gabriele, 140
Anti-Imperialist League, 190
Arabia, 94, 137, 142, 152, 154-55, 158, 162, 166-70, 311
Arabian Desert, 161
Arab League, 32-33, 170, 173, 309
Arabs, 9, 124-26, 158, 171, 173
Arab States, 120, 166-67, 170-73, 176, 312

315

Arabic, 172
Arab world, 121, 170, 307
Aragon, House of, 98
Aranha, Dr. Odvaldo, 58
Archangel, 119, 258
Arctic Ocean, 119, 184
Ardahan, 159
Argentina, 9, 11, 27, 64, 69, 74, 79, 81, 83-4, 86, 247, 293
Aristotle, 155
Armenians, 158, 165
Asia, 9, 43, 91-94, 119, 129-30, 156, 180, 185, 191, 198, 202, 210, 212-13, 216, 220-21, 225, 270, 290, 300, 307, 309, 311
Asia Minor, 157
Assyrians, 161
Aswan Dam, 173
"Ataturk," see Kemal
Athens, 30
Atlantic Charter, 28, 250, 261-62
Atlantic Ocean, 48, 75, 120, 129, 133, 172, 206, 234
Atomic weapons, 10, 101, 107, 125, 220, 248-49, 258-60
Attila, 228
Austin, Warren, 70
Australia, 34, 63, 93, 181, 186, 193, 206, 289; in SEATO, 33, 197
Austria, 21, 43, 108, 131, 134, 137-38, 140, 156, 164, 234
Austrian Empire, 93-4, 136-39, 214, 227
Austria-Hungary, 95, 135
Austro-Hungarian Empire, see Austrian Empire
Axis Powers, 46

B

Babylonians, 161
Baghdad, 156
Baghdad Pact, 33, 173
Bahrein, 152, 167, 169
Bali, 187
Balkan League, 137
Balkans, 43, 94, 119, 126; Mohammedans in, 21; Mongols in, 92
Baltic republics, 95
Baltic Sea, 109, 119, 130, 133, 140, 151

Bank for International Settlements, 281
Bao Dai, 194
Barbary States, 172, 309
Bataan, Death March of, 110
Battle of the Bulge, 105
Beirut, 163
Beirut University, 163
Belgium, 33, 94, 143, 153, 205, 207, 227, 251, 283; neutrality and World War I, 43
Benelux, 283
Berbers, 206
Bering Strait, 119
Berle, A. A., Jr., 71, 87, 262, 267
Berlin, 64, 104, 108; Communist blockade of, 113-14
"Berlin-to-Baghdad," 156
Bernadotte, Folke, 171
Bismarck, 46, 161
Black Sea, 91, 106, 120, 124, 152-53, 159
Blaine, James G., 66
Bliss, Tasker H., 139
Boer War, 10
Bohr, Nils, 101
Bogotá, Colombia, 59; Charter of, 72, 77, 80; Inter-American congress at, 72; Pact of, 77
Bolivar, Simon, 59, 65, 79
Bolivia, 15, 32, 74, 82, 84, 89, 283
Bolshevik Revolution, 95, 164
Borneo, 193
Bosnia, 93
Bosphorus, 91, 120, 124, 136, 153, 166
Braden, Spruille, 86
Brandeis, Louis D., 290
Brazil, 13, 15, 64, 67, 69, 73-4, 79-80, 83-4, 274, 276, 279, 292-93; area, 40; population, 40; resources, 40-41
Breslac, 164
Bretton Woods, 291
Briand, Aristide, 102
Britain, see England, Great Britain
Britannia, 202
British Commonwealth of Nations, 34, 56, 60, 63, 65, 153, 197, 204, 226
British East India Company, 270
British Empire, 29, 34, 42, 53-4, 56,

93-4, 123, 161, 163, 199, 201, 209-10, 214, 226-28, 290, 296
Brittany, 98
Broz, Josef, *see* Tito
Budapest, 9, 150, 216
Buenos Aires, 66, 259
Bulganin, 23, 97, 305
Bulgaria, 93, 95, 100, 103, 111, 131-33, 136-37, 139, 143, 146, 148, 152, 160, 228
Bunche, Ralph, 171
Burma, 93, 115, 223, 228-29, 289
Burgundy, House of, 98
Byrnes, James, 71
Byron, 136
Byzantine Empire, 22, 90, 93, 122, 126, 156; *see also* Roman Empire
Byzantium, *see* Constantinople, Istanbul

C

Cabell, James Branch, 260
Cairo, 121, 171, 259; Convention, 246, 263
Caesar, Augustus, 61
Calabrian, 232
Cambodia, 186, 190, 194-96, 289
Canada, 13, 15, 34, 63-4, 251, 258, 287, 289, 309-10; in NATO, 32; population, 73; radar line in, 8, 17, 299
Canton, 186
Cape Horn, 176
Caribbean, 15, 57, 297
Carnegie, Andrew, 243
Carthage, 51
Cartier, Raymond, 300
Caspian Sea, 159
Catharine the Great, 94
Cathay, 230
Catholic Church, Roman, 27, 99-100, 135, 242; and European unity, 21-2
Caucasus, 159, 165
Celebes, 193
Celtic, 98
Central America, 27, 57
Central Europe, 109
Central Powers, 44
Ceylon, 289
Chaka, 207

Chamberlain, Neville, 141
Chapultepec, 114, 263; Act of, 68-72; conference, 11
Charlemagne, 21, 99
Charles V, 23, 41, 101
Charles Martel, 21, 92
Chiang Kai-shek, 182
Chicago Air Conference of 1944, 11, 247-48
Chile, 74, 84, 293
China, 13, 15, 31, 33, 49, 69, 129-30, 161, 174, 178, 181-89, 192, 194-95, 197, 206, 209, 211, 213-14, 216, 221, 225-27, 262, 265, 271-72; area, 41; Communist success in, 115-16; conflicts with Soviet Union of, 117-18; Europeans in, 94; and Indo-China, 52; Japanese invasion of, 46; and Korea, 116; Mongolian Empire of, 92; population, 41, 73, 117, 181; resources, 41; and Soviet Union, 96-7, 107, 109; and U.N., 67-8
Chinese, 197, 206, 212-15, 232, 247
Chinese Nationalists, 183
Chosen, *see* Korea
Chou En-lai, 184
Christ, 155
Christianity, 25, 58, 99-100, 155, 157
Churchill, Winston, 28, 104-6, 111, 182, 234, 250, 261-62
Clemenceau, 95
Cliveden clique, 103
Cochin China, 194
Cold War, 62, 112, 266
Colombia, 81, 83-4
Colombo Plan, 278, 289-92
Colonialism, 180, 198-202, 210, 212, 216, 264, 290, 308
Columbia Law School, 9
Columbus, Christopher, 92
Communication, 9-10, 34-5, 147-48, 221, 228
Communism, 25, 127, 212, 216-17, 224-25, 230, 234-35, 253, 286, 299, 302, 305-6; in Asia, 191-92, 194, 198, 213; in China, 182-83; in Cyprus, 122; in Latin America, 84; and Mid-East, 178; in Mid-Europe, 108; post-war revolutions, 52; a religion, 22, 55; and sovereignty, 22-3; and supra-nationalism, 23;

theory of state of, 26-7; World
War II objectives of, 75
Communist Internationale, 51
Communist Party, see Communism
Concert of Powers, 95
Confederated States of America, 267
Conference of Berlin, 120
Congo, Belgian, 15
Congress of Vienna, 95
Constantinople, 22, 90, 93, 120, 122,
126, 138, 155, 157, 161-62, 164-66,
174, 178, 228; see also Byzantium,
Istanbul
Convention for Economic Coopera-
tion, 114
Cooke, Dwight, 185
Copts, 122, 157-58
Cordon Sanitaire, 95
Costa Rica, 72, 82, 84
Council of Europe, 32, 288
Council on Foreign Relations, 278
Croats, 98, 131, 139
Crusades, 161
Cuba, 42-3, 84, 214, 221, 293
Cyprus, 30-1, 122-23, 156
Czarist, see Russian
Czechoslovakia, 22, 67, 95, 108, 117-
18, 131, 135, 138-40, 142, 146,
148, 160, 171, 173, 192, 213-14
Czechs, 98, 131, 228

D

Dakar, 155
Danes, 99
Danube River, 153
Dardanelles, Straits of, 120-21, 124,
136, 151, 153, 156, 160, 162, 165-
66, 174
Danzig, 142
Darien, 116
Darius the Persian, 50
Declaration by United Nations, 11,
29, 105, 262
Decline and Fall of the Roman Em-
pire, 90
Defense, 217; international charac-
ter of, 16-17; political aspects of,
76; regional, and United Nations,
70-1, 218
De Lesseps, 161
Denmark, 119, 133, 143, 259

Dewey, Admiral George, 9
Dew Line, 299
Diaz, Porfirio, 271
Dickens, Charles, 224
Diebold, William, Jr., 278
Dien Bienphu, 195
Dingaan, 207
Disraeli, Benjamin, 93, 120, 156, 161,
199
Disarmament Conference of 1924,
Washington, 11, 45
Dniester River, 153
Dominican Republic, 66, 81, 84, 87
Don River, 153
Dumbarton Oaks, 67, 262
Dutch East Indies, 186, 193
Dutch Empire, 93-94, 187

E

East vs. West, 91-94, 118, 131, 191
East Europe, 133
East Germany, 109, 133
East Indian archipelago, under Dutch
rule, 93
E.C.A., see Economic Cooperation
Administration
Economic Cooperation Administra-
tion, 281
Economic and Social Council, United
Nations, 263
Ecuador, 84, 259
Eden, Anthony, 104
Egypt, 93, 121-22, 124-25, 151-52,
154, 157, 161, 164, 169-71, 214,
232, 250, 259, 270, 308, 311; an-
cient, 51; and Arab League, 32;
British control, 161-3; independ-
ence movement, 160; leader of
Moslem world, 157; population,
171; in World War II, 167-68
Einstein, Albert, 101
Eisenhower, Dwight D., 105, 108,
168, 248
Eleanor of Aquitaine, 20
Eliot, Charles W., 28
Elizabeth I, 20-21
Ems telegram, 46
Engels, Frederick, 159
England, 11, 20-1, 35, 99-100, 134,
225-26, 228, 241-43; nationalism
and supra-nationalism, 20-1

English language, 200
Eritrea, 152, 164
Erzegebirge, 108
Eskimo, 186
Essays on Leninism, 234
Estonia, 95, 131, 135, 138, 140-41, 146, 214
Ethiopia, 151-52, 207, 244
Europe, 11, 20-22, 66, 93, 101, 118, 126-27, 131, 140, 148, 152, 156, 169, 181, 207, 220-21, 223, 225, 229, 276, 290, 294-95, 300; boundaries, 98; organization of postwar, 106; population, 14; reconstruction, 107, 110; trade with Latin America, 73; U.S. concentration on, 64; unity, 101-102; and World War II, 43
European Coal and Steel Community, 33
European Defense Community, 42
European Payments Union, 280-81
European War, *see* World War I, World War II

F

Far East, 12, 15, 33, 121, 129, 152, 160, 162, 180, 214, 271; and Soviet Union, 107; and World War II, 46
Farouk, King, 171
Farson, Negley, 153
Fashoda, 270
Federation of Malaya, *see* Malaya
Feis, Dr. Herbert, 262
Fermi, 101
Figuéres, Jose, 84
Filipine, *see* Philippine
Finland, 95, 138, 140-44, 214
Fins, 98, 131
Fiume, 140
Florida, 43, 57
Food and Agricultural Organization, United Nations, 291
Formosa, 9, 116, 181, 183-84, 189
Four freedoms, 28, 102
Fourteen Points, 28, 250
France, 11, 20-1, 24, 33, 35, 43, 46, 57, 65, 93-5, 98, 100, 103-4, 107-8, 134, 138-39, 142-44, 153-54, 164, 167, 177-78, 184, 197, 205, 207, 211, 220, 225-27, 229, 253, 258, 265, 270, 294; Communist strike against, 112-13; fall of, 104; and Indo-China, 194-95; mandates of, 166; Marshall plan and, 112; in NATO, 32; and North Africa, 172; reconquered, 105, 144; and SEATO, 33; and Suez, 125, 175-76
Frankfort, Germany, 8
Franks, 227
Freedom, 236; supra-national values, 24; U.S. ideology, 51-2
Freedom from Fear, 28, 102, 220
Freedom of Information, 28, 102, 220
Freedom of Religion, 28, 102, 220
Freedom from Want, 28, 102, 220
From Isolation to Leadership, 39

G

Gandhi, Mohandas, 291
GATT, *see* General Agreement on Tariffs and Trade
General Agreement on Tariffs and Trade, 285
General Assembly, United Nations, 264
General Staffs, 220, 236, 313; British, estimate of end of war, 105; German, 43, 96, 141-42, 257; German, attack on Russia planned by, 103, 143; inter-American, 72; political objectives accepted by all, 108; Soviet, 112
Geneva, Conference of 1955, 49; Conference forms GATT, 285; Conference on Indo-China, 195
Georgians, 96, 159
Germany, 8, 21, 33, 43, 46, 64-5, 67, 92, 94, 96-8, 100, 103, 106, 108-10, 113, 119-20, 131, 133-38, 140, 142-46, 154, 156-57, 164-65, 167-68, 178, 181-82, 220, 227, 234, 253, 261, 270, 272, 286, 288, 294, 307; *see also* East Germany, West Germany
Ghana, 209
Gibralter, Straits of, 120, 153, 197
Goeben, 164
Goethe, 233
Gold Coast, 34, 209-10
Gomulka, 149

Good Neighbor Policy, 66
Goths, 91, 227
Governments-in-exile, 106
Grand Alliance of World War II, 11, 105, 144
Great Britain, 15, 24, 33, 43, 53-4, 63, 67, 69, 94-5, 98, 102-6, 120, 136, 138-39, 154, 156, 158, 164-67, 177-78, 183, 197-98, 204, 207, 209, 211, 253, 257-59, 262, 265, 270-71, 274-75, 282, 287, 289, 299, 303; Commonwealth, 34; and Cyprus, 123; and Greek war, 111; mandates of, 166; and Marshall plan, 112; in NATO, 32; and private property, 25-6; in SEATO, 33; and State church, 27-8; and Suez, 122, 125-26, 161-62, 171-76; and U.N., 67-8; see also British Empire, England
Greece, 35, 98, 100, 109, 114, 119-21, 124, 131, 133, 136-37, 140, 143, 146, 155-57, 173, 187; claims Black Sea Coast, 123, 165; Communist revolution in, 97, 111, 115, 146, 156; and Cyprus, 30-1, 122-23; independence movement, 136, 156; Italian attack on, 103-4; in NATO, 32; Truman doctrine and, 62-3, 71, 111-12
Greek Catholic Church, 155
Greek Orthodox Church, see Greek Catholic Church
Greeks, 158, 220, 225, 229
Greenland, 128, 208, 299
Green Pool, 284
Grew, Joseph C., 46, 214
Guam, 43, 57
Guerrillas, Communist, 106, 111, 115
Gulf of Finland, 100

H

The Hague, 243, 252, 263
Haiti, 32, 208, 276; U.S. intervention in, 66
Hamid, Abdul, 158, 163
Hanoi, 195
Hapsburg Austria, see Austria
Hapsburg emperors, 23, 147; Empire, 41, 135; House of, 98
Harding, Warren G., 261

Harvard University, 28, 35
Hashemites, 121
Hatta, Mohammed, 193
Hawaii, 57, 206
Hedjaz, 166
Hegel, 87, 231
Helen of Troy, 91
Henry VIII, 20
Herodotus, 91
Herzegovina, 93
Hindu Kush, 160
Hindus, 158, 200, 228
Hiss, Alger, 69
Hitler, Adolf, 9, 24, 45-7, 55, 67, 102-4, 110, 127, 134, 139-43, 157, 167-69, 229, 234-36, 252-53, 257, 261, 271, 296
Hitler-Stalin Pact, see Nazi-Soviet Pact
Hittites, 161
Ho-Chi-Minh, 195
Hoffman, Paul, 281
Hohenzollern Empire, 135-36, 147-48
Hohenzollern Germany, see Germany
Holland, see Netherlands
Hollandia, 187
Holy Alliance, 95
Holy Land, 20
Holy Roman Empire, 22, 101; see also Roman Empire
Honorius, 91
Hoover, Herbert, 235
House of Commons, 104
House of Lords, British, 27
Hughes, Charles Evans, 45, 257
Huk-Balahaps, 192
Hull, Cordell, 46, 51, 65-6, 211, 262, 278, 285
Hungary, 21-2, 24, 95, 103, 131, 135, 138, 141, 143, 146-50, 175, 214, 216-17, 225, 228, 306, 308, 312
Huns, 91, 228
Hussein, Emir, 121, 167
Hydrogen bomb, 9, 119, 258-59

I

ICAO, see International Civil Aviation Organization
Iceland, 8, 259, 299

Igorrotes, 189
ILO, see International Labor Office
Inca Empire, 82
India, 13, 15, 34-5, 56, 93, 117, 119,
    123, 160, 181, 184, 199-200, 202,
    204, 211, 221, 223, 226, 228-29,
    289; area, 41; population, 41, 73
Indians (American), 82, 89, 229, 232
Indian Ocean, 120, 151-52, 160
Indo-China, 33, 52, 94, 115, 180,
    183-86, 194-96, 198, 214, 221, 274
Indonesia, 151, 181, 187-88, 190,
    192-94, 202, 204, 211-12, 214, 289
Indus River, 160
Inner Mongolia, 33
Inonü, President, 167
International Bank, 291-92
International Civil Aviation Organi-
    zation, 247-48, 263
International Court of Justice, 252,
    263-64
International Labor Office, 263
International Monetary Fund, 291-92
International Telecommunication
    Union, 263
Iran (Persia), 119, 121, 123, 138,
    152-54, 156-59, 161; in Baghdad
    Pact, 33, 173
Iraq, 121, 152-53, 158, 166-67, 169-
    70, 214; in Baghdad Pact, 33, 173
Ireland, 98
Iron Curtain, 108, 111-12, 119, 147-
    48, 248, 306-307
Islamic, see Mohammedan
Israel, 9, 121-22, 124-26, 152, 155,
    158, 162, 166, 170-73, 175-78, 309
Istanbul, 22, 93-94, 120, 122-23, 151,
    153, 155-57, 162; see also Byzan-
    tium, Constantinople
Isthmus of Kamchatka, 180
Italy, 20-1, 94, 98, 100, 103, 132, 134,
    140, 154, 164, 168, 227, 229, 261,
    288; Communist strike against,
    112-13; and Marshall plan, 112; in
    NATO, 32; seizes Tripoli, 137
Ivan the Terrible, 221

J

Japan, 9, 129, 180-84, 188-91, 194,
    196, 205, 211, 214, 220, 227, 229,
    257, 271-72, 289; in China, 46;
population, 129; Russia defeated
    by, 95, 115; Soviet Union and, 107,
    109, 116; war with, 110, 112
Japan Sea, 129
Japanese, 188-91, 196, 198, 206, 212,
    271
Java, 187, 193
Jerusalem, 155, 157, 163, 170
Jessup, Philip, 255
Jesuits, 57
Jews, 96, 142, 158, 166, 169-71, 309
Jewish religion, 155
Jimenez, General Perez, 83
Jinnah, Mohammed Ali, 200
John XII, Pope, 22
Jordan, 152, 170

K

Kabul, 123
Kandahar, 123
Kansas, 8, 128, 259
Kars, 159
Kashmir, 152, 160
Katz-Suchy, Dr., 149
Kemal, Mustapha (Ataturk), 165,
    167
Kennan, George, 35, 216, 308
Kenya, 232
Keynes, Lord, 287
Khan, Genghis, 53, 92, 159, 225
Khan, Kublai, 92, 108
Khedives, 161
Khruschev, 23, 97, 148, 305, 308
Khyber Pass, 123
Kipling, 23, 87
Koran, 59
Korea, 185, 188, 190, 221, 254, 263,
    307; see also North Korea, South
    Korea
Korean War, 41, 44, 117-18, 211,
    304-5
Kremlin, see Moscow, Soviet Union
Kubitchek, Juscelino, 83
Kurds, 123, 158
Kurile Islands, 116, 180-81, 186
Kuwait, 152, 167, 169

L

Labrador, 15, 129
Lantané, John H., 39

Laos, 186, 190, 194-97, 289
Latin America, 27, 32, 65, 74-5, 78, 177, 204, 278, 286-87, 308, 310, 313; defense of, 76; faith of, 88; Organization of American States, trade of, 73-4; politics in, 79-80, 84-6; productivity, 88; unity in, 86-8; *see also* Central America, South America
Latvia, 95, 131, 135, 138, 140-41, 146, 214
Lawrence of Arabia, 164
League of Nations, 44, 102, 244, 261, 267; mandates, 166
Lebanon, 152, 158, 162, 166, 170, 214
Lenin, 55, 96, 138, 165, 182, 221, 307
Leningrad, 258
Leninism, 52, 55, 299; *see also* Communism, Marxism
Liberia, 207
Libya, 137, 164, 168, 170
Liechtenstein, 98
Lima, 75; Declaration of, 66-67
Lithuania, 95, 131, 135, 138-41, 146, 214, 228
Little Entente, 95
Livingstone, David, 209
Lloyd George, David, 165
London, 64, 125, 140, 221, 228, 275
Lords Spiritual, 27-28, 261
Lorraine, House of, 98
Louis XI, 225
Louis XIV, 225, 227
Lovett, Robert, 71, 114
Luxemburg, 33, 283

Mc

MacArthur, Douglas, 116

M

Machiavelli, 87
Macedonia, 132, 137
Maginot Line, 16, 142-43
Magsaysay, Ramon, 192
Magyar, 98, 131
Maine, battleship, 42
Malacca, Strait of, 186, 197, 249
Malaya, 15, 74, 93, 115, 180, 186, 188, 190, 194, 197, 283
Malayan Federation, *see* Malaya

Manchuria, 181-82; 184-85; 188-89; Japanese hegemony in, 95; Soviet Union and, 115-17
Manila, 189
Mansholt, 284
Mao Tse-tung, 116, 183-85
Marco Polo, 231
Marco Polo Bridge, 271
Marmara, Sea of, 92, 153
Marshall Plan, 112-14, 280-81, 287-89, 290-92
Marshall, General George, 71, 114, 287
Mau-Mau, 232
Marx, Karl, 95, 159, 221, 224
Marxism, 22-3, 55, 215, 236, 269; *see also* Communism, Leninism
Mary, Queen of Scots, 20
Mary Tudor, 101
Master Race theory, 142, 229
Mecca, 155
Medea, 91
Mediterranean, 92, 114, 119-22, 124, 133, 136, 151-53, 158, 162, 168-69, 173, 176, 206, 250, 261
Mein Kampf, 234
Metternich, 102
Mexico, 32, 57, 64, 66, 69, 221, 223, 229, 270, 308
Mexico City, conference in, 68
Middle East, 94, 125-26, 130, 137, 140, 150-51, 154, 156, 160, 163-64, 166, 168, 172-73, 199, 206, 234, 253, 266, 286, 294, 311-12; population, 162; *see also* Near East
Mid-Europe, 126, 130, 134-36, 139, 141-45, 151-52, 159-63, 168, 171, 173, 178, 195, 229, 234, 307, 311-12; Hitler plans control of, 103; objectives, 134; population, 98, 108, 133; revolts in, 149-50; Soviet Union controls, 108-109, 146-47, 156; and Turkey, 137
Mikhailovitch, 143
Mohammed, 155, 231
Mohammedanism, 155, 157-58
Mohammedan world, 151, 178
Mohammedans, 21-2, 24, 59, 92, 126, 132, 155, 200, 231
Molotov, Vyacheslav, 51, 103, 116, 141
Monaco, 13, 98

Mongolia, 185; *see also* Outer Mongolia, Inner Mongolia
Mongols, 92, 131, 158, 225
Monroe Doctrine, 66
Montenegro, 139
Montevideo, 66
Montreal, 247, 263
Montreux Convention, 124
Montgomery, 157, 168
Morgenthau, Hans, 35
Mormons, 274
Morocco, 8, 9, 151, 172, 211, 299, 308
Moscow, 9, 51, 62, 103-104, 108, 112, 116-18, 128, 133, 143, 146, 149, 156, 160, 173-74, 179, 184, 191, 212-13, 216, 221, 228, 247, 259, 307; Declaration, 262; *see also* Soviet Union
Moslems, *see* Mohammedans
Mosul, 176
Mukden, 188
Munich, 140
Murmansk, 119
Muskat, 167
Mussolini, Benito, 45, 55, 58, 140, 143, 244, 253, 261
Myrdal, Gunnar, 300

N

Naguib, Mohammed, 171
Nagy, Imre, 149
Napoleon, 22, 95, 102, 116, 127, 148, 156, 301
Nasser, Gamul Abdul, 125, 169, 171-73, 175, 250, 253, 257
Natal, Brazil, 75
National Academy of Science-National Research Council, 268
NATO, *see* North Atlantic Treaty Organization
Nazi Germany, *see* Germany
Nazism, 142, 234; appeal to German-Americans, 58; political warfare, 75-6; theory of state under, 26-7; U.S. opposition to, 45
Nazi-Soviet Pact, 97, 102-103, 141, 146
Near East, 43, 64, 74, 118, 121, 154, 158, 169, 174, 176, 216; *see also* Middle East

Negroes, 207-10; 232; Mohammedans, 155
Nehru, Jawaharlal, 160, 201
Nepal, 289
Nestorian Christianity, 158
Netherlands, 16, 94, 99, 109, 133, 143, 153, 190, 192-93, 202, 205, 211, 214, 227, 243, 283-84
New Guinea, 186, 193
New York, 114, 197, 221, 239, 275
New Testament, 268
New Zealand, 34, 63, 93, 205, 289; in SEATO, 33
Ngo Dinh Diem, 195
Nicaragua, 66, 72, 81, 84
Nietzsche, 229
Nigeria, 34, 209-10
Nile, 157, 168, 173
Nirvana, 27, 234, 238
Norman Conquest, 20
Normandy, landings in, 48
North Africa, 151, 168, 172, 270; Mohammedans in, 21, 178; in World War II, 48
North America, 57
North Atlantic Treaty Organization, 32, 34, 63, 65, 70-2, 114, 119-20, 126, 176, 212, 217, 236, 263, 272, 289, 300-1
North Korea, 33, 116, 182-83, 186, 212
North Pole, 128
North Sea, 99
Novaya Zemlya, 259
Nye, Gerald P., 256

O

Occupation, zones of, 108, 110
OEEC, *see* Organization for European Economic Cooperation
Office of European Economic Cooperation, 288
Okhotsk, Sea of, 180
Okinawa, 189
Oman, 152, 169
Oppenheimer, Robert, 101
Oregon, 43
Organization of American States, 27, 32, 59-60, 63, 65, 72, 236, 274; defense, 74-77; functioning, 80-86; population, 73; resources, 73-4;

search for ideology, 77-80; trade, 73-4

Organization for European Economic Cooperation, 32, 280, 288

Orinoco Valley, iron ore in, 73

Otranto Strait, 132

Otto the Great, *see* Otto of Saxony

Otto of Saxony, 21-22, 101

Outer Mongolia, 33, 117

P

Pacific Ocean, 46, 48, 94, 110, 115, 118, 181, 205, 225

Pakistan, 34, 56, 119, 123, 152, 154, 158-60, 199-200, 202, 226, 228, 289; in Baghdad Pact, 33, 173; in SEATO, 33, 197

Palestine, 166, 169-70; *see also* Israel

Paley Report, 49

Panama, 65-6

Panama Canal, 64, 177, 186, 249

Pan-American Union, 65-66, 72

Pan-European Wars, 102

Pan-Slavism, 137

Paris, 9, 11, 64, 100, 112, 114, 125, 194, 221, 227; Peace Conference, 136, 165

Parliament, British, 142

Parran, Thomas C., 247

Parsees, 229

Pashtuns, *see* Pukhtuns

Paz, Gainza, 310

Pearl Harbor, 9, 46, 49-50, 105, 110, 211, 214, 257

Peiping, 92, 118, 183-84, 212, 216, 221, 228, 247

Peking, *see* Peiping

People's Republic of China, *see* China

Pericles, 99

Peron, Juan, 27, 81, 84, 86, 310

Perry, 188

Persia, *see* Iran

Persian Gulf, 152-54, 160, 162, 168-69, 172, 176

Persians, 158

Peru, 74-5, 82, 276

Pétain, 24

Peter the Great, 94, 96, 221

Philip II, 23, 101

Philippine Islands, 33, 43, 93-4, 115, 181, 186, 189-92, 198, 211, 214, 226, 228; in SEATO, 33, 197

Piccolomini, 90

Pius II, Pope, 90

Pizarro, 82

Place de la Concorde, 11

Plantagenet, House of, 20, 23

Point Four program, 216

Poitiers, 21, 92

Poland, 9, 22, 95, 98, 100, 103, 110, 117, 131, 135-36, 138-41, 145, 149, 175, 214, 217, 223, 225, 302, 308, 312

Poles, 98, 228

Pope John XII, 22

Pope Pius II, 90

Port Said, 125

Portsmouth, New Hampshire, 188

Portugal, 57, 94-5, 129, 153, 205, 207, 227

Portuguese Empire, 59, 94

Potsdam Conference, 109-12

Poznam, 148-49

Prague, 131, 140-41

Puerto Rico, Commonwealth of, 57

Pukhtuns (Pashtuns), 158, 160

Q

Qatar, 152

R

Red Army, 139

Red Sea, 120, 151-54, 162, 164, 174-75, 206

Rhine river, 105, 133, 144, 153, 177

Rhine-Main-Danube Canal, 153

Ribbentrop, 103, 141

Richard Lionheart, 20

Richard III, 20

Richelieu, 225, 227

Rio Branco, 79

Rio Doce Valley, iron ore in, 74

Rio Grande, 67, 80, 86-7

Rio de Janeiro, 11; Treaty of, 32, 59, 68, 70-72, 263

Roberts College, 162

Roberts of Kandahar, 123

Rockefeller, Nelson, 68-71

Rocket warfare, 119

Rocky Mountains, 274

Roman Empire, 22, 24, 91, 93, 98-9, 122, 161, 225, 228
Romanoff, House of, 95, 135
Rome, 13, 56, 64, 91, 100, 132, 221, 225, 227, 234, 240-42; capture of, 91; Christianity and, 99-100; laws, 58, 99; Legions, 99; religion, 58; Republic of, 51; universality, 99
Rommel, 157, 168
Roosevelt, Franklin D., 11-2, 28, 45-6, 66, 68, 70, 105-6, 182, 190, 220, 250, 261-62
Roosevelt, Theodore, 188
Rosenberg, Alfred, 235
Rouen, France, 20
Roumania, 95, 100, 103, 131-32, 135-36, 138-39, 143, 146-47, 228
Rousseau, Jean Jacques, 221
Rozas, 83
Ruhr Basin, 133, 295
Russell, Bertrand, 55
Russia, 35, 43, 63, 92, 94-7, 100, 104, 123, 134-36, 138, 147, 156-57, 159, 161, 164-65, 168, 174, 182-84, 188, 212-16, 227, 231, 234, 247, 286, 311, 313
Russian Central Asia, 92, 159-60
Russian Empire, see Russia
Russo-Japanese War, 10, 95, 109, 189, 270
Ryukyu Islands, 181, 189

S

Saar, 295
Sahara Desert, 206-7, 211
Sakhalin, 116
Salk vaccine, 36
Salonika, 132, 134
Samarkand, 159
San Francisco, U.N. conference at, 70-71, 262
San Marino, 98
Santos, President, 68
Saracens, see Mohammedans
Sarajevo, 138, 164
Sarmiento, 79
Saud, Ibn, 166-67
Saudi-Arabia, 121, 152, 154-55, 157, 166-67, 169-70, 214, 299
Savoy, House of, 98
Schweizer, Albert, 232

Sears, Roebuck & Company, 275-76
SEATO, see South East Asia Treaty Organization
Self-determination of nations, 138, 214, 234
Semetic race, 158
Serbia, 136-37, 139
Serbs, 98, 132, 139
Sèvres, Treaty of, 165
Shakespeare, 21
Shantung, 181-2, 271
Shaw, George Bernard, 256
Shaw, T. E., see Lawrence
Shell Oil Company, 294
Shiites, 157
Siam, see Thailand
Siberia, 117, 162, 180-81, 185
Sinai peninsula, 125, 175
Singapore, 93, 180, 186, 188, 190, 197-98
Sinkiang, 185
Skoda munitions, 192
Slavic, 98
Slavs, 131-32, 159, 184, 229
Slovenes, 98, 131-32, 139
Smith, Adam, 222-23
Smyrna, 165
Somoza, 84
South America, 11, 15, 27, 35, 57, 64, 69, 75, 128, 154, 169, 229, 275
Southeast Asia, 64, 271, 283, 286
South East Asia Treaty Organization, 33, 197, 217
South Korea, 116, 186, 211, 213-14, 265
South Pole, 128
Sovereignty, 13, 15, 17, 19, 155, 218; and supra-national values, 24; and Suez, 177, 311
Soviet Foreign Office, 105, 118, 121, 173
Soviet Union, 13, 15, 17, 22-3, 31, 39, 47, 49, 51-2, 54-5, 67, 69, 92, 100, 102-6, 115, 119, 123, 126-27, 131-33, 141, 143-45, 152-53, 161, 167, 209, 213, 217, 223, 225-26, 235, 246, 257-59, 262, 265-66, 272, 280, 295-96, 300, 303, 305-8, 312; area, 40; in Asia, 33, 180-81, 183, 185, 187, 195; Berlin blockaded by, 113-14; and China, 96-7, 107, 109, 115, 117-18, 184;

early hostility to, 95; Europe threatened by, 21; and Geneva conference, 97; Hitler attacks, 46, 140, 143; and Japanese war, 107, 109-10, 116; and Manchuria, 115-17; and Marshall plan, 112-14; Mediterranean outlet sought by, 114-15, 119-21; and Mid-East, 74, 159-60, 177-78; in Mid-Europe, 133-36, 144, 146-47, 149, 156; Montreux convention and, 124; opposes Organization of American States, 71, 79; policy change of, in 1944, 105-6; political war objectives, 107-9, 144-47; population, 40, 184; revolts against, 148-50; and Suez, 121, 124-26, 173-76
Spain, 21, 23, 57, 92, 94-5, 134, 154, 178, 189, 223, 229, 261, 270
Spaniards, empire-builders, 57
Spanish Empire, 16, 43, 58-9, 93-4, 214, 226-27
Spanish American War, 9, 10, 43, 57
Sparks, Edward J., 89
Sparta, 91
St. Peter, 29
Stalin, Josef, 9, 23, 50-1, 92, 96-7, 103, 118, 139, 141, 143, 145, 148, 182-83, 229, 234-35, 246, 248, 252, 257, 305, 308
Stalingrad, 105, 157, 259
Stanley, Sir Henry Morton, 209
State Department, see United States, Department of State
States, sovereign, 25, 30-1, 234, 255, 312; defense, 16-7; defined, 13; internal pressures, 19; international relations of, 31; self-sufficiency, 14-5; sixteenth to nineteenth century, 14
Staten Island, 197
Statute of Westminster, 56
Stettin, Germany, 108-9, 111
Stettinius, Edward, 69-71
Stettin-Trieste line, 109, 111
Stevenson, Adlai, 248
Stikker, Dirj, 284
Stilicho, 91, 221
Stockholm, 221
Storey, Moorfield, 190
Straits of Magellan, 87
Streicher, 235

Stuart, House of, 20, 23
Students, exchange, 35
Sudan, 151-52
Suez Canal, 9, 34, 36, 120-21, 124-26, 152-54, 161, 168-69, 173-78, 186, 249-50, 253, 263, 311
Suez Canal Company, 125, 161-62, 173, 175, 177, 250, 253, 311
Sukarno, 193
Suleiman the Magnificent, 93, 178
Sumatra, 180, 186, 193
Summit Conference, see Geneva Conference of 1955
Strasbourg, 221; University of, 100
Sunnites, 157
Sun Yat Sen, 181
Supra-nationalism, 33, 41, 90, 177, 205, 223, 245-51; communism, 22-4; examples, 20-2; values, 24
Sweden, 119
Switzerland, 131, 285
Sylvius, Aeneas, 90
Syria, 125, 152, 158, 166-67, 170, 174-76, 214

T

Tadjik, 158-59
Taiwan, see Formosa
Talleyrand, 102
Tamerlane, 92, 159
Tashkend, 159
Teller, 101
Temushin, see Genghis Khan
Teschen, 139
Texas, 154
Thailand, 185, 190, 195-97, 259, 289; in SEATO, 33, 197
There Is No Asia, 185
Thirty-eighth parallel, 116, 185
Thrace, 134, 137
Tibet, 33, 185
Tientsin, 186
Tigris-Euphrates Valley, 152
Timur, see Tamerlane
Tito (Josef Broz), 11, 115, 146, 149, 174-75
Titoism, 149
de Tocqueville, Alexis, 39
Tokyo, 198, 212, 221
Tonking, 194; Gulf of, 184, 186

Toussaint L'Ouverture, 208
Toynbee, Arnold, 87, 91, 93-4
Trade and Payments in Western Europe—A Study in Economic Co-operation, 1947–1951, 278
Transjordania, 121, 166-67
Trans-Siberian Railroad, 116
Transylvania, 138
Trebizond, 99
Trieste, 108, 111, 119
Triple Entente, 95
Tripoli, *see* Libya
Troy, 91
Truman Doctrine, 62-3, 71, 111-12
Truman, Harry S., 63, 70, 111, 146, 254
Tunis, 168
Tunisia, 172
Turcomen, 159
Turks, 90, 93-4, 131, 157, 170, 220, 229
Turkey, 63, 94, 119-21, 124, 126, 151-53, 156, 158-59, 161-64, 167-68, 173, 189, 214, 227; in Baghdad Pact, 33; and Cyprus, 30, 122-23; empire, 132, 135-36; empire dismantled, 137-39, 166; in NATO, 32
Turkish Empire, *see* Turkey
Turkistan, Soviet, 160

U

Ukraine, 104, 135
Ukrainians, 98
Undergrounds, 121, 191, 195-96, 198; Western vs. pro-Russian, 106, 145-46
Union Pacific Railroad, 26
Union of South Africa, 34, 207-10, 255
United Kingdom, *see* Great Britain
United Nations, 31, 36, 62, 67, 114, 118, 120, 127, 160, 193, 209-10, 214, 236, 239, 247, 249, 251-52, 254, 262-68, 274, 291, 310; charter, 69-70, 231, 262; Committee on Disarmament, 258; Dumbarton Oaks, 67; and NATO, 32; and Organization of American States, 69-72; and Palestine, 170-71; San Francisco conference of, 70-71, 262; Security Council, 67-9, 183, 254, 264; and Suez, 125, 176-77; in World War II, 29
United Nations Relief & Rehabilitation Administration, 287
United States, 8, 13, 24, 29-30, 49, 51-52, 54, 56, 58, 61-63, 78, 100-4, 119-20, 127, 129, 142, 149, 154, 159, 165, 168, 173, 179, 181, 187, 189-91, 198, 203, 206, 212, 214-15, 217-18, 220-21, 223, 226, 228-29, 235-36, 239, 251, 257-59, 261-62, 265, 270-76, 278, 280-85, 287-89, 292-306, 308-11; Arab-Israel conflict, 118; and British Commonwealth, 60, 63; and China, 183; Congress of, 11, 190, 256; Constitution of, 59, 283; defense, 8, 16-7, 75-6; Department of State of, 13, 31, 36, 42, 69-71, 86, 103, 129, 151, 247; as Far East power, 43, 46, 94; imperialism, 56-7, 59, 94, 211, 214; interdependence of, 10, 73-4, 86; and Korea, 118, 213, 254; and Latin America, 59-60, 65-7, 88-9; and NATO, 32, 63; and Organization of American States, 27, 63, 65, 72-3, 79-89; population, 14, 40, 73; productivity, 40, 47; Public Health Service, 247; public opinion in, 7, 8, 48; and SEATO, 33, 197; self-sufficiency, 14; and sovereignty, 19; and Suez, 125, 173-76; Supreme Court of, 59, 265-66; and U.N., 67-8, 105; world leadership of, 9, 39-40, 44, 48, 50, 65; and World War I, 43-5, 120, 138-39; World War II, 105-106, 110, 112
United States Steel Company, 26
UNRRA, *see* United Nations Relief and Rehabilitation Administration
Ural Mountains, 98
Ural River, 98
Uruguay, 82, 84
U.S. v. 14 Diamond Rings, 59
Utah, 84, 274
Uzbek, 159

V

Vandals, 91; Pannonian, 228
Vandenberg, Arthur, 70-1

Vargas, Getulio, 83
Vatican, 13
Vatican State, 13
Venezuela, 15, 73-4, 81, 83-4
Versailles, 225; Peace Conference, 44, 138-39, 164; treaty of, 11, 95, 99
Vichy government, 24
Victoria, Age of, 282, 314; Empress of India, 93, 199
Vietnam, 186, 190, 194-96, 212, 214, 274, 289
Vienna, 64, 91, 93, 131, 133, 179; Congress of, 95
Vietminh, 33, 183, 186, 190, 194-97, 213
Vladivostok, 120, 181, 185
Vlöri, 132, 174-75
Voice of America, 24, 247
"Volunteers," 126, 176, 253, 313

W

Wahabites, 157
Wall Street, 212
War, political character of, 75-6, 107-9, 144
Wars of the Roses, 225
Warsaw, underground crushed, 145
Washington, 81, 86, 103, 105, 111, 143, 211-12, 262; North Atlantic treaty signed at, 72, 114
Weber, Max, 233
Welles, Sumner, 65, 103, 143, 244
Wends, 98
West vs. East, 91-94, 118, 131
Western Europe, 26, 43, 48-9, 63-4, 71, 98, 102-3, 119, 121, 124-25, 134, 136, 153-54, 161, 169, 172, 175-76, 178-79, 220, 235, 250, 258, 284-85, 289, 308, 312; and Asia, 91-4; boundary of, moved, 109; Convention for Economic Cooperation of, 114; and Latin America, 74; and Marshall Plan, 112, 114; and Pacific war strategy, 110; population, 98; reconstruction, 108, 110; unity of, 32, 41-2, 99-100, 127, 133
West Germany, 113, 119
West Indies, 11, 57

West Ukraine, 139
White Citizens Councils, 206
White House, 105, 262
White Sands, New Mexico, 107
WHO, see World Health Organization
Wilhelm II, 47, 102, 120, 140, 165, 270
William the Conqueror, 20
Western Hemisphere, 11, 47, 60, 64, 66-67, 79, 129, 169, 215, 227, 278, 309
Wilson, Woodrow, 11, 28, 39, 44, 48, 95, 102, 138, 165, 214, 244, 250, 261
Winant, John G., 104
Woods, Sam., 143
The World Against the West, 91
World Bank, see International Bank
World Health Organization (WHO), 247
World War I, 16, 39, 43-5, 51, 62, 93, 95-96, 99, 102, 123, 134, 137-38, 156-57, 162, 164, 166-68, 171, 181, 204, 214, 234, 244, 250, 261, 271, 281, 297-98, 311
World War II, 9, 11, 13-5, 24, 32, 45-6, 48, 51, 56, 64, 67, 75, 96-7, 102, 105, 120, 132-33, 139, 144, 157, 167-68, 182, 188, 190, 202, 211, 214, 219, 234, 246-47, 260-61, 278, 282, 291, 295, 307
World War III, 75, 119, 127, 307

XYZ

Xerxes, 51, 61
Yalta Conference, 69, 106, 109-11, 146
Yalu River, 116
Yellow Sea, 186, 188
Yemen, 152, 167, 169-70
Yoshida, 46
Young Turks, 163
Yugoslavia, 76, 91, 93, 95, 98, 103-4, 111, 114-15, 119, 124, 131-33, 135-36, 138-40, 143, 146, 149-50, 173-75, 220, 225
Zion, 163, 170, 177
Zionists, 170, 172
Zulus, 207